Bea Vidacs

Visions of a Better World

Bea Vidacs

Visions of a Better World

Football in the Cameroonian Social Imagination

LIT

Cover photo by Bea Vidacs

Bibliographic information published by the Deutsche Nationalbibliothek
The Deutsche Nationalbibliothek lists this publication in the Deutsche Nationalbibliografie; detailed bibliographic data are available in the Internet at http://dnb.d-nb.de.

ISBN 978-3-643-10431-1

A catalogue record for this book is available from the British Library

Fresnostr. 2 D-48159 Münster
Tel. +49 (0) 2 51-620 320 Fax +49 (0) 2 51-922 60 99
e-Mail: lit@lit-verlag.de http://www.lit-verlag.de

Distribution:

In Germany: LIT Verlag Fresnostr. 2, D-48159 Münster
Tel. +49 (0) 2 51-620 32 22, Fax +49 (0) 2 51-922 60 99, e-mail: vertrieb@lit-verlag.de

In Austria: Medienlogistik Pichler-ÖBZ, e-mail: mlo@medien-logistik.at

In Switzerland: B + M Buch- und Medienvertrieb, e-mail: order@buch-medien.ch

In the UK: Global Book Marketing, e-mail: mo@centralbooks.com

In North America by:

Transaction Publishers
New Brunswick (U.S.A.) and London (U.K.)

Transaction Publishers
Rutgers University
35 Berrue Circle
Piscataway, NJ 08854

Phone: +1 (732) 445 - 2280
Fax: + 1 (732) 445 - 3138
for orders (U. S. only):
toll free (888) 999 - 6778
e-mail: orders@transactionpub.com

Contents

Acknowledgements

People rooted for the completion of this manuscript on three continents. I first wish to extend my thanks to my friends and associates in Cameroon; without them this work would not have seen the light of day. Football people constitute a very special group and many Cameroonians consider the sport theirs. I owe special thanks to the following: Abdou, Akoa, Bayam, Bob Baugnie, Djob Tjomb Marc, Essono Pie, Roger Happy, Himoug, Cyrille Mbang, Engelbert Mbarga, Mbah, Colonel Moume Liberté, Jean-Marie Ndjetkeu, Nguidjol, Jean-Michel Njelezeck, François Njike, Amos Ngankou, Alain Ntamag, Jacques Noumi, Jean Manga Onguéné, Jean-Pierre Sadi, Sado, Santa Maria, Célestin Tapa, Daniel Tchakougang, Dominique Wansi, Youdom, and Zé Essola. I thank them for having shared with me their enthusiasm for and expertise on football.

Many Cameroonian intellectuals outside football circles also welcomed me heartily, expressed interest in my work, and helped me in small and large matters with hospitality, stimulating conversation or office space. Among them, I owe special gratitude to: Emmanuel and Emma Chiabi, Jacqueline Ekambi, Ambroise Kom, Flavien Ndonko, Paul N. Nkwi, and Antoine Socpa. I owe my first steps in the world of Cameroonian football to André Ntonfo. Thanks are also due to Mitzi Goheen as well as Milton and Judy Krieger, who received me with collegial friendship in the field. I would like to extend special gratitude to His Excellency, Jeanvier Fayeu, who extended his friendship to me both in Yaoundé and in the village. I thank him and his circle of friends: Alhadji, Alphonse, Boniface, Jean-Paul, Maurice, and M. Pierre for having included me at the very beginning and shared their thoughts and opinions with me.

A second round of thanks is due to friends, colleagues, and institutions in the United States. First of all, I wish to thank the Wenner-Gren Foundation for Anthropological Research which supported my doctoral research in 1994-1995, and made the updating of the material and the completion of the manuscript possible by awarding me a Richard Curley Hunt fellowship.

The Anthropology Program of the City University of New York, Graduate Center provided a stimulating intellectual environment, very good mentors and colleagues. I think with special gratitude of Professors Vincent Crapanzano, Michael Blim, Louise Lennihan, and Jane Schneider. Among my colleagues, I am grateful for endless conversations, advice, and support to Diana Agosta, Hugo Benavides, Julia Butterfield, Gerald Creed, Carmen Ferradas, Alcira Forero-Pena, Alfredo Gonzalez, Murphy Halliburton, Trenholme Junghans, Carmen Medeiros, Allyson Purpura, Aseel Sawalha, Jonathan Shannon, Suzanne Scheld, Robin Sheriff, and Ian Skoggard. Bernice Kurchin deserves endless thanks for her help and advice over the years.

Last, but not least, I am grateful to family, friends, and colleagues in Hungary. I will forever be thankful to my parents who steadfastly supported me in all my undertakings and to my brother and his family who patiently waited for the end result. Among my colleagues and friends in Hungary, I owe thanks to János Bali, Zoltán Fejős, Kata Jávor, Éva Pócs, Zsuzsa Szarvas, as well as Gábor Vargyas. I am especially grateful to Mihály Sárkány and Péter Somlai for their unflagging interest in my work and for critical advice on numerous occasions. Naturally any failings of the work are mine alone.

CHAPTER I

INTRODUCTION: OF TEARDROPS AND FOOTBALLS

There is a mural in Douala, the economic capital of Cameroon. It is to be found in an abandoned looking open space that is closed off from a main road by a fence. Behind it, a little way off, is a cemetery with many tombs from the 1880s with German names, a reminder of Cameroon's first colonizers. On the opposite side of the road sits Douala's cathedral, another reminder (if one is needed) of the foreign influences on Cameroon. The mural is decidedly modern, non traditional, and yet it is unmistakably African; one could even say Cameroonian. It is colorful, angular, full of rhythm, with various styles mixed in. Among the dancing swirls of color, elongated figures seem to jump up and down, the abstract–geometrical style mixing successfully with a figurative style, as symbolic representations of emblematic African objects appear. In the midst of all this movement and angularity, there is a football player depicted in a much more realistic, graffiti style than the rest of the mural. His foot reaches out. It has just kicked the ball away; the tension in the athlete's leg is still full. The ball itself is the traditional football, where pairs of rectangular leather strips alternate in a crosscut pattern rather than the more "up-to-date" hexagonal patches. Teardrops roll down the "face" of the football. This work will attempt to explain what those teardrops mean.

Cameroon reached the quarterfinals of the 1990 World Cup for football [1] and thus created world history, being the first African team ever to have arrived at such a high level in the competition. On the way there, it beat Argentina, holder of the title, thus creating a mega-sensation in the world of football. The significance of this victory for all Cameroonians, and all

[1] This book deals with the sport known as soccer in the United States, everywhere else in the world the game is know as football, and I will use the latter term throughout.

Africans, and arguably for all Third World peoples as well, was enormous. Yet, despite the glory, dignity, pride, and satisfaction that Cameroon's 1990 World Cup participation brought (and Cameroon has been victorious in other events as well, most notably winning the African Nations Cup four times,[2] which the junior team also won in 1995, and in 2000 the gold medal at the Sydney Olympics), those teardrops are justified.

WHY SPORTS?

A common reaction to my subject matter is to think that football in particular or sports in general are not a subject for serious inquiry.[3] I myself fall into this trap in as much as I have heard myself say jokingly that the good thing about my topic is that, unlike many other colleagues who write about famine, war, rape, exploitation small and large, my topic is "fun!" Certainly, it is fun, and much of my fieldwork was spent among people who love football, discussing various fine points of the game, watching it, critiquing it, reflecting upon its nature, and its contradictions. What could be more fun? Much of this happens in bars while drinking beer, munching peanuts or fried termites in various stadiums or in taxis, or basically anywhere where one gets to talk to people in Cameroon. In the end, of course, it has to be realized that the form both my fieldwork and the game itself take, should not blind us to what is really going on. Football is thoroughly embedded in Cameroonian social realities; football life is no more fun than the social realities of which it is part. (I should hasten to add that it is no less fun, either.) Too often, Western commentators tend to see Africa in a dramatic light, where life is one of doom alone with no room for either hope or lightness (Chabal 1996, Gordon and Wolpe 1998, Kaplan 1994, Rieff 1998). And if there is lightness, it is often seen as a sign of immaturity. Curiously enough, these are the same terms in which nineteenth century European travelers saw Africa as well (cf. Pratt 1992).

Of course, enjoyment is an important part of the experience. People attend matches to forget about their troubles, to relax, to think of something else than the daily grind. But there is also intrinsic joy in seeing the game,

---

2 In 1984, 1988, 2000, and 2002.

3 Cf. Vidacs 2006, on possible reasons for the reluctance of Africanist social science to take the subject of sports seriously.

not only because it makes one forget one's troubles, but because it is interesting to watch and is aesthetically pleasing. It is a game of strategy with constant surprises and a variety of possibilities. When done well, it is also almost humorous with feints and dribbles; it is dramatic.

Why people play it is a somewhat different matter, because at least these days football is a means to riches. Like most other spectator sports that have become big business, the real stars of football are millionaires. Thus, most young Cameroonian would-be players dream of becoming stars in Europe, or even in Latin America. Does the fact that sport is a means to an end, take away from the enjoyment? I do not know the answer to this question, but I suspect, yes, to some extent. Certainly, coaches, elderly fans, and former players would say that they used to play for the sheer fun of it, whereas today's players only know how to make demands. Actually, all sides make enormous sacrifices in order to make football happen in Cameroon, and this includes the players as well. Probably there still is fun in the game, despite the means-to-an-end aspect of it. Part of this comes from the game itself, and of course, from the joy of accomplishment, of mastering the technique, of doing something well, of winning, yes, winning.

THE POSTCOLONIAL AS CONTEXT AND CONDITION

Although I am writing about football, the very fact that football as a symbolic construct can be seen to encompass all aspects of life in Cameroon, and all aspects of life encompass football means that I deal with a larger set of issues than what merely pertains to football. The larger context of this study is the postcolonial condition. I am using the postcolonial condition as shorthand for contemporary life in Cameroon, but by doing so I also presuppose a number of factors as the context for my study, and more importantly, for the lives of the people about whom I am writing. This includes the fact of Cameroon having been colonized, and as a result being an "underdeveloped" country. Its current economic and political life is to a great degree both internally and externally structured by its relationship to its erstwhile colonizers and by its unequal relationship to the "developed" world in general. These parameters constitute the framework within which the country exists and through which its inhabitants see themselves and carry out their daily lives. It also means that the majority of Cameroonians are poor; and poverty structures and limits people's possible fields of action. The postcolonial condition also means a set of internal circumstances that though conditioned by the external, have an autonomy of their own. I am trying to steer away from an overly deterministic view of the postcolonial, where all the ills that plague Cameroon are seen to derive from external factors. I am also trying to steer away from an overly pessimistic view of the internal life of Cameroon, even if Afro-pessimism seems to be one of the reigning ideas of our days. Cameroonians themselves are often given to these pessimistic views, both in everyday discourses on the streets of Cameroon and among intellectuals inside and outside the country.

Achille Mbembe's discussion of the postcolonial is a scathing critique of the postcolonial condition in which the state locks itself, and the population that is forced to coexist with it, into what he has labeled "zombification," seen as a mutual inability to get out of an impasse, and the collusion of all parties in maintaining this impasse. Mbembe, of course, is fully aware of the continuing effects of the colonial past on these practices (cf. Mbembe 1984, 1986, 1996), but his concern is to try to understand the nature of the postcolony and to see by what means the postcolonial state, ruler, and ruled, continue to stay the way they are. According to him, both sides collude and the process of domination–opposition becomes much more complex than a simple dichotomy between ruler and the ruled, and collaboration and resistance (cf. Mbembe 1992, 2001). Mbembe argues that being locked into this kind of a mutual understanding renders the postcolony impotent, and in fact, prevents any change. He writes:

> ... the postcolonial relationship is not primarily a relationship of resistance or of collaboration but can best be characterised as convivial, a relationship made fraught by the very fact of the *commendement* and its "subjects" having to share the same living space. Precisely this logic – the necessary familiarity and domesticity in the relationship – explains why there has not been (as might be expected from those so dominated) the resistance or the accommodation, the disengagement or the "refusal to be captured", the contradiction between overt acts and gestures in public and covert responses made "underground" (*sous maquis*). Instead, this logic has resulted in the mutual "zombification" of both the dominant and those apparently dominated. This zombification means that each has robbed the other of vitality and left them both impotent (*impouvoir*). (Mbembe 2001: 104)

Mbembe has been criticized for overstating his case and not proving it in a systematic way, and also for being overly pessimistic.[4] Mikael Karlström (2003) in a sustained criticism of Mbembe's 1992 celebrated article (republished in a slightly changed form in his 2001 volume) faults Mbembe for his radical pessimism and for according too much power to the state and too little autonomous thinking to the population at large, and thus denying the "possibility of critical or oppositional consciousness" (72). I sympathize with Karlström's point of view and certainly much of what I have to say about football and Cameroonians' reactions to their government during the mid-1990s supports his views. Writing about Ugandans, he argues that lampooning and "mobilising a local discourse of social morality and political accountability ... provides them with critical leverage against their rulers" (Karlström 2003: 72). In the case of football in Cameroon – and the difference is perhaps more attributable to the subject matter of what we are analyzing than to a difference of opinion – the models of "social morality and political accountability" that people are upholding are mostly foreign, but in the Cameroonian case too, bespeak of "critical consciousness" even if they cannot always be regarded as resistance in an active sense. Cameroonian expressions of this critical consciousness have changed over time. As I will discuss it in Chapter VII, in 2006, after a long period of political stalemate, people changed their attitude from one of principled mental (if not actual) resistance to one of self-conscious self-deprecating irony, which turned inside-out earlier discourses of football. They still maintained a critical edge, but one that was more ambiguous than before and often seemed to be directed at the people themselves. I assign this change in attitude to the depoliticization, which has been taking place in Cameroon, partly under the impact of what is described by most observers as a conscious policy on the part of the government to divert people's attention away from politics and partly under the impact of the consequent loss of hope in the possibility of change any time soon.

My interest in Mbembe, however, is on a more "ethnographic" level, in the sense that on the one hand, I find his depiction of Cameroonians' predicaments eminently recognizable and thought-provoking. He gives

---

[4] Cf. Public Culture 1992 special issue, which was devoted to reactions to Mbembe's article, for example Coronil 1992, see also Coquery-Vidrovitch 2002.

more of a sense of the lived experience of Cameroonians than almost any author I can think of. On the other hand, the notion of zombification captures the frustration of people caused by marshalling all their resources, making sacrifices, planning, and plotting – that I have seen many a time in Cameroon – which then seem to come to nothing. Although Mbembe uses the phrase "each robbed the other of vitality" in his characterization of zombification, this is not, strictly speaking, an apt description because on the level of everyday life in fact this zombification (perhaps neutralization would be a less suggestive but more precise term) is accompanied by feverish activity by all concerned, and zombification is only the result of this activity, not its mode.

THE ECONOMIC CRISIS

As described in the next chapter, Cameroon has been undergoing an economic crisis since 1987. The repercussions of this crisis have been manyfold on the lives of Cameroonians. Achille Mbembe and Janet Roitman (1995), analyzing its meaning to Cameroonians, demonstrate that in many ways it undermined Cameroonians' sense of certainty about an orderly progression of things in their lives (cf. also Ferguson 1999, Mbembe 1997, Ndjio 2005, Vigh 2006). In attempting to give a multifaceted image of the crisis as lived experience, of "the way in which the crisis is inscribed in the everyday urban landscape" (Mbembe and Roitman 1995: 327), they describe examples of breakdown in Cameroon from the deterioration in the state of the roads in many neighborhoods of Yaoundé, to the disintegration of cars (I can attest to the veracity of their description, every item of clothing I owned while in Cameroon sooner or later got torn or otherwise damaged in the many taxis I took), to the breakdown in public services such as electricity and water, garbage collection, the decay in factories, and the large number of abandoned buildings in a state of half-completion, where weeds and criminals thrive. This generalized breakdown is also true for football. It is true for football infrastructures and for equipment. It is true for the everyday unfolding of football, the relationships between people, the organization, and results of matches, all the way up to the level of the national team (see especially, Chapter III, for local level competitions, and Chapters V and VI, for the international level).

Mbembe and Roitman (1995) argue that the uncertainties that such a situation brings into people's lives lead to the development of what they refer to as "new forms of rationality" (339). By this, they mean that people have to find innovative ways to survive under these circumstances. Their emphasis is not so much on corruption, though obviously corruption is an integral part of these practices, but rather on a mentality where everybody has to arrange things, where "things no longer exist without their parallel. Every law enacted is submerged by an ensemble of techniques of avoidance, circumvention and envelopment which, in the end, neutralize and invert the legislation" (340).

This is not so unusual, the combination of oppressive regimes and poverty together bring about such "maneuvering." In a Hungarian[5] pop song from 1970, the singer, who claims to have finally learned the ropes after an earlier state of naïveté, sings "I didn't know [until now] that next to the large gates there are smaller doors where people actually enter."[6] This line echoes nicely the idea that under certain conditions, things are never what they seem, and in order to succeed one has to know one's way around.

What I am after in discussing Mbembe and Roitman's article in such detail is to pinpoint how people perceive the possibilities for and constraints upon action. Mbembe and Roitman go on to argue:

> There is hardly a reality here without its double. Hence acting efficaciously requires that one carefully cultivate an extraordinary capacity to be simultaneously inside and outside, for and against, and to constantly introduce changes in the reading and usage of things, playing, in this way, with the structures and apparatuses, capturing them where possible and eluding them where necessary, and in any event, amputating them and almost always emptying them of their formal and designated functions so one can better restore them with those that correspond best to desired goals and expected gains. (Mbembe and Roitman 1995: 340)

---

5 Throughout this work, examples taken from Hungary will crop up. This is because I am a Hungarian, and inevitably my experiences of having been brought up in a country which was/is in many ways similar to third world countries (single party, autocratic rule, censorship, a pronounced inferiority complex towards "Europe") shapes my understanding of my Cameroonian material. In fact, football has had great social and political significance in Hungary too (cf. Bali 2001, Hadas and Karády 1995, Hadas 1999, Handler 1994, Zsolt 1978).

6 Szörényi and Bródy 1970.

These practices and techniques are so common as to have become routinized, although they are publicly condemned. This kind of improvisation is also apparent at all levels of football: in the borrowing of uniforms; last minute hiring of coaches; falsification of licenses; last minute creation of teams, etc., which I will discuss in greater detail in Chapter III.

ETHOS/WORLDVIEW/IDEOLOGY

French anthropologist, Christian Bromberger (1994a, 1994b,1995, as well as Bromberger et al. 1995), who has undoubtedly produced the most nuanced anthropological study of football to date, argued that football is a worldview in the sense that it helps people explain their world, their experiences, and their place within the larger scheme of things. Positing that football is a worldview implies that it is a reflection of the reality of people's lives, but I will argue that in the Cameroonian context (and most likely elsewhere too); football is more than just a reflection of the world. As a symbolic construct, football is inherently ambiguous and carries multiple meanings. Bromberger would subscribe to this notion, but I would like to go one step further and suggest that in addition to reflecting the world as it is (with all its contradictions and cleavages), football is also a way for people to envision how the world should be. For this reason, it can hold out at least the illusion of a potential for transforming the very reality it reflects. In this sense, then we can ask whether football is a worldview or an ethos. If we follow Geertz's (1973) distinction between the two concepts, then football has a dual character: it is both a worldview and an ethos. In Geertz's formulation ethos is the ideal and worldview is the real. By this token in Bromberger's view, football is a worldview (it describes/reflects how the world is), but I am suggesting that there is another dimension to football in that it also serves as an ethos (how the world should be). Despite what Geertz says about the synthesized nature of the two, I would put the stress on the contradictions between them. Of course, Geertz sees worldview as people's "most comprehensive ideas of order" (127), whereas Cameroon, if we follow Mbembe, is disorder!

In analyzing the meaning of the crisis for Cameroonians, Mbembe and Roitman (1995) make a case for the tension being caused by "the unbearable discrepancy that exists between publicly announced reality and that other constantly changing, unstable and uncertain, quasi-elliptic realm that is consistently pursued and always dissipates, often emerging only after a long and exhausting bargain" (342). There is likewise an "unbearable discrepancy" between what I have dubbed football as ethos and football as worldview in the previous paragraph. As attested by satirical writing, cartoons, popular music, and other forms of popular humor[7] Cameroonians seem quite capable of being cynical about "publicly announced reality." When it came to football, at least during the 1990s, the counterpart of "publicly announced reality" was what I have dubbed football as ethos and this ideal was cherished, not ridiculed; it was what held out hope to many. If people ridiculed something in football, it was the worldview side, the side that reflected people's reality. A further irony is that, at least in part, this ethos derives from the ideological arsenal of modern sports as they came into being in nineteenth century Europe, with, among others, notions of fair play, discipline, and building character (Baker 1987, Bourdieu 1978, Guttmann 1994, Mangan 1986, 1987, Ranger 1983). But instead of being seen as an external imposition it is internalized.

Bromberger's formulation does not talk about how football also allows people to question their world and their place in it, and in some ways it creates at least the illusion, and sometimes the reality – however momentarily – of transforming this world. It is this promise of the transformative possibilities held out by football that I would argue holds in great part the attention of so many people.

AN ANSWER TO ZOMBIFICATION?

Having studied football in Cameroon for more than two years, I had ample occasion to experience along with the football teams I worked with, and the people I came into contact with the absurdities and the incalculabil-

[7] Cf. Mbembe 1997 and Schneider 2004 on political cartoons, or the taped and widely heard satirical pieces of comedians such as Tchop-Tchop and Antonio in Cameroon. For social criticism through popular music, see Essono 1996 and Nyamnjoh and Fokwang 2005. This type of humor is not unique to Cameroon; see for example Comi Toulabor's work (1981, 1991) on similar type of humor exercised in Togo about the powerful, and especially about the president of the country or George Ogola's (2005) analysis of a cartoon series in Kenya. For an analysis of how football appeared in the discourses of Cameroonian comedians during the 1990s, see Fandio 2004.

ity of life in Cameroon. As we shall see in the ensuing chapters, these are present on all levels of the game and frustrate people's attempts to work efficiently and achieve their desires. Naturally, Cameroonians are not uniform in how they relate to football, and as a first approximation, we need to distinguish between three broad categories: football people or the practitioners of football (players, coaches, former players, club presidents, referees, and other officials); the bulk of the population of ordinary people; and the power wielders, those Mbembe termed the *commendement*. None of these categories are hermetically sealed. They can and do overlap greatly. For example, a low-ranking police officer in certain respects is part of the power structure of Cameroon, but in other respects is part of the powerless, and of course, he can also be part of football circles. Intellectuals also can straddle all three categories. As Eyoh (1996) has cogently pointed out talking about Africa in general, intellectuals are by definition of their level of education assimilated into the modernity represented by the state and are potentially if not actually, part of the power structure of the modern state. By ordinary people, I mean approximately what Jean-François Bayart (1993) means by "little people." The core meaning is their relative lack of access to power, although due to links of patronage based on ethnic ties or on some other form of voluntary association, in some instances even the powerless have (or think they have) access to power. Football people are also a not too clearly defined category, since other than people actively engaged in the actual practice of the sport a very large segment of the male population [8] of Cameroon can claim some connection with football other than that of being a "mere" supporter. Football people often refer to themselves as "*les sportifs*" and juxtapose this term to that of "*les profanes*." But the two categories are elastic, their inclusiveness varying situationally. Nonetheless, we need to keep in mind that along with other identities, which category a person belongs to is going to influence both his/her (though it is mostly his) perceptions of, attitudes to, and opinions about football.

Those who participate in football can be seen and see themselves in a heroic light. They perceive themselves as wanting to create something: something concrete, something real, a better future, a good team, that everyone will remember and that will be the talk of the town. Coaches very

8 I will discuss women's position in the world of football below.

often claim that they do not train football players, but "Men," in an "old-fashioned," pathos-filled sense. As an ideal, at least on the level of desires and will, in Cameroon football represents an antithesis of the zombification, inertia, and impasse of the postcolonial condition, described so vividly by Mbembe and others. In practice, the general state of Cameroon constantly frustrates this desire, and one could subscribe to Mbembe's thesis and recognize in football the zombification he talks about, mirroring the general state of affairs of the country.

Football being a reflection of its context demonstrates many of the ills of Cameroonian society: falsification of names, ages, match results, betrayal of trust, stealing each other's players, etc. Where football differs from the rest of Cameroon is that at least on the level of the imaginary it presents an alternative, a place where unlike the impasse that Mbembe and Roitman are talking about, and Mbembe describes so vividly in his 1992 article (where he posits the notion of zombification), efficacious action is possible (cf. Castoriadis 1987, Crapanzano 2004, Gaonkar 2002, Taylor 2002, Vigh 2006). Thus, in some ways the world of football can be regarded as more "real" and more predictable than the "real" world. Of course, under the guise of being a break from the "real," football at the same time helps legitimize and reproduce the very conditions from which its practitioners hope to escape.

Partly people's perception of football as a space for efficacious action and a more equitable world comes from the structure of the game. Unlike the rest of Cameroon, in football there are seemingly clear rules, whose application or interpretation may be contested, but even then they are there unequivocally stated. Thus, people often bring up the 17 Laws of the Game as posited by the world governing body of football, FIFA, as the epitome of the clarity and permanence of the game. Theoretically, at least, there is no shadow world behind football. Naturally, the state's rules are also seemingly clear and as I cited from Mbembe and Roitman above, Cameroonians find or need to find a way to subvert them, and so they do with football. But a goal is a goal is a goal. What the game represents at least on an ideal level is in stark contrast to what Mbembe and Roitman describe for Cameroon.

This space for efficacious action also comes from the game's overall organization itself. A championship is a series of away and home matches against a set number of adversaries; each match is a world of its own, and each match presents a unique opportunity to prevail over the adversary of the moment. Even if a match is lost, there is always hope that the next one can be won, you can think of a solution, reinforce the team by recruiting a new player, develop a new strategy, have better luck, or have a different referee assigned who will not be so blatantly against you, or who will actually favor you. The structured nature of both a match and of a championship, the repetitiveness, despite the infinite variety of the actual game itself, lends an air of certainty and calculability, which is otherwise lacking in Cameroonians' lives. If it is Wednesday during the championship season, you know that you will be in the stadium, you know that there will be a match, you know that there are certain people you will find there, and you can also know what their reactions are going to be. Rituals of repetition in a world where there are no certainties are extremely comforting.

Although football is often the embodiment of both local ethnic and local national identity, at the same time, it is perceived as a way to transcend local identity and to change people's reality, both on an individual and collective level, in both concrete and symbolic ways. Local identity (being poor and downtrodden is an identity for many) is often defined in terms of local constraints, and football is seen as a way of changing these constraints, a way of revising history (personal, ethnic, and national). This process is full of internal contradictions and countervailing tendencies, but football as an ideal – a representative of the potential of Cameroonians, a space where they can be better than others, where a different set of (better) values apply – is used rather self-consciously by Cameroonians themselves. The fairytale like fact that a small, poor, downtrodden African country can beat the "great countries" of the world at their own game gives a lot of satisfaction to people in Cameroon and in Africa, giving people a recognition that is otherwise lacking (cf. Monga, C. 1990a).

WHOSE WORLDVIEW?

Christian Bromberger emphasizes that beyond crystallizing identities, football represents something fundamental to the people who watch it. In his view, the association between modernity and football takes on great significance. Following Ehrenberg, he sees in football the symbolic representation of the fundamental values of modern society, which he identifies with democracy. According to Bromberger (1994b), football celebrates merit, symbolizes such values as team work, solidarity, division of labor, and collective planning "in the image of [the] industrial world which originally produced it" (285). Although it allows for performance and competition among equals, due to the intervention of chance events, it also represents "the uncertain fate of man in the world today" (Bromberger 1994b: 284). This presents a more sophisticated reformulation of the idea, which is quite common in the sport sociology literature, that sports are attractive to people because they "present the human drama."

Bromberger is talking about European societies, and the world that is reflected in "his" football is the world of post-industrial Europe. Thus, his conclusion in another article (Bromberger 1995: 311): "In the light of football's complex and contradictory properties, one is perhaps justified in seeing this sport, which is neither pure spectacle, nor an established ritual, as *symbolic of an epoch in which the classificatory landmarks of collective life have become confused*." (emphasis added)

Cameroon is not quite the same as Europe. This rather obvious fact begs the question of whether football presents the same drama to Cameroonians as to Europeans, and to a great extent the answer is bound to be no. That said, Cameroon is not as removed from Europe or from modernity as one might think.

The modernity question deserves a little detour. As Robert Thornton (1996) explains:

> Because of their different relations to power, Modernism and postmodernism have quite different meanings and values in the Third World. Despite the fragmentation of modernism in the West, the aporias of reason, the politics of pastiche, the crisis of authenticity and the pervasive presence of simulacra, the Third World appears to be embracing modernism and modernisation as never before... For the most part, this appears to be true of African élites as well [as of Asian élites which he discusses first], who are not only still modernising but seem to be set to continue their commitment to modernisation well into the future. The postmodern anxieties of the postindustrial West seem irrelevant to them. (137)

The embracing of modernity is not limited to élites, but rather represents a hope of a better future to most people, even if this wish to join the modern crowd is often expressed in a consumerism of wanting to have a hold on the external emblematic features of modernity (cf. Friedman 1990, Gandoulou 1989, Meyer 1998). That it also goes deeper than that can be seen in the comment that I heard from a woman, of not much education, living in a small village, who – rejecting someone's appellation of a man as being important for having been to Paris – exclaimed "What is Paris? You have to work there just as much as you have to work here, if you work hard in the village, you have everything." She added as an afterthought, "All we lack is development: we need electricity, a paved road, and drinking water." When modernity means the hope of the fulfillment of such basic needs, rejecting modernity is impossible. Though on the level of infrastructure, Africa is behind Europe, it cannot be argued that Africans are not modern. What they do is to straddle the modern (and even the postmodern) and the traditional, sometimes subverting one with the other (Cf. DeBoeck 1996, who shows the ability of both traditional chiefs and the "modern" Mobutu government to mutually subvert each other). This modernity is represented by Europe (and North America) and the attitude of Africans to Europeans or whites is highly ambiguous (cf. Nyamnjoh and Page 2002 for a discussion of young Cameroonians' attitudes to whites). For example, Cameroonians are aware of their colonial past and neocolonial present and see many of the ills of the post-colonial period to be emanating from their continuing (unequal) relationship to Europe. Thus, the attitude is part distrust verging on hate. It is also part admiration and a wish to emulate in order to obtain the emblematic values of Europe (cf. Bashkow 2000, Vigh 2006). Coupled with this is a wish to be recognized by the larger world as actors in their own right and on an equal footing.

THE LEVEL PLAYING FIELD

Bromberger argues that the meritocracy evident in football (that is to say its modernity that he identifies with democracy) can be derailed by the intervention of chance events, so that the better team does not always win. He limits this mostly to what happens on the pitch, while in Cameroon, the way things can go wrong has a much wider scope (see Chapter III). In his view, this is what gives tension to the game because it both symbolizes and humanizes the vagaries of life. This is no doubt true in Cameroon as well, but there is another dimension to the question. The ideal of the level playing field is very seductive. On the one hand, it represents a space where it is possible to do something, to have achievements that are real as opposed to Mbembe's simulacra. On the other hand, in the more conventional sense of the term, it implies that the better team should win, regardless of external realities, i.e. the relative socio-economic and political strength, the symbolic (and real) capital of the participants. Thus, football can be seen as providing an opportunity to invert the actual power relationships reigning in the world. This is a moralizing concept in both of its senses. In the first sense, it is a negation of the postcolonial condition – instead of despair and inability to act – it affirms the possibility and efficacy of action. In the second sense it is also a moralizing concept where virtue (superior ability) is and will be rewarded, and the revenge of the underdog becomes possible, thus providing an opportunity for justice to be done, not just in sport, or football, but in the larger context of the world. The meaning of the level playing field is fraught with contradictions, which is one of the main sources of the tension and excitement of the game. The main contradiction is of course that by positing the "level playing field" in the second sense, it is claimed (consciously or unconsciously) that the game is outside the framework of the everyday, real relations of power. At the same time, the significance and meaning of the game, or of a particular match, or competition, derives precisely from the fact that it is reinserted into this larger framework and gains its significance and meaning from the outside world.

In order to appreciate the significance of football to Cameroonians, we need to understand what it means to its practitioners and fans. During the 1990s, people presented football as a *model for* themselves and their society, and they attributed to it the (mostly imagined) potential to transform their reality, while at the same time in the practice of football, they recreated a *model of* their society which seemed to doom them to failure. By 2006 – under the circumstances of a political stalemate and the non-qualification of the national team for the World Cup of that year – people's attitudes to the sport had shifted considerably. Instead of holding football to be a sacrosanct realm as they did earlier, they collapsed the ideal and the real and were poking fun at both.

FOOTBALL AND IDENTITY CONSTRUCTION

One of the characteristics of football is that it lays bare the fundamental cleavages in a society through the crystallization of identities. I use the plural advisedly because depending on the context, different identities may come to the fore. Unlike most Africanists, I talk about nationalism and ethnicity in conjunction with each other and not as separate issues. Football allows us to examine the phenomena of identity formation and identification on various levels of inclusiveness: from the local, through the regional, national, continental to the global, as part of a continuum. Sports competitions are segmentary in nature, on different levels of the competition the identities being mobilized by the sport can be more or less inclusive, ranging from village to ethnic group to region to nation to continent. Economic conditions (rich–poor), race (black–white), historical circumstances (colonized–colonizer), and current or past political relationships also give rise to intense identifications. These identities are not necessarily exclusive, but rather vary contextually, and more than one of them can be at play at a given moment. It is also clear that these identifications at different levels often do not seem to be contradictory to those people who think them.[9]

In sport sociology, studying the role of football (and other team sports) in the crystallization of identities has become a minor industry. One has a sense of *déjà vu* after reading a dozen of these studies, where sport will either unite or divide people in particular ways, where the sentiments deployed and mobilized follow well-regulated grooves. Football can indeed lead to the crystallization of different sets of identifications according to the level of competition. Although I examine the question of identity formation through football, the point has relevance beyond sports sociologi-

---

9 As Chinua Achebe puts it: "Poor me, you might think, what kind of life can result from the interplay of such an array of forces [referring to the many, contradictory roots of his identity]? Is the poor fellow stretched by competing claims on a painful rack of rival antagonistic identities? I regret I cannot report any intolerable stress or excitement. Perhaps it is my Igbo inheritance which comes to my aid by upholding so insistently the notion of plurality. Where something stands, something else will stand beside it ... Igbo culture teaches the necessity to cope with the impossible and to enjoy it if you can. Which is one other reason perhaps why I can be so excited and so frustrated about being a Nigerian" (quoted in Ranger and Vaughan 1993: 20). At times, of course, identities can become not just contradictory, but calcified into exclusive antagonisms, as in the case of Yugoslavia, or Rwanda, and many other places.

cal concerns. I am more interested in making the point that an awareness of national belonging and the existence of nationalist sentiment (of which football happens to be a very good example) is just as much part of the Cameroonian landscape of ideas as in the case of other nations. This goes against the grain of much of the literature in which Africans tend to be seen as "ethnics" and Westerners (especially Europeans) as "nationalists." One of the few early exceptions to this trend is Ulf Hannerz's (1987) article, in which he calls for acknowledging the existence of particular national cultures within Africa and argues that manifestations of these are most readily found in various forms of popular culture. More recently, in light of the persistence of boundaries despite ethnic pressures to the contrary, Crawford Young (2002) has advocated for a reconsideration of the relevance of the nation on the continent, concluding that "territorial nationalism is surprisingly resilient in Africa" (17), and pointing out that these sentiments are also deeply ingrained in the population at large. But most authors in fact have considered African nationalism in the context of the anticolonial struggle only, and have framed what has since been happening in ethnic terms, very often only making fleeting reference to the fact that there is some kind of "nationalist" notion in the minds of Africans. Significantly for this book, this reference is often made, not surprisingly, in connection with football (on Africa in general cf. Bayart 1993: 248, Fabian 1998: 137-138, Fardon 1996: 142; for Cameroon see for example Fisiy and Goheen 1998: 398).[10]

10 In recent years social scientists have began to pay more attention specifically to sports and football in Africa, although anthropologists who are increasingly interested in popular culture have mostly left sports – including football – alone. The importance of football is also attested to by the recent appearance of Armstrong and Giulianotti's (2004) edited volume on the subject, and the special issue devoted to the sport in the German Africanist journal *Afrika Spectrum* (2006). The discipline most concerned with sports within African studies has been history (Alegi 2004, Deville-Danthu 1998, Fair 1997, 2001, 2004, Martin 1991, 1995, Ranger 1987), most often dealing with the role of sports in imposing the values of the colonizers and the way Africans have in turn made use of sports to contest colonial power. Political scientist, Michael Schatzberg, has devoted several articles to examining football discourses as eminent examples of the coexistence of different kinds of understandings of political causation: scientific/rational, religious/spiritual, and sorcery (cf. Schatzberg 2000, 2001, 2006). The question of the use of "juju" or sorcery in football has been discussed in a pioneering article by Scotch (1961), as well as by Anne Leseth (1997), and Patrick Royer (2002). No doubt because

In the concrete case of football through the medium of radio and television coverage the sport can serve very much the same functions in helping citizens imagine the nation as Benedict Anderson has argued for the novel, or print capitalism. This is also due to the structure of national competitions (encompassing the whole country), and the nature of international or especially world competitions, such as the World Cup (which pit countries, races, continents, and even economic conditions, such as First World vs. Third World, against each other). But in this case, the nation and the world, the global system, are being imagined simultaneously.

MY PLACE IN THE FIELD

No matter how we look at it, I was a curiosity first and foremost, closely watched and never allowed to forget that I was white. Being a woman must also have influenced my work in ways I cannot even imagine. Football in Cameroon is a male sport. This is true even if there is a women's version of the national championship and the Challenge Cup, and there are a handful of female referees and even a few female coaches. (On the varying level of acceptance and reception of women's football in three African societies, see Saavedra 2003.) Women's football does not command much respect, although "hard core" football buffs (the true *sportifs*) will watch female football if there is nothing else on offer. But the highest praise a female player can receive is that "she plays like a boy." Women can be football fans too, but in a limited way. Their support is most evident in their presence at the

---

of the importance of sports to the anti-apartheid struggle, South Africa has garnered the largest number of works on sports in general and football in particular (see among others Alegi 2004, Black and Nauright 1998, Odendaal 2003). Football as part of local level politics in urban or rural milieu or on the level of the nation has been the subject of several studies (Baller 2005, Goerg 2002, Mehler 2006, Ralph 2006, Sarro 1999). Less directly concerned with what happens on the continent itself have been studies of Africa's relationship to FIFA, such as evidenced by Paul Darby's work (2002, 2003, 2005). Sugden and Tomlinson (1998) also devote a separate chapter to the question in their volume on the organization. A new line of inquiry, reflecting a growing trend on the ground, is the interest in the migration and trade of African football players (Bale 2004, Lanfranchi and Taylor 2001, Poli 2006, Poli and Dietschy 2006). Finally, in recent years, a body of work is emerging on the implications of the sport for peace-building, development, and human rights (see for example, Armstrong 2002, 2004a, 2004b, Giulianotti 1999b, 2004, Hognestad and Tollisen 2004, Richards 1997.)

stadium or in front of TV screens in bars when the national team plays, or when there are village level championships, which function somewhat differently from official football. Interestingly, in 1994 when the Indomitable Lions did not do very well at all in the World Cup, and in a program entitled "*Bonjour l'Amérique*" Cameroon Radio and Television (CRTV) opened the airwaves for the public to express its frustration, a surprisingly large number of women contributed. Not only that, many of them expressed some of the strongest statements and opinions. This is why, if someone were to count the number of contributions that I quote from women and compare them to those quoted from men, it would seem that women are almost equally concerned with football as men. This is not so, but the strength of these women's statements, and the depth of their passion often made their remarks more "quotable" than those of men. It seems likely to me that since it *is* unusual for women to be involved in football, if a woman did feel the urge to contribute, it meant that her determination and conviction to have her point heard was much stronger than that of a man.

Many of my contacts came about in a snowball kind of way – I met one person, through him, I met others, through them, I met yet others. Some people understood the importance of my work to be to tell the world how Cameroonians suffer. Many others thought that my work would help improve the lot of Cameroonian football by concrete suggestions. I cannot possibly fulfill all these expectations; at best, I can hope that the end result is going to be recognizable if incomplete.

Others thought that I was there to recruit players, discover talent, and get them a contract in "Europe." Or alternately, I was seen as a possibly useful source of equipment, procurement being a perennial problem in the lives of many a team. [11] I navigated these demands as best I could. Clearly, I had no way of fulfilling the first expectation, though probably there were many people who did not believe me when I said so. The second problem was even greater since in the eyes of everyone, despite being a "poor graduate student," I was objectively (if only comparatively) rich (cf. Geertz 2000,

[11] It is often remarked that football could become so popular in the world precisely because it requires so little equipment and on some level, this is true. However, during my 1994-1995 fieldwork even the necessary minimum for serious play was beyond the means of most Cameroonian teams, or stretched them to their limits. (See Chapter III.)

Nyamnjoh 2005). I did what I could by way of helping, but my efforts were to a large extent insignificant, and mostly limited to my close associates. [12]

In the early 1980s, I did fieldwork in a small eastern Hungarian village on strategies of choosing godparents (Vidacs 1985). One of the most shocking experiences I had early on in my fieldwork then was when one morning at about seven o'clock, or perhaps earlier, I was awakened by a knock on my door. It was my hostess. They were preparing to harvest maize that morning with a group of relatives, friends, and neighbors, and she wanted to get something from a closet in my room. I had already gone with them the previous day, and had other plans for the day. Groggy from sleep, I went to open the door in my nightgown. Besides the familiar figure of my hostess, there were three or four other black-clad women as yet unknown to me. One among them, looking positively demented (as I later found out she was in fact mentally retarded, but I did not know that at the time), jumped on me, as my hostess was marching past resolutely, and kissed me on both cheeks. This done and my hostess having retrieved whatever she had wanted to get, they all retreated, leaving me completely floored. I spent the next couple of hours getting over the shock, the shock of having been inspected, intruded upon, and my privacy invaded at a moment when I was nowhere near prepared for it. Eventually, I concluded that the need to retrieve the item was a mere excuse and the need to wake me and get into the room was dictated by sheer curiosity on the part of the visitors, the wish to look at the exotic guest in her lair. The fact that I was in my nightgown only made it more interesting.

The experience was somewhat akin to what Elenore Smith Bowen (Laura Bohannan) described in *Return to Laughter* when she was mobbed by the market women at the beginning of her fieldwork (Bowen 1964: 18-22). I had already read the book at the time, though I don't remember making an explicit connection, but conscientious fieldworker that I was, in addition to being shocked by the experience, I was in turn equally shocked at being shocked. Eventually, I came to the conclusion that part of the shock was that I was completely unprepared for being the object of curiosity and

[12] During the mid-1990s, the price of a pair of not very good quality football boots ranged between $30 and $50 and a set of jerseys (for 15 players including substitutes) around $1000-1500 in the United States. Football boots get worn out especially fast.

speculation, for being seen as some kind of an "Other." I assumed far more commonality with the villagers than they were willing to grant me. I stayed with a middle-aged, childless couple, and questions as to where I went, what I had done, whom I spoke to, when was I going to get home, were constantly showered on me. My own parents had never subjected me to such inquisition, and I felt the control to be irksome. Even though I was doing fieldwork in what was purportedly my own culture, in fact the dividing lines were surprisingly sharp. One of the main lessons I came away with was that, despite the relative homogeneity of Hungary, it was illusory on my part to have thought that I was doing research in my own culture. I kept expecting it, but I kept finding that it was not so. Obviously, class and urban vs. rural differences loomed large.

I also supposed that had the same experience happened to me in an "African village," I would have expected it, and thus been able to cope with it better. In turn, when I was doing fieldwork in Cameroon I was in a different situation, yet there were similarities. Apart from a few trips to the countryside, I spent the overwhelming majority of my time in Yaoundé, the capital of Cameroon, "hanging out" in a variety of circles, most of which related directly to football. I followed the work of several football teams, attended the matches of an "Old Boys' Club" (commonly known as 2-0), attended international, first, second, and third division matches, casting half-an-eye on women's football as well as on a village championship. There were weeks when apart from training sessions and friendly matches, I easily saw five or six official matches. In this, I was conforming to what the most avid insiders of Cameroonian football do. No match is ever the same, there is always something new to see. In addition, as long as it lasted, I belonged to a loose circle of friends – in the neighborhood where I lived – on a street corner where people gathered every night at a newsvendor's stand. I also had friends in academia and attended the women's group of my host's village association.

The football circles mostly overlapped each other, and after a while, I was known to most people who would be there even if I could not identify all of them. People knew my business, or certainly thought they did. One of my constant problems was that players assumed that I was going to be able to help them get a contract in Europe in a professional club, and I suspect that they thought that my refusal was somehow lack of goodwill on my part. It was difficult to convey the notion that academics have little power and influence in the world of sports. I can only imagine how many people knew me and of me on the streets of Yaoundé; certainly I was familiar to the football players who trained, played, or just simply hung out in the *Omnisports* area (as the neighborhood around the main stadium of Yaoundé is known), those spectators who congregated around any of the third division teams, the administration, and leadership of all these teams, people who worked at the Federation, people who sat in the section of the stadium, where I usually sat with my friend and principal informant, Coach Nguidjol. Still others knew me from my "hanging out" at the newspaper vendors', as did university students, where I typed up my tape recordings, the community of Anglophones with whom I attended the Etoug Ebe Baptist church, taxi drivers, barmen, cigarette vendors, waiters, newspaper vendors, people in my neighborhood, and so on and so forth.

Getting a taxi at certain times of the day in Yaoundé was a next-to impossible task, especially to a neighborhood like the one where I was living, which was quite far away from the center of town and on the way there, the road was very bad in places. One evening when I was waiting interminably for a taxi to take me home, a friend remarked wryly "underdevelopment is bad." When I asked why in particular, he answered, "They refuse to take you because the road is bad, and that is due to underdevelopment." However, quite often, what happened was that after waiting quite hopelessly for a long time, some complete stranger would grab me and push me into a taxi, joining me, naturally, because she or he knew me from the neighborhood and was more adept at grabbing the chance than I was. I was greeted as "*présidente*" (the feminine version of *président*), which, other than "coach" (the English word is the one that is used in "Camfrench") is the most common (often honorific) way to address someone who is involved in football, all over town by people whom I did not seem to know, but who obviously knew me.

During my fieldwork, Yaoundé had approximately one million inhabitants, thus the seemingly huge number of people who knew me was miniscule compared to the number of people who did not. In some respects I was never accepted, I never became completely enmeshed in the social life of the city. Consequently, one of my overwhelming memories of this field-trip, surprisingly similarly to my fieldwork in Hungary, is that of being the "Other." But of course, a Hungarian woman is the "Other" in Africa and in a Hungarian village in very different ways. In both places, I stood out immediately as different. In the Hungarian village, because of the small size of the village, everyone did actually know who I was, even if despite my repeated attempts to explain, many of them never knew quite what I was up to. In Yaoundé, everyone knew that I was a foreigner, white at that, and probably most people's immediate assumption was that I was French. But overwhelmingly, I was identified as "*la blanche*" (whitewoman), this was a label I could not escape, which irked me constantly, and drove home to me day in day out that I was viewed as different, that I was being noticed. It gave me a feeling that I could never just be, that I was always being seen and remarked upon. People who knew me accepted me (although perhaps I flatter myself), but even they could never quite let go of my obvious difference, and used me adroitly as a foil in various discussions about the state of the world, the role of blacks and whites in history, in the present, and in the future. I was constantly drawn into debates, both to chart some kind of a separate place for myself, as other than "*la blanche*," as someone who was not personally responsible for all the misdeeds of whites in history, nor for all of the wondrous inventions of "white science," what Cameroonians half-jokingly refer to as "*la magie des blancs*": as myself, someone with a genuine interest in what was going on in Cameroon. People seemed equally interested in what I had to say. In a world limited by poverty and underdevelopment, I clearly had seen things and been to places that they had only heard about or seen on TV and my stories, my opinions were news, and thus at the very least, entertainment. I tried to explain in vain, I am afraid, that not all was well in the United States, that there was poverty and injustice aplenty there too. That American colonialism, advocated by some friends in a debate as possibly better than what they had known, would be no better than what they were familiar with ... I also overstepped some boundaries, my sheer presence at the stadium, on and near the football pitch being already surprising. As I noted above there are very few women in Cameroonian football and the sport remains an essentially male domain, where women are only admitted grudgingly and have to prove that they love football and know it. As part of the life of *les sportifs,* I entered bars where women should only enter rarely and in the company of men, drank beer very cautiously with men because while they would urge me to drink, they would be the first to be shocked were I to get drunk. (This actually would have been the same in Hungary where it was also almost impossible to refuse a drink, but female drunkenness is frowned upon.)

I fear that I will disappoint most of my informants in that other than recording and interpreting what their life is about, which I hope to be able to do faithfully I am unlikely to come up with practical solutions to their problems. In their view, that is what is needed, but I know what they do not seem to know – that not many people lend an ear to a social scientist – and I am not even likely to be able to come up with a solution.

I worked closely with a third division team, participating rather fully in its life, attending practically all training sessions during a six month period, going as far as (using my feminine skills) cooking meals for the team prior to matches. I also became "honorary member" of and regularly took part in the life of one "Old Boys' Club." Contacts I made through it led to my entry into a village championship, hampered, however, by the fact that I could not speak the language of the village. I conducted my research in French and English, the two official languages of Cameroon. Football brings together people from many ethnic groups and the language used (in the French speaking part of the country) is French. This of course also meant that I could be excluded when people switched to their own language, which did happen from time to time. Had I been able to speak one of the almost 300 Cameroonian languages, I would have done a very different fieldwork, since I would have been automatically identified with the group whose language I spoke, and I too would have inescapably identified with the group. (As things stood I was identified to a greater or lesser degree with the various people I worked with, thus the team I worked with was seen as "my team.") As a result of working in football and in Yaoundé and in the different contexts enumerated above, I came into contact with a variety of people from different ethnic groups, and formed close ties with some of them, and some enduring friendships.

In the course of establishing these friendships and doing my fieldwork, I had occasion to hear people's opinions about tribalism, and heard their complaints and grievances against others in a more varied and "multivocal" way than I would have had had I been closely involved with only one ethnic group. Hearing these grievances, and being the outsider in a multiple kind of way, I could see how they were right, how those expressing them had some just cause against the others. Yet hearing the other side, I could also see their justice, their resentment, coming to the uneasy and ambivalent conclusion that everybody was right and everybody was wrong. I might add that I also heard people explain the justice of the cause of some other tribe or grouping than their own, thus although "tribalist" discourse was alive and well in Cameroon, there were instances where people were able to see the others' point of view. This fact of multiple personal identifications on my part led to the interesting constellation that, unlike anthropologists who work in a more traditional rural setting, I do not have "a" tribe. In other words, my setting, my unit of analysis is Cameroon – not Anglophone Cameroon or Francophone Cameroon, not Bamileke-land, not the Bassa, not the Douala, but the whole of Cameroon. I am talking about Cameroonians in general, their attitudes to football, their opinions about life, the importance attached by them to football and the intertwining of football and politics. Yet my knowledge is grounded in these personal contacts, interviews, observations, and half-caught conversations.

Other sources of my information come from radio and newspaper coverage. *Bonjour l'Amérique*, the call-in radio program originally put in place to garner support for the national team during the 1994 World Cup – when things did not go as well for the Indomitable Lions as people would have wished – became a forum for the expression of people's bitterness and proved to be a gold mine. Cameroon has witnessed the proliferation of newspapers since the beginning of the 1990s, and I rely on these sources too.

As Christian Bromberger (1994b: 282) put it: "... when one attempts to trace football's latent functions one finds multivalent, fluent, and contradictory processes which defy any single or reductive interpretation." Football can be discussed in innumerable ways. What follows is going to be just a few slices of the cake; the totality is so vast, so intricate, and has so many layers that any one analysis can only approximate it at best. Football has many meanings to any one individual, and the meaning also varies from individual to individual. At the same time, certain meanings crystallize in particular ways so that in some instances, I can talk about the consensus of Cameroonians, with the proviso that there are always dissenting voices.

CHAPTER II

"AFRICA IN MINIATURE": CAMEROON IN A NUTSHELL

Cameroon is situated in either Central or West Africa. This statement already indicates the historically determined ambiguities that surround such definitions. The origin of this particular ambiguity is to be found in the country's divergent colonial history. Although the coastal Duala had long-standing relations with the British, Cameroon was first colonized in 1884 by the Germans who concluded treaties with some Duala chiefs, and thus gained a foothold in the area. Following Germany's defeat in World War I, the *Kamerun* colony was divided between Britain and France as a League of Nations Mandate, the larger, eastern, part came under French control, while the smaller, western, part was administered by Britain as part of Nigeria. On the eve of decolonization, the two territories of British Cameroon voted in a plebiscite to decide whether they wished to belong to Cameroon or Nigeria. The southern part of the area voted to be "reunified," and join in a federation with French-speaking Cameroon, the entity known as *La Républlique du Cameroun*. Its inhabitants have retained a separate identity signaled by the term Anglophone. Thus the ambiguity of the geographical positioning of Cameroon can be resolved, if we realize that Anglophones think of their country as being part of West Africa, while Francophones think of it as being part of Central Africa. The significance of this difference is that West Africa, at least in the minds of those who think of Cameroon as properly belonging to that region, signifies English-language use, whereas belonging to Central Africa would, in their eyes, signify French-language use.

"AFRICA IN MINIATURE"

Cameroon is often described by Cameroonians as "Africa in miniature."[1] This is a stock phrase learnt in school, and I heard it on countless occasions. What the term signals is that the country encompasses great geographical, ecological, and cultural variety. From the point of view of ecology, it ranges from the rain forest region in the south through savanna to semiarid and even arid areas in the north. In terms of topography, Cameroon spreads from the Atlantic Ocean to Lake Chad, and boasts of the highest peak of Western and Central Africa (Mount Cameroon), which is an active volcano. High plateaus and hills in the western half of the country provide dramatic vistas and fertile lands on steep slopes. The population and its traditional economic occupations are equally varied and present a variety of "textbook" ecological adaptations within the confines of the country. We can find fisherfolk in the south, hunting–gathering Pygmies in the rain forest; as well as slash-and-burn cultivators in the savannah region; and Bororo cattle-herders in the north. The colonial period left its stamp on the economic activities of Cameroon's peoples. In addition to small-scale agriculture (which produces the main export crops of the country: bananas, coffee, and cocoa), there are large-scale estates of tea, rubber, palm oil, and cotton, especially in the west and north. Political systems comprise almost all known forms of political organization from bands through acephalous kin-ordered societies to highly hierarchical kingdoms, all of which intermingle with the structures of the modern state. Islam and Christianity, in addition to traditional religions, are also present and structure the social relations of modern Cameroon.

Cameroon's triple colonial history (Germans (1884-1916), French, and English (1916-1960/1961)) divides and unites its peoples in complex ways. The reader should keep in mind these multiple divisions and crosscutting experiences. In the following account, I will be referring to Cameroon's regions by the names of its ten provinces (which came into being in 1983, superseding what were six provinces): Extreme (or in some translations Far) North, Adamawa, North, North-west, South-west, Littoral, West, Center, South, and East. The first three constitute what sometimes is referred to

[1] Interestingly, the same metaphor was used by the 19th century Hungarian geographer János Csaplovics (1822), when he characterized his country as "Hungary is Europe in miniature." I thank Mihály Sárkány for calling my attention to this.

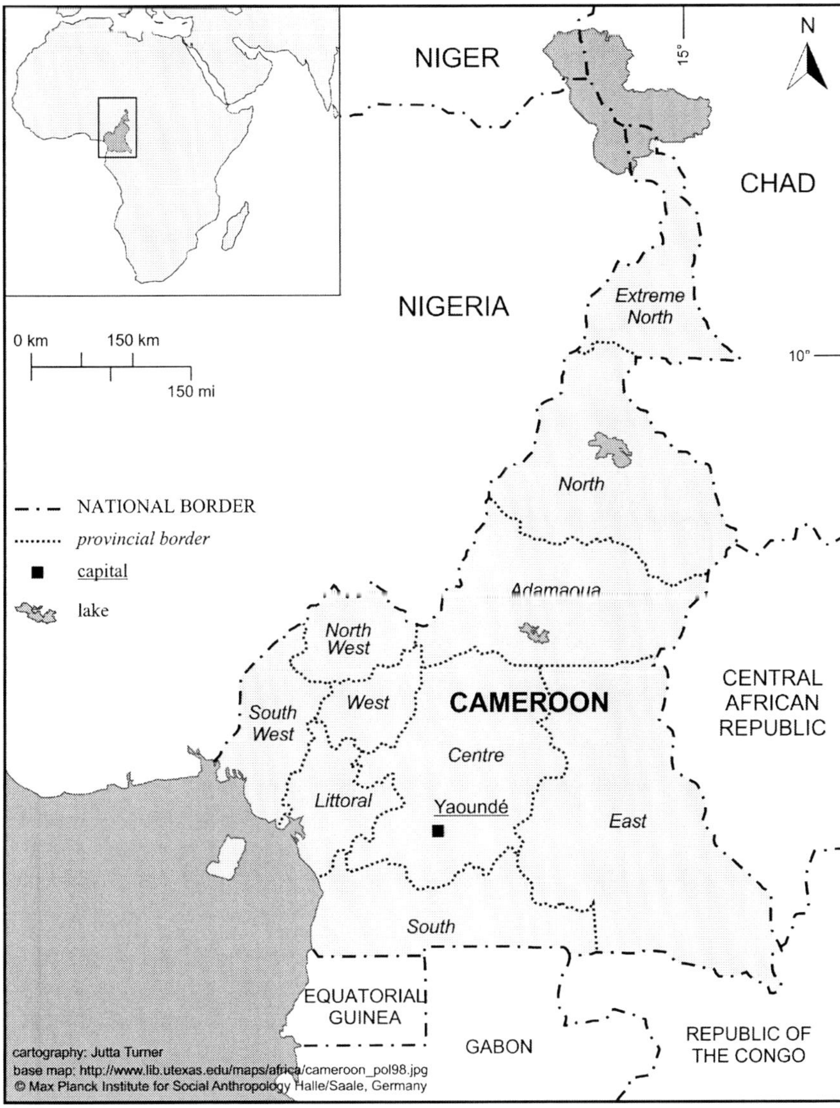

NIGER
CHAD
NIGERIA
15°
N
10°
0 km
150 km
150 mi
Extreme North
North
Adamaoua
North West
West
South West
CAMEROON
Centre
Littoral
Yaoundé
East
South
CENTRAL AFRICAN REPUBLIC
EQUATORIAL GUINEA
GABON
REPUBLIC OF THE CONGO
NATIONAL BORDER
provincial border
capital
lake
cartography: Jutta Turner
base map: http://www.lib.utexas.edu/maps/africa/cameroon_pol98.jpg
© Max Planck Institute for Social Anthropology Halle/Saale, Germany

as the Grand North (*Grand Nord*), and this is the Muslim area. However, not all of the population in the north follows Islam, and there are Muslims to be found in other regions as well in part because of recent migrations and in part because Islam had exerted its influence on various chiefdoms in earlier times too.

The North-west and the South-west provinces are the areas which had been under British control after the end of the German colonial period, and as a result, their population is English-speaking. This area sometimes is referred to as Southern Cameroon, because it was the southern part of the British-controlled territory. The same area is sometimes referred to in the literature as Western Cameroon, especially between 1961 and 1972, when the former British and French parts of the country were reunited into a federated state, the constituents of which were referred to as Western and Eastern Cameroon, respectively. Due to these historical complications, the territory comprising the West Province is in fact to the east of the North- and South-west provinces. The North-west province and the West Province together comprise most of what is known as the Cameroon Grassfields, which is a cultural area where similar hierarchical kingdoms have been arbitrarily divided by English and French language use. To facilitate the task of the reader, and because the names of the provinces do not correspond to self-evident geographical categories, I attach a map of Cameroon.

Cameroon's ever increasing population stood at about 18.5 million in 2008. During the 1994 World Cup, journalists spoke of eleven million "breathing as one" in their support of the national team. In 1998, when a similar reference spoke of thirteen million, a man listening to the broadcast on the street exclaimed: "So, we are 13 million now!" In 1976, the population was officially stated to be 7,663,246 while in 1987, it was 10,493,655. According to a 1993 publication of the Ministry of Planning and Territorial Management (*Ministère du plan et de l'Aménagement du Territoire*), which provides figures by province, in 1987 a little more than 40 percent (4,206,575) of the population lived in the three northern provinces (the former *Grand Nord*), while about 20 percent (2,075,390) resided in the two "Anglophone" provinces. There is a rough correspondence between ethnic belonging and province, but these numbers can only serve as approximate guidelines to ethnic distribution in Cameroon.

Apart from the fact that statistical figures are often incorrect and easily open to manipulation (for example Anglophones will claim that they comprise 25 instead of 20 percent of the overall population), we have to keep in mind that considerable population movement has characterized Cameroon since colonial days and before, and settlers and traders, as well as civil servants originating from different regions can be found almost everywhere. To mention just the most obvious examples, due to land shortage at home, many Bamileke (West Province) have fanned out to different regions of the country, where they may have been established for several generations (Joseph 1977, Malaquais 2002, Socpa 2003). The same is true of the two major cities of Cameroon, Yaoundé and Douala, whose inhabitants considerably boost the population size of their respective provinces, Center and Littoral, comprising some three million people. However, these cities have an ethnically mixed population, which in recent years has led to claims and counterclaims of belonging and exclusion (cf. Ceuppens and Geschiere 2005, Eyoh 2004, Geschiere and Jackson 2006, Geschiere and Nyamnjoh 2000). According to the same publication, the rate of urbanization in Cameroon rose from 28.5 percent to 37.8 percent between 1976 and 1987; by 2008 it reached 57%.[2] This is significant because football is essentially an urban phenomenon. It is also important to recognize that a far greater number of people than indicated by these figures are likely to have been exposed to city life, as people move back and forth between urban and rural areas with great regularity both on a temporary and permanent or semi-permanent basis.

THE ETHNIC PICTURE

As can be gathered from the foregoing, like most African countries, Cameroon is multiethnic. It has become a truism of anthropology that "tribes" and "ethnic groups" are very much the result of manipulation. The pre-colonial "tribal" flux was in many ways altered by colonial rule, tending to freeze otherwise fluid relationships between groups, bringing into

---

[2] The figures are taken from the 2008 World Population Data Sheet of the Population Reference Bureau. By comparison, the Central African region has a 41 percent rate, while Europe a 71 percent rate, and Central America a 70 percent rate. See www.prb.org/pdf08/08WorldDataSheet.pdf (accessed August 2, 2009).

existence groups that had not existed before and at times privileging certain ones among them (cf. Berman 1998, Lentz 1995, 2000, Ranger 1983, 1993, Southall 1970, for Cameroon cf. Eyoh 2004, Geschiere 1996, Monga, Y.D. 2000, 2001). The subsequent juggling for power within the newly created post-colonial states has led to different constellations of the reorganization of ethnic loyalties. What is clear is that the fluid and changing nature of ethnic categories has not stopped, and newer and newer redefinitions of various groups continue. In fact, Geschiere and Nyamnjoh (2000) argue that the more recent autochthony-allogeny discourses are vaguer and more open to manipulation than earlier ethnic categories.

For Cameroon, it is generally claimed that the country has nearly three hundred ethnic groups, based on language use, although it is not very clear how many of these are separate languages and how valid this division really is.[3] In the following discussion, I will concentrate only on some of the main groups that are important from the point of view of my discussion of the political realities of the country and of football. As mentioned above, one of the main cleavages in Cameroon is between Anglophone and Francophone. There are also significant differences between Muslim North and Christian South, although these categories often hide more differences than they highlight.

The categories of Anglophone and Francophone are not quite comparable, even if they both denote colonial heritage in language use. The term Anglophone is used in Cameroon for a variety of peoples who have undergone one particular form of colonization. But obeying the rules of minority/majority relations, while Anglophones are highly conscious of their identity as English speakers (the connotations of which will become clearer as we go along), Francophones seldom employ French language use (also the result of colonization) as a rallying point or point of self-reference. To a great degree – and despite the official policy of French–English bilingualism – since French is the majority language, its speakers remain unmarked,

---

3 Estimates of the number of ethnic groups in Cameroon vary, their number is often put between 200 and 250, practically every source giving a slightly different number. With regard to the difficulties of giving a precise number see, LeVine 1971: xx–xxi. The Summer Institute of Linguistics lists 286 languages for Cameroon ("278 are living languages, 3 are second languages without mother-tongue speakers, and 5 have no known speakers"). See Lewis 2009.

their majority status being signaled by this very lack (Konings and Nyamnjoh 2003, Wolf 1997, 2001).

A. H. M. Kirk-Greene (1980) has argued that due to the small number of colonizers actually on the ground, in some ways, colonial presence was insignificant in the everyday experience of the vast majority of Africans. The Cameroonian case, however, demonstrates that apart from larger, well-known changes in the economic orientation and power structure of African societies associated with colonialism, on the level of everyday practices, different colonial cultures meant significant differences in lifestyles and attitudes. Thus for example, in Cameroon the difference between English speakers and French speakers goes well beyond language use. In the everyday practices of people's lives, there are real and imagined differences between the two populations. The differences function as ethnic rather than purely linguistic markers, especially as far as English speakers are concerned. In daily life, these differences range from a different educational system, through a different legal system, to practices such as eating a different kind of bread (square loaf vs. baguette).

Political philosophy is another area where the two colonial powers left their mark on Cameroon. Joseph Takougang and Milton Krieger (1998) argue (and they would be in agreement by and large with Mazrui and Tidy's (1984) discussion of the different kinds of consequences of British and French colonization) that some of the division between Francophones and Anglophones comes from a different conception of the role or rather the nature of the state (see also Mazrui 1983). That is to say, Francophones (in keeping with received French notions of centralization) prefer a much more centralized state, whereas Anglophones favor decentralization. To these very real differences, we should add Cameroon's post-independence political history (discussed later) where the Anglophone minority has suffered a number of political setbacks, thus compounding their sense of separateness and difference. (There are political differences, as opposed to philosophical ones, as well, since clearly decentralization would also enable Anglophones to regain some of their lost autonomy vis-à-vis their Francophone compatriots; cf. Eko 2003, Eyoh 2004, Konings 1996, 2004, Konings and Nyamnjoh 2003, 2004, Mbuagbo 2002, Takougang 2003.)

An important feature of the division according to language is that a whole plethora of groups get lumped together under the heading of Anglophone, and the internal identity of these groups is rarely scrutinized. Francophones do not acknowledge the internal sub-units of the group known as Anglophone because they "don't care," and being in the majority, do not know much about their Anglophone compatriots. Anglophones, because they see themselves as being disenfranchised and marginalized, do not question it either.

However, since the mid-1990s, some cracks have developed in Anglophone unity along the fault lines of the two provinces, they inhabit, reflecting differences in economic and political history, as well as cultural makeup, and the success of the Biya government in driving a wedge between the two provinces. The 1996 appointment of Peter Mafany Musonge from the South-west Province as prime minister in the place of Simon Achidi Achu from the North-west Province was seen as evidence of this by most commentators (cf. Eyoh 1998b, 1998c, 2004, Konings 2004, Mbuagbo and Akoko 2004, Nyamnjoh and Rowlands 1998, Takougang 2003, Takougang and Krieger 1998). The other factor is that the northern part of Anglophone area is culturally part of the Cameroon Grassfields with its fairly distinct set of cultural characteristics, encompassing the Francophone Bamileke, yet there are many ways in which the Bamileke and the Anglophone groups are being distanced from each other. In the eyes of non-involved Cameroonians, during the 1990s, one common insult to be hurled at these groups was to call them "Anglo-Bami." Anglophones, together with many other Cameroonians, dislike and resent the Bamileke, while the Francophone Bamileke do not see much of a commonality with Anglophones at all.

The Bamileke who occupy the Western Province of Cameroon constitute a significant group in the country in their own right (cf. Hurault 1962, Tardits 1962, Warnier 1984). Like many other ethnic groups in Africa, the Bamileke have been constructed as an entity as a result of colonization (cf. Geschiere (1996) for a discussion of the constructed nature of the Bamileke as a group). The term Bamileke unites a large number of groups, who live in highly hierarchical societies. However, these are fairly independent units, which do not constitute a centralized whole, all the more so as there are language differences between them. It is also important to recall that since the beginning of the colonial period, the Bamileke have been migrating to other parts of the country, seeking to escape land shortage at home, and to settle as cultivators and traders all over Cameroon. They are considered to be the most economically dynamic group in Cameroon, and are widely thought to be dominating the economy. This is resented by many, and they are often constructed as the enemy within the ethno-political landscape of the nation. This has repercussions in football as well. With the economic crisis of the late 1980s and early 1990s, Cameroonian football witnessed a remarkable rise in the number of Bamileke teams in the First Division. In addition, as the Bamileke were being marginalized in the political domain, they began to derive increasing satisfaction from this prominence in the domain of football. On the national level, however, this expansion of Bamileke teams has led to a diminished supporter base for those Bamileke teams that earlier stood for the entire region, especially *Racing de Bafoussam*, which in 2006 descended into the Second Division.

The advent of multiparty politics during the early 1990s has exacerbated the problem. As many Bamileke gravitated toward the main opposition party, the Social Democratic Front (SDF), they became more and more openly pitted against the Beti of the southern region (Center and South Provinces) from which Paul Biya, the president, hails. As Eyoh (2004: 104) argues, "[a]cross the nation, including the domains of opposition, political competition came to be increasingly framed as contests over local citizenship and rights to political representation." In effect, what this means is that the local (autochthonous) population questions the right of "strangers" (allogenes) to participate in the life of the locality, especially when it comes to fielding candidates for political office. The Biya regime encouraged these tendencies in order to break the opposition's hold over the popular imagination. The 1996 constitution, in a drastic departure from earlier attempts at nation-building, codified these ideas, by protecting the "indigenous" population against encroachment by outsiders (cf. Geschiere and Nyamnjoh 2000, Jua 2001, 2004, Monga, Y.D. 2001, Socpa 2003, 2006).

The Beti as a group are of even more recent origin, consisting of ethnic groups which until recently were seen as separate entities (Bulu, Ewondo, Eton, Etoudi, etc.) and the term Beti was a linguistic term, describing the interrelated languages of these various groups. Some of their representatives are among the autochthonous inhabitants of Yaoundé, the capital of Cameroon. Their emergence under the collective name Beti dates to the 1982 rise to power of Paul Biya, who is a Bulu. In recent years, the Biya regime has increasingly tried to put more and more administrative power into Beti hands (to counter what is seen as Bamileke economic dominance), and in the ethnic charges and countercharges that are now rife in Cameroon, both groups accuse each other of ruining the country.

The Bamileke see the Beti as lazy and using their closeness to power to enrich themselves at the expense of the country, while the Beti accuse the Bamileke of likewise enriching themselves and selfishly promoting their own interests. In response, the Beti often point out that not all of them by far benefit from the Biya regime (cf. Anonymous 1998, *Collectif Changer le Cameroun* 1992, Ondoa-Etoa 1994). The relationship of the two groups has become more and more bitterly antagonistic since the beginning of multipartyism in Cameroon, a trend that Geschiere (1996) following Lonsdale (1992) has characterized as "political tribalism."

The Bamileke have also migrated in great numbers to the port city of Douala, which is the economic capital of the country. Although numerically insignificant, the Duala people were the first to be in contact with Europeans.[4] They concluded the first treaties with the German colonizers (and even earlier with the British), and for a while controlled trade and other relations with whites. As gatekeepers, the Duala both benefited from close contact with Europeans and suffered the first negative consequences of colonialism (cf. Austen and Derrick 1999, Joseph 1977). According to Lynn Schler (2005), Douala has been multiethnic from the start of the colonial period because, being the economic capital of Cameroon it attracted a large number of immigrants. Thus already by 1930, the Duala became a minority in the city (Schler 2005: 96-97). The town has long been considered the seat of popular political discontent in the country, and it is regarded by many as the most politically radical of Cameroonian cities. This was the case at least until the 1990s, when the Anglophone town of Bamenda (the provincial capital of the North-west Province) became the epicenter of popular challenges to the government.

4 According to Richard Joseph's (1977: 15) estimate, they numbered "a mere 45,000," but Yvette Monga (2001: 205) claims that they had never numbered more than 20,000.

Since the mid-1990s, the Duala have been the driving force behind the Sawa movement (People of the Water), which unites them with several other groups from the coastal area, and even cuts across the Anglophone–Francophone divide by incorporating peoples from the Anglophone Southwest Province. Yvette Monga (2001) argues that the Duala elite has taken this road to offset their numerical disadvantage and regain their waning political influence, but at the same time, they have to carefully negotiate with other members of the group lest the latter leave the "coalition" and choose to emphasize their particular identities. The main effect of the movement seems to be to prevent the Bamileke and other migrants from gaining political prominence in the area. It is part of the recent growth of autochthony discourses in Cameroon. As mentioned earlier, this discourse has also been encouraged by the government especially with the provisions of the 1996 Constitution, which – adroitly and cynically using the discourse of human rights and indigenous rights – grants preferential rights to the autochthonous population. Especially prominent has been the question of whether people can stand as political candidates and participate in the electoral process, if they are not "sons of the soil" in a given area. Monga and other authors (Geschiere and Nyamnjoh 2000, Konings 2004: 302, Vubo 2006) maintain that the government has encouraged the rise of such an overarching Sawa identity for political ends of its own.

Another important cleavage in Cameroon is between the Muslim North and the Christian South. The northern areas of Cameroon were overrun by the Fulbe (sing. Fulani) as part of the Islamic jihad led by Uthman dan Fodio, from present-day Nigeria in the early part of the nineteenth century. In the general upheaval of those times, the Fulbe managed to conquer the area and to establish semi-independent *lamidates*, which owed allegiance to Yola, and ultimately the Sokoto Caliphate, both in present-day Nigeria (Azarya 1978, Fardon 1988, Mohammadou 1988). The autochthonous peoples of the area were either conquered and became incorporated into the *lamidates* as more or less slaves or escaped to mountainous areas, and were thus able to hold onto their independence. During and even after the colonial period, these peoples were forced to abandon their strongholds and have been gradually incorporated into the *lamidates*, which more often than not meant their conversion to Islam and their taking on a Fulbe identity.

Thus colonial domination had the effect of extending the power of the Fulbe over groups that up until then had managed to remain independent (Bayart 1985: 26). The non-converted, non-Fulbe population is referred to as Kirdi, which means pagan, clearly a stigmatizing label, which at the same time encompasses a wide variety of culturally distinct groups (Burnham 1972, 1996, Gausset 1999, Regis 2003, Schultz 1984). As a result of Ahmadou Ahidjo's rise to power as the first president of Cameroon, his native region, the North, achieved great political significance in the first two decades after independence which also facilitated the process of fulbeization. Following the end of Ahidjo's rule, the pressures for the Islamization of the Kirdi population have decreased (cf. Gausset 1999, Schilder 1994, 1997, van Santen 1997). Due to their demographic weight, northerners remain an important bloc of the Cameroonian political landscape. [5]

COMPARATIVE COLONIAL ASSESSMENTS: THE GERMANS AND THE FRENCH IN CAMEROON

The first phase of German colonialism, like the first phase of all colonial conquests, was bloody, especially as there was vigorous resistance in various parts of the territory (cf. Joseph 1977: 31-38, Lobé 1977, Mbono Samba Azan 1976). The overall assessment of the German colonial period is contradictory. Besides the essentially violent nature of the conquest, the Germans are seen, both by Cameroonian and foreign scholars, as well as by Cameroonian public opinion, to have done quite a lot in a relatively short time. In terms of infrastructure, they established plantations, built roads, schools, hospitals, and churches, many of which still stand today. As Cameroonians had an opportunity to experience French as well as British colonialism following the Germans, there developed a kind of

[5] Interestingly, in current Cameroonian parlance, the Northerners are often dubbed Hausa (the dominant and culturally similar population of Northern Nigeria), which is a misnomer. Another noteworthy factor is that the flowing, embroidered robes of the Fulbe aristocracy are becoming one of the "national" costumes of Cameroon, in as much as people of all ethnic backgrounds, if they can afford them, are likely to wear them, especially, on festive occasions. In fact, less richly embroidered versions, using less material, can be seen on poorer people as well, on ordinary occasions. Thus, these robes which used to be exclusive markers of Fulani, Northern, or Muslim status, no longer serve as such.

comparative colonial assessment according to which, the Germans were better than the French. As Victor T. LeVine (1964: 37) puts it, "... for many Cameroonians, the Germans shone in the distorted light of retrospection; their administration seemed that much the better for being past, and hence that much more available for disparaging comparisons with the current regime." The regime LeVine refers to is French colonialism, and he is alluding to Cameroonian complaints about French rule. However, more than thirty years after LeVine wrote these words and thirty-five years after the official end of French rule, in 1995, I still heard many comparisons favoring the Germans over the French. One of my friends, a carpenter, remarked one day that if a German comes to Cameroon even for a year, he will buy proper furniture, whereas a Frenchman may spend several years in the country and still only invest in (much cheaper) bamboo furniture. He then added, "You just have to look around, the Germans built everything while they were here, but what did the French build? Nothing!" His words are borne out by Joseph (1977: 21), who points out that until after the Second World War the French added very little to the already existing (German-built) infrastructure of Cameroon. The same sentiments continued to crop up in 2006 as well, thus this assessment of the Germans can be seen as part of Cameroonians' common font of knowledge about their country.

We also have to realize, however, that apart from divisions, this history also helped to create a sense of national consciousness among Cameroonians. The "original" German Protectorate of Kamerun served as the basis for proto-nationalist and nationalist aspirations during the French era, providing not only a comparative perspective for Cameroonians, but also a unit to which to aspire. As Joseph argues:

> The thirty years of German rule in the Cameroons, 1884 to 1914, were of fundamental significance in the emergence of Cameroun – or *Kamerun* – nationalism. The very fact that the Cameroons were once ruled by a people other than the French was a prima facie argument against the permanency of French rule. This notion took concrete form in the resuscitation of the German name *Kamerun* for 'Cameroons' during the years of the nationalist struggle for independence and reunification. (Joseph 1977: 20)

Cameroonians who escaped from the harshness of French rule often fled to British Cameroons and Joseph also remarks that some of these "were later to constitute a core of activists demanding unification of the two Cameroons as a means of freeing the French sector from French rule" (Joseph 1977: 29, see also Ardener 1996, Takougang 2005).

THE POST-WAR RISE OF NATIONALISM AND THE CREATION OF INDEPENDENT CAMEROON

After World War II, the French allowed greater political autonomy in Cameroon, including the creation of a large number of political parties and trade unions. Cameroonian delegates were elected to the French Assembly for the first time (although on the basis of a very limited franchise), and a Cameroonian Territorial Assembly was also established. Despite these concessions by the French, the post-war period saw a rise in nationalism, as elsewhere in Africa, which culminated in the *Union des Populations Camerounaises* (UPC) rebellion, led by Reuben Um Nyobe. Although the UPC grew out of trade unionism and had Marxist overtones, it was a genuinely nationalist movement spearheaded predominantly by members of the Bassa ethnic group. The UPC pushed for independence and unification (or in Cameroonian parlance reunification) with British Cameroons at the same time. The Bassa people in the south-western area of the country live along the Sanaga River Valley. Although, due to the activities of the American Presbyterian Mission they had a high level of education, they suffered some of the worst ravages of colonialism. According to Joseph, they resisted unsuccessfully the German penetration and when the Germans began constructing the *Mittelkamerun* railway through their area, the worst excesses of forced labor affected the local population. During the First World War, the area was part of a war zone for two years. After the war, when the French resumed the building of the railway that the Germans had begun, their experiences again were among the harshest in the territory. Eventually, the Bassa's economic survival was threatened by the decreasing importance of their main product, palm oil and palm nuts. No wonder then that the Bassa became the main force of the post-World War II anti-colonial struggle and the leaders of the UPC rebellion.

The banning and suppression of the UPC in 1956 led to an armed guerilla war. Um Nyobe died in the *maquis* (underground) in 1958, most likely betrayed by one of his close associates. His body has never been recovered. Following his death, the struggle was continued mostly by the Bamileke wing of the UPC, which was first suppressed bloodily by the French, and then, following independence, by Cameroon's first president Ahmadou Ahidjo and his government.

The memory of the UPC rebellion and its bloody suppression has left indelible marks in Cameroonian popular memory, and it could be argued that the trauma of those times has acted to prevent the appearance of further armed conflict in the country (cf. Bayart 1985). At the same time, both Joseph and Bayart, as well as Mbembe (1986), have argued that because of the derailing of the UPC rebellion, all subsequent Cameroonian governments have lacked legitimacy at least in the eyes of part of the population. Mbembe, in an especially insightful analysis of folklore relating to Um Nyobe among the Bassa, has shown that, at least in the eyes of the Bassa, as long as the body of Um Nyobe has not been properly buried, there is no possibility of reconciliation.

Ahmadou Ahidjo, a northerner, but not of aristocratic background, rose to be the prime minister as a compromise candidate in 1958, and he was seen by many as an insignificant character, probably to be replaced soon. Ahidjo turned out to be an astute politician who managed to unify the country by creating, as Bayart (1985) calls it, a hegemonic alliance, at the same time neutralizing the opposition of traditional rulers and appeasing most of the radical elements. It was under his rule that the country became independent in 1960, and the following year, after the plebiscite held in the British Trust Territory of the former Kamerun, he presided over the reunification of Southern Cameroon (the northern part having voted to remain in Nigeria) and Cameroun, creating a Federal Republic, thus fulfilling (and co-opting) one of the cardinal demands of the nationalist movement.

AHMADOU AHIDJO AND HIS LEGACY

As Ahidjo consolidated his power, his rule became more and more autocratic, and the UPC movement, which by now had deteriorated into a desperate guerrilla war waged mostly on Bamileke territory, was bloodily suppressed. Ahidjo also created the *Union Camerounaise* (later *Union Nationale Camerounaise*), which then ruled the country in a one-party system. All political dissent was clamped down on, very often in the name of national unity. The connection between the two was such that Bayart views "national unity" as a guise for political oppression (cf. Bayart 1978, 1985, 1986). Sport was also pressed into service in the creation of this national unity (cf. Mokeba 1989, Nketcha 1990/1991), slogans and newspaper commentary pointed to the need for interethnic co-operation in sport, and by extension in the country in general. In 1970, the then minister of Youth and Sports, Michel Njiensi, tried to reorganize football by decree on a non-tribal basis; disbanding teams, reducing their numbers, and regrouping them according to administrative districts within the towns of Douala and Yaoundé. The attempt caused such a public outcry that President Ahidjo, who was absent when the decree was issued, reversed it upon his return to the country (cf. Bayart 1973: 128, Ntonfo 1994a: 63-67). Following this, the minister was dismissed and imprisoned without trial for a year. Ntonfo (1994a) remarks wryly that "the Minister found out at his own expense that the official discourse was not made to be put into practice" (66).

While all Cameroonians agree that Ahidjo ruled with an iron hand and that political oppression was ever present in the country during his rule, the propaganda and slogans of the time actually resonated among the population. Thus one of the stock phrases Cameroonians are apt to use, not surprisingly in connection with football, is "*l'impossible n'est pas camerounais*" (the impossible is not Cameroonian, that is to say, nothing is impossible for Cameroonians), which is attributed to Ahidjo. This defiant phrase which clearly serves to urge people to overcome difficulties, at the same time treats Cameroon the country as an unquestionable unit, where the attitude of defiance applies to each and every person without regard to ethnic origin. Everybody is Cameroonian. Another oft-cited recurring slogan is Ahidjo's insistence on "*l'autosuffisance alimentaire*" (food self-sufficiency), which again acts as a defining feature of Cameroonian identity, indicating that they are capable of providing for their most basic needs through their own labor and without foreign interference. In fact, in recent years with the continuing economic crisis, and the political disillusionment in President Biya, there has been something of a nostalgia for Ahidjo's times, often expressed in quoting these slogans and expounding on their wisdom.

The Ahidjo regime's economic policies were rather astute and ensured that throughout his reign Cameroon counted among the most reliable African countries, where the growth of the economy was at a steady pace of 6-7 percent. As Mbembe and Roitman (1995) explain, this fact contributed to a sense of Cameroonian self-definition according to which, people had a clear vision of the future where their living standards were supposed to rise, and there was a sense of movement forward. Thus part of the nostalgia for Ahidjo's regime is not only nostalgia for a sense of order which is characteristic of many truly oppressive regimes, but also for this (both real and potential) prosperity experienced during his time and for this sense of progression toward a better future. When the economic crisis hit Cameroon in 1987, according to Konings (2004: 290), people were apt to blame the Biya regime for it.

One of the major events of Ahidjo's regime was the dismantling of the federal system and the creation thereby of a unitary republic. This took place in 1972, and to this day it is seen by Anglophones as a betrayal as it significantly weakened their autonomy and continues to be a thorn in their side. Despite being a measure to "unify" the country, it has exacerbated the division between Anglophones and Francophones and created an abiding sense of alienation in Anglophones. The Anglophone complaints range from economic underdevelopment, through discrimination based on language use to political exclusion. "Reunification" and the hastily organized plebiscite that preceded it reinforced Anglophone perceptions that they were being recolonized all over again. Especially after 1990, these grievances have become much more pronounced and gained a voice with the political liberalization that took place following the introduction of multiparty politics discussed later (cf. Eyoh 1998a, 1998b, 2004, Konings 1996, Konings and Nyamnjoh 2003, 2004, Nyamnjoh and Rowlands 1998, Takougang and Krieger 1998).

In a surprise move, quite unique in Africa, President Ahmadou Ahidjo announced his retirement from power in 1982. In 1975, Ahidjo had restored the position of prime minister, a post held by Paul Biya, a Bulu, from the

South Province and as constitutionally foreseen it was he who stepped into Ahidjo's shoes.[6]

THE BEGINNINGS OF THE BIYA-ERA

Biya first had to stabilize his power and to mark himself as different from his predecessor. Although he first appeared as a reformer, over time his rule became increasingly autocratic. His initial promises of liberalization came to nothing, although individual freedoms increased somewhat and such measures, as for example, allowing multiple candidates in elections, were welcome and helped him consolidate his power.

Biya had re-formed the ruling party under a new name (from *Union Nationale Camerounaise*/Cameroon National Union (UNC/CNU) to *Rassemblement Démocratique du Peuple Camerounais*/Cameroon People's Democratic Movement (RDPC/CPDM)) and propagated new slogans. His "New Deal" program was to bring political liberalization and social and economic improvement to Cameroon and called for "rigor, moralization, and integrity" in public life. He claimed that the country had moved to a new level of national unity, from the slogan of "national unity" of the Ahidjo era, to that of "national integration."

The Ahidjo regime had played a careful game of ethnic balancing in most appointments, although even that system has had its critics. Thus for example, in post-facto analysis, Ndiva Kofele-Kale (1986) criticizes Ahidjo's policies of patronage of certain members of certain ethnic groups as having led to the politicization of ethnicity. Subsequently, several authors have argued that the appearance of ferocious ethnic competition and enmity in Cameroon since the 1990s has its origins in the policies of the Ahidjo

6 There has been quite a lot of speculation about Ahidjo's motivations in stepping down all the more, so as he quickly seemed to have changed his mind. He is supposed to have influenced the hatching of two aborted coup attempts against Biya (Bayart 1989, DeLancey 1989, LeVine 1986). The first of these significantly happened at the final of the Cameroon Challenge Cup, in June 1983; and the second, a plot by northern military officers, on April 6, 1984. These events, apart from an extensive clamp-down on northern elements in the higher circles of power, seem to have substantially influenced Biya's attitudes, and according to Takougang and Krieger, may have been at the root of his growing tendency to surround himself with a circle of trusted fellow-Betis (albeit in the extended sense of the term).

regime (for a detailed analysis, cf. Eyoh 2004, Takougang 2003). Although the Biya regime's ethnic policies continued the trend of co-opting elites from each region of Cameroon, Biya's rule has been increasingly marked by the passing of real power into what is seen as Beti hands (Anonymous 1998, *Collectif Changer le Cameroun* 1994, Derrick 1992, Eyoh 1998b and c, 2004, Jua 1993, Krieger 1994: 607-608, LeVine 1986, Takougang 1993: 95-97). In retrospect most analysts think that the Ahidjo regime was genuinely trying to create national unity, whereas the Biya regime's policies, especially the 1996 Constitution, promote local interests at the expense of those of the nation. The fostering of ethnic competition and discord is seen as one of the president's maneuvers to consolidate his power, following the political upheavals of the early 1990s (Geschiere and Nyamnjoh 2000, Jua 2005, Konings 2004, Monga, Y.D. 2001, Takougang 2003).[7]

Meanwhile from about 1987, the economic prospects of Cameroon have deteriorated due to a combination of factors. According to Takougang and Krieger, in addition to a decline in oil revenue, there was a fall in export crop prices which was made even worse by a decline in agricultural production due to drought. Capital flight coupled with corruption rounds off the picture. Under the Biya regime, corruption worsened and this began practically at the outset. The government tried to introduce austerity measures, but to no avail, and in 1988, the Cameroonian Government was forced to turn to the World Bank and the International Monetary Fund (IMF). The implementation of Structural Adjustment Programs only made the lot of ordinary people even more difficult. During the early 1990s, civil servants' salaries were drastically reduced and as the crisis deepened, the government withheld several months' salaries to be paid at a later point, in some cases several years later.

MULTIPARTY POLITICS DURING THE 1990S

1990 saw the rise of multiparty politics in Cameroon. Contrary to what the Biya government claimed, the move for multipartyism rose out of popular

[7] Cf. also the special issue of the opposition newspaper *Le Messager* on the occasion of the twenty-third anniversary of Paul Biya's rise to power, which compares the achievements of the two regimes, concluding on the whole that the Biya regime's accomplishments lag behind those of his predecessor (Dossier, *Le Messager*, November 7, 2005).

resistance, and the government only served to rubber stamp what was already happening on the ground. This was in concert with demands for "democratization" elsewhere in Africa and fitted into the larger context of the end of the Cold War. Ordinary citizens (not just intellectuals), emboldened by the fall of the oppressive regimes of Eastern Europe and the release of Nelson Mandela, demanded greater democracy at home, while at the same time Western powers began to pressure African governments in the same direction (cf. Chabal 1996, Joseph 1999, Konings 2004).

In Cameroon, the first signals of something new emerging came out of Bamenda, the capital of the Anglophone North-west Province, where the first (and it turned out main) opposition party, the SDF, was formed in May 1990 by John Fru Ndi. It is often claimed by his detractors that Fru Ndi was an insignificant bookseller prior to his rise to eminence. However, he had been the leader of the Executive of PWD Bamenda, the most important Anglophone football team, which has consistently, if not entirely steadily, maintained a presence in the First Division of Cameroon's National Championship. The team carries the hopes and aspirations of most Anglophones (cf. Mokeba 1989: 126-131, 225). Prominence in football always offers the possibility of the social capital thus gained being converted later into political capital, and Fru Ndi's case is rather suggestive in this respect.

The formation of the SDF served as a catalyst and several new parties were formed. The most important among them were Bello Bouba Maïgari's *Union Nationale pour la Démocratie et Progrès*/National Union for Democracy and Progress (UNDP/NUDP) and the *Union démocratique du Cameroun*/Cameroon Democratic Union (UDC/CDU) which was created in the Sultanate of Foumban in the West Province. Predictably most of the new parties were created along ethnic lines, thus the UNDP was a party of northerners, while the UDC mostly attracted people from the West province, although quite a bit of Bamileke support went to the SDF. Other parties followed, and eventually Biya had to legally institutionalize multiparty politics, which he did at the end of that year (Monga, C. 1990b, Takougang and Krieger 1998: 102-110). This added a new impetus to the creation of further parties. The SDF remained the most important of them, but among the newly created parties was the resuscitated UPC, only to be divided later on. The proliferation of parties was such that within a few months there were at least two dozen, and by mid-1995, Takougang and Krieger (1998) report the existence of 109 parties (154ff). Takougang and Krieger characterize the emerging picture as follows:

> Some [parties] were ephemeral or so localized and clearly opportunistic as to count for little beyond the registry paper, others resulted from the CPDM fishing the multiparty waters to create satellites and thus complicate politics to its own benefit, still others emerged from disputes the new parties could not contain. (Takougang and Krieger 1998: 123)

The demonstrations organized by a group of university students in Yaoundé, the so called Parliament, were also significant for the radicalization of the country. The group's members primarily criticized university life, which under the ongoing economic crisis has deteriorated like everything else in Cameroon, but the students' popular discontent "threatened to support and join democratic openings in the city" (Takougang and Krieger 1998: 124). When eventually troops went in and shot at student demonstrators, several students died. Augustin Kontchou Koumegni, the Minister of Information, announced on the public media that there were no deaths (*Zéro mort*/None dead). The phrase *Zéro mort* became the sobriquet for Kontchou who was subsequently the target of much scorn and dislike, and in general, was considered to be a liar. These events helped radicalize the population all over the country.

During the summer of 1991, in the continuing wave of demands for democratization which swept most of Francophone Africa, a coalition of opposition parties, National Coordination of Opposition Parties and Associations (NCOPA), similarly to opposition forces elsewhere, demanded the holding of a Sovereign National Conference. This would have brought together representatives of civil society, opposition parties, and the ruling party to discuss the political future of Cameroon and air grievances in the tradition of the African palaver (cf. Eboussi Boulaga 1993, Robinson 1994a and b). When Paul Biya declared the Sovereign National Conference groundless ("*sans objet*") and unnecessary, the opposition parties called for a national strike, the so-called "*villes mortes*" or "ghost towns." All economic activity was to cease, except for two days a week. In Takougang and Krieger's characterization:

Spontaneous street demonstrations, market and other economic boycotts became trenchant, fully organized civil disobedience which for three to six months, depending on the locale, made massive rallies and other highly visible challenges to state authority Cameroon's dominant features. They spread from provincial capitals of North West, South West, West and Littoral Provinces, ... Their grievances were old and new, including traditions and grudges dating back to precolonial, colonial and *maquisard* times, and more recent language, ethnic, and other forms of marginalization. Rural people either joined actively or were drawn into the movement, some reluctantly by threats. "Villes mortes" held firm in all parts of these four provinces for at least ten weeks, longer but with some slippage in Douala, until Christmas in Bamenda and Bafoussam. (Takougang and Krieger 1998: 127-128)

Though it never spread to the entire country, the movement largely paralyzed the economy, and had it attained its goal, the opposition would have won more than just the right to constitutional debate. *Villes mortes*, apart from being the most glorious example of the emergence of civil society in Cameroon, also divided the population. As noted by Takougang and Krieger earlier, in the strongholds of the opposition the strike was maintained by force at times. Elsewhere (in six other provinces), it did not take hold, or did so only sporadically, and reinforced already existing cleavages or created new ones (cf. Jua 1993, Nyamnjoh and Rowlands 1998). After the fact it is easier to see the cleavages, but Takougang and Krieger's assessment of the 1991 situation is apt:

Even in this most hostile environment [of Beti and regime-dominated Yaoundé] ... , dissenting forces were in touch and mobilizing by 1991. They linked widely separated terrains, and began a process whereby lines of class, ethnicity, and religion presumptively dividing their leaders from leaders, followers from followers, and leaders from followers, were modified by a basic literacy and common experience in opposition politics. (Takougang and Krieger 1998: 140)

The regime, however, did not remain inactive for long. Apart from repressive measures, such as refusal to deal with the opposition and large-scale media misrepresentations of the opposition's goals, it managed to divide the opposition and appease the population. This was accomplished above all by scheduling legislative elections for February 16, 1992, and inviting the representatives of the opposition for individual consultations with the prime minister. This eventually led to the Tripartite Conference in October

1991, where "members of the government, leaders of opposition parties, and 'notables' (most of these were CPDM partisans)" met (Takougang and Krieger 1998: 141). The conference ended with the signing of the so-called Yaoundé Declaration by the majority of the then legalized parties (forty out of forty-seven), but not by the most significant opposition party, the SDF. In the eyes of many, this fact de-legitimized the entire conference, but nonetheless the Yaoundé Declaration put an end to *villes mortes*, and life returned to "normal" in Cameroon. Obviously, this weakened the position of the opposition considerably.

The 1992 (October 11) presidential elections took place in this climate, and amidst widely suspected electoral fraud, Paul Biya won by a narrow margin against John Fru Ndi, the chairman of SDF, who ran as the representative of a coalition of opposition parties. The elections were widely referred to in Cameroon as the "stolen elections," a disparaging reference to electoral fraud (Jua 1993, Krieger 1994, Takougang and Krieger 1998). Although people did not necessarily like Biya any better for it, a certain kind of grudging admiration for him, for the amount of power he wields, sprung up in the minds of those members of the society, who were not necessarily for him, but who were not adamantly for the opposition. Those who were clearly for the opposition hated Biya with a vengeance. On New Year's eve 1994, as the president's televised New Year speech was reverberating on the streets of Yaoundé, one of the members of the informal group of friends, who gathered around my street corner newsstand exclaimed with feeling that he wished Biya were dead. Somebody else answered with great solemnity that no, he did not wish that, he rather wished that Biya lost his power and would have to continue living and suffer the indignities of not being able to make ends meet on a government salary.

The above mentioned ethnic and political cleavages became more pronounced as a result of the elections. Jua (1993) gave a detailed account of Beti fears and threats on the local Ewondo-language radio during the electoral campaign, which used the language of "ethnic cleansing," both feared and threatened by the Beti (cf. Azeyeh 1994: 58-59, who after outlining his multiethnic origins and multiple background explains that he had always thought of himself as Cameroonian, but since 1985-1992 one had to be from "somewhere"). Apart from this exacerbation of "political tribalism," the disappointment caused by the elections resulted in widespread disillusionment, while the economic crisis continued unabated. For the time being, the regime's hold on power was tenuous at best, but on the surface Biya managed to retain his power and had the continued support of the French Government, and thus of the IMF and World Bank. Bitterness against him was rampant during my fieldwork (1994-1995).

THE CONSOLIDATION OF THE BIYA GOVERNMENT AFTER THE DEMOCRATIC CHALLENGE

When discussing the post-1992 period, most authors agree that the Biya government began a slow process of recovery and re-establishment of its hold over the country. The 1994 devaluation of the CFA franc [8] deepened the economic crisis, making the economic situation of a population which felt that it was already on its knees even worse. The local elections, due in 1993, had been postponed several times. They only took place in early 1996, and despite the RDPC's ability to control (and rig) elections, mayoral elections in urban councils showed an even split between the RDPC and the SDF with some places going to the UNDP of Bello Bouba. However, the results of the elections were revoked administratively, and government appointed delegates replaced the elected ones, amid some protests (cf. Takougang and Krieger 1998: 197-198). The results of subsequent elections further demonstrated the staying power of the Biya regime. Takougang (2003: 441) points out on the basis of the results of the 1997 presidential and 2002 legislative elections that, "it could be argued that President Biya and his regime are more firmly entrenched in power today than they were on the eve of the pro-democracy movement in Cameroon." Besides being able to manipulate elections, President Biya's regime also adroitly used other methods to neutralize opposition parties at first through intimi-

---

[8] The CFA franc is the currency used in France's former African colonies, as well as in Equatorial Guinea and Guinea Bissau. Currently, in the case of the countries of Central Africa (including Cameroon), which unite into the Central African Economic and Monetary Community (CEMAC), the abbreviation stands for *Coopération financière en Afrique centrale*. In the case of West African French-speaking countries, united in the West African Economic and Monetary Union (UEMOA), the abbreviation stands for *Communauté financière d'Afrique*.

dation and later employing divide and rule tactics, especially between the two Anglophone provinces. These strategies have been accompanied by government co-optation of opposition politicians and taking advantage of and/or actively encouraging internal squabbles leading to splits within the more important parties (UPC, SDF, and UNDP) (cf. Konings 2004, Mbaku and Takougang 2004, Takougang 2003). In addition to this, Nyamnjoh and Rowlands (1998) demonstrate that the Biya regime foments another process, that of neutralizing political parties by encouraging the "politics of the belly" through increasing the role of elite associations in rural areas.

FOOTBALL: THE INTERTWINING OF SPORTS AND THE STATE

Apart from the question of the potential for the exploitation of the sport for political purposes and the political challenges it may present, which I will discuss in Chapter V, the Cameroonian state is at the interface of the local and the global practice of football. To begin with, the state physically structures football in Cameroon, in as much as at different levels of competition the administrative units of Cameroon determine what units are pitted against each other, thus concretizing and crystallizing both the local and the national, making these abstract categories real in the minds of people. Thus, the First Division championship encompasses the entire country. In order to ascend to it, the champions of each of Cameroon's ten provinces (Second Division) compete in the *interpoules* competition for the three places that become vacant as the last three of the First Division are relegated to the Second Division. The Third Division (*la ligue*) competition is carried out on the level of the lowest administrative division of the country, that is to say, the *département* or district. Winners of these championships accede to the Second Division through the so-called *interligues* competition, which brings together all the *ligues* of a province.

Recently there have been attempts to refashion the championship. First, its structure was altered as an experiment in 2004: instead of sixteen teams, the First Division was augmented to eighteen teams only to be lowered again two years later. In October 2007, the championship was again reformed. It was renamed "MTN Elite One" (after MTN, the mobile phone company, which in recent years has begun to sponsor football in the country, just as on the continent), and it is planned that starting in September 2008, the number of teams will be reduced to fourteen. This change is accompanied by the introduction of a second tier of elite football baptized "MTN Elite Two," organized into three zones: Zone I, comprising Adamawa, North, and Extreme North Provinces; Zone II, including Center, South, East, and West Provinces; and Zone III consists of the teams of the Littoral, North-west, and South-west Provinces. The Second and Third Divisions retain their function of serving to organize football on the provincial and departmental level, respectively. It is to be seen how the new formula is going to work as it will impose far greater costs on the higher tier of teams of the former Second Division than before, as they will have to travel much farther than they used to. For the new system to work the funding has to be in place because the teams cannot be expected to cover the travel expenses on their own. According to my informants although the Federation does provide funds to the teams, the amount is insufficient.

The structuring role of the state is also present on the international level of the game, where countries and continents compete against each other. Football in Cameroon is a local manifestation of a global phenomenon, and it is only through the state that Cameroonian football can take place on the international level. Because the state provides the funds for the participation of the national team in international competitions, and because the state stands for Cameroon, international participation is unimaginable without it. The state is also in charge of setting sports policy for the country, although both football practitioners and outsiders complain about the inadequacies of these policies. The performances of the Indomitable Lions recreate and fill with meaning the category known as Cameroon, and while the state claims credit for victories, these claims do not go unchallenged by the population. This intertwining of the state and football both on the international level and the national and local level, as well as the symbolic nature of the sport, allows for polyvalent, sometimes competing, sometimes converging meanings to be attributed to the sport, and thus give us glimpses of how Cameroonians see themselves in different contexts from the local to the global.

It is one of the clichés of sports sociology and journalism that belonging to *Fédération Internationale de Football Association* (FIFA), the international governing body of football, is as much a mark of being a sovereign country as belonging to the United Nations; in fact FIFA has more members than does the UN (Duke and Crolley 1996: 2, Sugden and Tomlinson 1998: 9). Being accepted on an equal basis (all members have an equal vote) can be seen as a confirmation of the sovereignty of a country and as conferring legitimacy on it. Thus, participation in the world of international football (as well as in other international bodies) is also constitutive of the entity known as Cameroon.

In fact, the members of FIFA are not the countries but rather the football federations of the countries. The Cameroonian football federation, *Fédération Camerounaise de Football* (Fécafoot), was created on the eve of independence in early 1959 (cf. Tsanga 1969). Soon after independence (in 1962), Fécafoot was accepted into FIFA. The task of the Federation is to oversee all competitions in the country and to represent Cameroon on the international stage. In addition to being a member of FIFA, the Federation also belongs to *Confédération Africaine de Football* (CAF), which oversees continental competitions. Although, in theory FIFA only deals with the Federation of a country, in the case of a country such as Cameroon, where the state takes an active role in the sponsoring of the national team, and where football is closely intertwined with politics, this separation of powers is somewhat illusory. As a result, the sporting federations, although ideally independent bodies, in fact are under government control. Thus in many ways, they could be harnessed to the interests of the government, all the more so as their employees are civil servants.

The other task of the Federation is to organize and oversee the orderly progression and daily running of football in Cameroon. This includes granting and administering licenses, establishing and coordinating the calendar of championships, designating officials for matches (referees, commissioners, and match delegates), homologation of matches, establishing sanctions, and collecting fees and fines. The employees of the Federation, as opposed to its officers, are civil servants, who at the time of my fieldwork in 1994-1995 had not been paid for almost a year.

The Ministry of Sports and Physical Education (MINSEP, earlier called Ministry of Youth and Sports (MINJES)) is the body which sets overall state policy on sports. This organ of the government has often been locked into debate with the Fécafoot over which one of them had jurisdiction over the country's most important sport, football. This has led to several confrontations over the years between the two organizations. FIFA often acts as a third party to these debates as well as to those occurring between the Federation and the government.

In 1995, the whole of Cameroonian football ground to a halt when the Association of First Division Clubs organized a strike to request a portion of the monies that were due Cameroon from FIFA for the country's participation in the 1994 World Cup. Every country that participates in the World Cup gets a certain amount of money, allocated in accordance with their length of participation, that is to say a country which went farther than the first round was allocated a larger sum, and the largest amount went to the winner. The presidents demanded a percentage of this money for the clubs of the First and Second Division and made some other demands as well. When their demands were not met, they refused to resume the championship which was in its midpoint break. The resulting stalemate brought all ongoing competitions to a halt, and the government stepped in to put a Caretaker Committee in the place of the Federation. Despite this decisive action, which had is own attendant problems with FIFA over the question of its legitimacy,[9] the championship in which the team I worked with the most closely participated, was held up for two months with disastrous consequences for the team. The struggles of the team and the vision of its owner–founder are the subject of the next chapter.

[9] In 1999, a similar incident took place in Hungary. When the government tried to dismiss the head of the Federation, FIFA intervened.

CHAPTER III

THE DAILY LIFE OF FOOTBALL

Football and its images are ubiquitous in Cameroon. Walking around the streets of Yaoundé, one sees young men and boys in faded football jerseys; a little boy of perhaps seven in a faded yellow T-shirt, with a handwritten inscription, "Thomas Nkono No. 1" (Thomas Nkono being one of the two great goalkeepers of Cameroon during the 1980s; bars named *Bar des Sportifs, Sports Bar, Sifflet d'or, Bar des amis sportifs*; and the many taxicabs which in the 1990s carried Roger Milla's name (he is the acknowledged genius and most renowned player of Cameroonian football). As new stars rise, new symbols of football appear. In the first decade of the twenty-first century, undoubtedly, Samuel Eto'o is the greatest star, and replicas of the Cameroonian national team's football jerseys can be seen on young men and boys displaying Eto'o's name. Others prefer to declare their admiration for him by wearing a replica of his "No. 9" jersey with the characteristic colors (blue and claret) of his Spanish team, Barcelona.

Lest we think that this ubiquity is only limited to the cities, although football *is* an urban phenomenon, Cameroonians, like other Africans, regularly go back and forth between town and village. In July 1997, on the way to a small village in the West Province, I saw a match being played, and was told that this was a match between "children" returning to the village for the school holidays from town. [1] In the village itself, there was as yet no electricity, and very few of the amenities of modern life were in evidence. However, in one of the houses that I had an opportunity to visit, a faded 1982 calendar, which had been the centerpiece of a journal, displayed the 1982 incarnation of the Indomitable Lions. In another house next to a

1 These villages are rather remote as they are off the main road along a dirt road, which carries one deeper into the interior, and cars rarely travel the road as far as the village I was visiting. Those who wished to go there often had to make the twenty-five km trip or part of it on foot.

framed photograph and other personal memorabilia displayed on the wall, there was a photograph of Thomas Nkono from a sports journal, and an article about the Lions' 1982 participation in the World Cup of Spain. I was to see the framed photograph again the next day, displayed in the "*funérailles*" (reburial) of the "ancestress" of the house.

Walking around Yaoundé, one would also see football being played everywhere. Football people in Yaoundé complain frequently that there are not enough football pitches, and doubtless, in light of the demand they are right. Apart from the Ahmadou Ahidjo or *Omnisports* Stadium, which is also "the" national stadium since this is where international matches (as well as First Division matches) are played, I have attended matches or training sessions at twelve other venues, and my research assistant could enumerate twenty-five, adding that doubtless there were others he forgot. In addition, inside the most crowded neighborhoods, wherever there is a little space, *ad hoc* teams will suddenly appear, especially during school holidays, and take over for a match or a mini-championship; kicking the ball rain or shine, appreciating the joy of the game. On a little side street in a residential area, I once saw a group of six- to ten-year-olds playing with abandon and among them – to my horror – a little girl with an eight-inch kitchen knife in her right hand; clearly she had abandoned her kitchen duties, just for a minute, to join in the melee. She held the knife down, behind her back, so as to keep it "safe," but the sight was hair-raising anyway.

People stop to watch all games. Neighborhood *inter-quartier* championships will gather their own crowds, and the organizers might even be able to collect some money from the spectators. Village championships in urban areas also have a built-in audience in the members of the village, who will come together as much to see each other as to see the game. Spectators of these matches too may be asked to pay a hundred francs [2] to watch the game. The "social occasion" nature of these village championships explains why there are an almost equal number of women among the spectators, which is never the case when official teams play.

---

2 At the time of my research in 1994-1995, 1 US dollar equaled about 500 CFA francs, a loaf of French bread (baguette) cost 100 francs, and a taxi ride cost 125 francs. Taxis function as public transportation in Yaoundé. There used to be a bus company, but it folded early in 1995.

But people will stop to see training sessions too, especially if a practice match is in progress. The *Stade Annexe* of the Omnisports stadium of Yaoundé lies along a main road, and it is perhaps two to three meters below the road level. During my 1994-1995 fieldwork, on any given morning or afternoon when teams played friendly matches, it was common to see people standing on the road, looking down onto the dirt pitch, and watching the game intently. Quite often a car or two also stopped; its passengers, captivated by the game, getting out to watch. In the summer of 1995, when the Football Federation was suspended by the Ministry of Youth and Sports and a Caretaker Committee took over the direction of football in Cameroon, one of its first actions was to organize a match between the *anciens gloirs* (old stars) of Douala and Yaoundé. Without any special advertising *Stade Annexe 1* drew an enormous crowd, people standing three deep (there were no stands as this was primarily a training ground, although Third Division official matches were held here too, as well as matches of the forever failing junior championship). Another row of people sat atop the fence enclosing the stadium. Looking at the scene from outside the stadium, I spotted a pair of crutches propped up against the fence, its owner watching the game perched up high.

FOOTBALL PITCHES: "MUD, DUST AND OTHER WILD GRASSES"

The football pitches of Yaoundé as well as of the rest of Cameroon are by all accounts in a terrible state. None of them have turf, which means that either the players play in dust or glide uncontrollably in the mud ... and I have seen a team with better boots winning the already lost match, because it started raining and the hitherto leading team's players had started gliding uncontrollably. Some football grounds tilt noticeably in one direction giving a definite advantage to the team trying to score downhill. (Luckily at half time the teams change sides!)

The Ahmadou Ahidjo Stadium is one of the two stadiums in the country to boast natural turf; the other one is the Reunification Stadium of Douala. A third stadium, where international matches can be, but are rarely, played has synthetic turf in Garoua (the capital of Adamawa Province, hometown of Cameroon's first president), but reportedly in 1994, the turf was in an advanced state of deterioration (cf. Ntonfo 1994a: 137). The same can be said of the turf of the stadiums of Yaoundé and Douala. In a highly ironic passage, Ntonfo characterizes the state of Cameroonian stadiums as follows:

> Under these conditions it is not surprising that a stadium with "real turf" sometimes becomes a handicap for a number of players used to playing-grounds that the unsuspecting observer could easily mistake for a wasteland, ill-kept cattle pens, grass-less pastures for goats or for an inaccessible swamp where two goals have been erected for the occasion.
>
> The first thing to learn on this type of terrain consists of mastering the forever uncertain trajectories of the ball. And for players who had learnt and practice the craft in such an environment, who know that you have to go left to be sure to capture a ball that seems to be going right, that a hump or a puddle – a suddenly appearing new player quickly identified – can redirect it, for players who take advantage of such partners – unrecognized by the CAF and even less by FIFA – as mud, dust and other wild grasses, for such players then, to find themselves on "real turf" can present a sizeable handicap. (Ntonfo 1994a: 133)

Ntonfo is not exaggerating. On one occasion when two Second Division teams were playing a Cameroon Challenge Cup match at the Ahmadou Ahidjo Stadium, the grass had not been cut and had grown so high that the coach of one of the teams instructed his players to forget about any tactical advice they had been given because it was impossible to play according to any kind of plan in such high grass. In 2005, the Minster for Sport and Physical Education decided that only the national team should play at the Omnisports Stadium, which meant that First Division matches were relegated to *Stade militaire*, which, although it was supposed to have been refurbished for the purpose, showed little improvement. There is no grass on it, and after a rain part of the terrain becomes flooded. This stadium belongs to the military and until the construction of the Omnisports Stadium for the 1972 Cup of Nations, it hosted the First Division championship of Yaoundé. Second Division matches have been held on it all along.

The sorry state of the stadium and the return of the championship to it, led one of the members of the 2-0 to remark bitterly, "It is unacceptable that I played the championship on this pitch when I was 17, and the championship still takes place here when I am over 70!" In the days after

Cameroon's elimination for the 2006 World Cup, the following comment appeared in the opposition newspaper *Le Messager*:

> How can we comprehend that this country to which football has given almost everything in the last thirty years, does not have any infrastructures in which it can be practiced. During his reporting of the match [on October 8, 2005 against Egypt] a colleague from CRTV-television said at a given moment that the match was taking place at *Stade militaire* of Yaoundé. Certainly this was a slip of tongue, but nonetheless revelatory of the fact that for the practice of national football the point of reference in the great capital of Cameroon, forty-five years after independence, is no other than *Stade militaire* which is anything but a football stadium. (Ngatsing 2005)

In fact for much of the time period of my initial research, the Yaoundé stadium was suspended by FIFA for international matches because of a plethora of problems. The suspension began on October 30, 1993, and meant that international matches were to take place in Douala instead of Yaoundé. As one journalist wryly put it, this was thanks to the fact that the FIFA inspection team did not think of going to Douala and inspecting the stadium there (Messang 1995a). Charles Nguini also expressed the same sentiment. Recalling the report of FIFA's representative, which led to the suspension, he gave the following list of deficiencies: "The worn out installations, the non-functional changing rooms and toilets, the tiny, insufficient and non-functional press cabins. And he was even indulgent" (Nguini 1996: 145). In 1995, from February 15 until April 9, not even local matches could be played because of work undertaken to re-build the athletic track in preparation for an athletic competition. This had disastrous consequences for at least one team, *Fogape*, discussed below.

In Europe or Latin America, clubs have their own stadium where they receive their opponents and where they can train. In Yaoundé, all teams trained wherever they could and used the Omnisports Stadium as their receiving stadium, and not even the supposedly fabulously rich Second Division team of *Olympic Mvolyé* owned its own terrain (cf. Vidacs 2001). *Tonnerre*, one of the oldest and most prestigious teams of the country, only established its headquarters in 1999, but still does not have its own pitch.

This discussion of the state of the stadiums of Cameroon partly calls attention to the fact that the infrastructures of football, despite the sport's elevated status and the country's multiple successes in the international arena, essentially reflect the general breakdown characteristic of the country. People often contrast football's reputation with the realities they see (literally) on the ground. Cameroonian commentators measure themselves against a mental template of how things are elsewhere. These bitter and often ironic statements are not limited to journalists and intellectuals, but all football people, and even the general public are keenly aware of the stark difference between the amenities at their disposal and the "norm." They know of this through watching TV, which apart from broadcasting the matches of the World Cup, also broadcasts the more important European competitions, especially and significantly, the matches of the national team of France. Football people also avidly read the French football magazine, *France Football*, and no doubt take some of their ideas from it. Most likely the contrast between people's everyday reality of football and that of what they saw on TV explains the frequent (self-deprecating?) laughter which accompanied the little carts that were employed during the 1994 World Cup to carry injured players off the playing field in the United States. By contrast, in Cameroon even a stretcher is a luxury and in most matches an injured player either hobbles off the field by himself, or is carried off by the two medical officers. In the first decade of the twenty-first century, another point of comparison is emerging – that of other African countries. In 2005 and 2006, several of my friends and informants remarked that elsewhere in Africa one can find better (and more) stadiums than in Cameroon, and that in other African countries (such as for example Côte d'Ivoire) much more substantial financial means are put at the disposal of clubs than in Cameroon.

AMATEURISM: PATERNALISM BY ANOTHER NAME

Football in Cameroon until now has been essentially amateur. This is not necessarily in the sense of adhering to the lofty ideals of Pierre de Coubertin, but much more so, it has been due to local realities. The ideals of amateurism were based on aristocratic principles, and were predicated on sportsmen not needing an income from sport as they had independent means (cf. Bourdieu 1978).

Indeed, in Cameroon the reverse has been the case. Apart from amateurism having been codified in the regulations of the Federation, it was in effect enforced by the lack of means on the part of clubs and those who organized teams. Recollections of former players indicate, on the one hand, that in the past many players were "taken care of" by the president of their club, either through being given a job, or being able to live in the president's household, or having their rent or their meals paid for on a regular basis. It is of course difficult to tell how widespread these practices were, as some of these recollections may be rosier than the reality was. On the other hand, it is also said by these same former players that they played just for the fun of it without expecting anything in return. This is a reference to monetary recompense since in-kind rewards were clearly available, and the juxtaposition these former players are making also has to do with the fact that by the mid-1990s players expected or at least would have liked to have monetary recompense. When they did not get it, which was often the case, they grumbled, and when the moment was opportune went on strike.

To some extent, the practice of in-kind recompense for football survives even today, but it is becoming rarer, and increasingly players have to fend for themselves. Some players are aware of this. A young goalkeeper explained to me in 1995, that he had studied catering because he realized that in order to be able to pursue a football career he needed a profession, which could provide him with a secure income. Others, however, are less lucky and clear-sighted and they eke out an existence, often having to rely on the unreliable bounty of club presidents. As mentioned in the previous chapter, during the first decade of the twenty-first century, a new pattern is emerging where the mobile phone company "MTN" officially sponsors the championship. In fact MTN's sponsorship is not limited to Cameroon; it goes up to the level of CAF. The national championship has been renamed after MTN as has the African Cup of Nations competition. In the case of Cameroon, some of these changes will only take effect in the 2008 season, and it remains to be seen how these changes will transform the game. However, parts of the sponsorship program were already in effect in 2006, and in interviews I conducted then, presidents, coaches, and even officials of the Federation privately, professed to be skeptical and presented a story different from what could be read in the newspapers. All concerned claimed that the funds were insufficient, and in any case they disappeared before reaching those who they were supposed to help, that is to say the teams.

During the mid-1990s, even players of the First Division did not have the luxury of a guaranteed income. The few teams which are sponsored, or owned by state or parastatal companies, constitute an exception. Most notable among these is *Cotonsport de Garoua*, which won the national championship nine times between 1997 and 2008, and is sponsored by the parastatal company "Sodecoton," but there are other "company teams" that are in the Second and even the Third Division. However, often the fortunes of the team and its players are closely related to those of the company which assists them. For example, *Fogape*, the team of *Fonds d'Aide et de Garantie aux Petites et Moyennes Entreprises*, was such a team. It did indeed rise to the First Division in 1994, but due to the failure of the enterprise was forced to forfeit the championship less than a year later, albeit under somewhat unusual circumstances. Fogape's forfeiture happened in 1995, amid the general chaos of the suspension of the Fécafoot. At least according to some commentators, the forfeiture was the consequence of corruption by some teams of the capital, which in order to manage to stay in the First Division needed the reshuffling of the results which was one of the side effects of the premature departure of the team from the championship (Nguini, 1996: 99-103). The club's problems were also compounded by the closing of the Ahmadou Ahidjo Stadium, its receiving stadium for repairs. The teams of the capital, among them Fogape, chose Douala as the place where they would receive their adversaries because no suitable stadium was to be found anywhere nearer. This increased their expenditures significantly, and no doubt contributed greatly to Fogape's inability to finish the season (cf. Nguini 1996: 142-147).

Other than these exceptional company teams, most football clubs were run on a more or less voluntary basis and team presidents had great difficulty meeting their financial obligations just in paying the requisite fees (such as affiliation, license fees, fines, and the like). Equipment presented a special problem, jerseys, boots, and even balls (both for training purposes and matches) were too expensive for most Cameroonian teams to afford, especially on a consistent basis. Consequently jerseys could be rented for a fee, from enterprising and wealthy individuals or from better off players, as could boots, or players were urged to fend for themselves in finding boots and matching socks for a match. Match balls could be borrowed as a favor from a better off team or an individual.

As the leadership of teams consists of volunteers, who more often than not maintain the team out of their own pockets, the team's ability to pay players on a regular basis is often strained. Even when the supporters of a club organize a collection to help defray the costs of an away match, or to assist with the payment of bonuses, or to buy equipment, the task is difficult, and such attempts rarely, if ever, yield enough. This is not a lack of goodwill for the most part, although there are plenty of accusations of certain individuals enriching themselves at the expense of the players. However, there are quite a few stories of others becoming paupers as a result of having "loved football too much." In 1995, two members of the 2-0 were commenting on the lot of the president/owner of a team that rose meteorically to the First Division within a few seasons during the mid-1980s. One of them said, "Look at Maître. X (a lawyer), he used to have three cars, and now he walks to work!" The implication was that the president had lost his wealth due to having (literally) invested too much in football. By the time this conversation was taking place, the team had sunk back to the Second Division and was about to be relegated to the Third Division. They just barely finished the season without forfeiture and the team folded after that. The ongoing economic crisis in Cameroon meant that people's resources were stretched to their limits in all aspects of life, thus any disposable income was required in many directions.

In addition to the economic crisis, there is another factor influencing the nature of the remuneration of players and officials. Cameroonian life, and thus football too, is pervaded by patron–client relationships. Even professional relationships outside of football are filled with rituals of respect and an air of paternalism where a clear *quid pro quo* is hidden under expressions of respect and bounty. Although patron–client relationships are often seen as associated with ethnicity, in the case of football, these ties often unite people from different ethnic groups. Thus, these patron–client relationships can also be regarded as an adaptation to modern and especially urban situations, where they increase the power of the patrons and provide – at least in theory – a modicum of security for clients, often across ethnic lines (cf. Barnes 1986, Wolf 1966).

Accordingly, coaches refer to their players as their children, players to coaches as their fathers, a newer team to a better-established team as their big brothers, etc. But these relationships go beyond rhetoric and mean among other things that players and coaches are not paid on a regular, contractual basis. Most players do not have a fixed income from playing. Some players are paid "a signature bonus" for signing with the club, but often they too find that the generosity of the club subsequently dries up, and their payments become just as haphazard as of the rest. At minimum, players need to be given transportation (taxi) money. They usually get this, as otherwise they would not be able to go to training sessions. In principle, players are always promised a bonus for matches, but whether they get it or not depends on the possibilities of the moment: it may be late or never forthcoming. Very rarely do they get money for training (and if they do get it, it is referred to as a bonus rather than as pay). When they actually get paid, the payment appears not as a due but as the bounty of the giver. Commenting on this state of affairs Ntonfo (1994a: 77) poses the rhetorical question of whether Cameroonian football players receive alms or a salary? The same is true of coaches. They too only get paid from time to time as the pocket (and/or whim) of the president allows it. This kind of situation means that there is nothing either a player or a coach can expect as his due. Everything is at the discretion of the president or one of his associates (who is almost invariably accused of pocketing some of the money).

The paternalistic relationships lead to ambiguities. Since payments are not fixed, players and coaches can never be sure of what form and magnitude their recompense will take, and more importantly when it will materialize. Another source of ambiguity in these relationships comes from the fact that people go back and forth, rather skillfully between acting in the more contractual and the more paternalistic mode. My friends complained bitterly about these practices, often expressing a very clear preference, at least to me, about their wish for things to be more businesslike. For example, one of my friends, a highly qualified coach, told me that he was constantly being asked to train various teams, but he kept refusing because "it is not right" ("*c'est pas normal*"), that they should expect him to work for nothing. However, these same people at other times would act in the same paternalistic mode that in other contexts they disapprove of.

THE TRIALS AND TRIBULATIONS OF COACHES

My most important informant, Coach Nguidjol, the coach and owner of the team I worked with most closely in 1995, told me that he started to play football out of disappointment when he – the eldest boy in his family, orphaned when he was about twelve, and obliged to stop school – had saved money for his younger brother's education, and the latter had refused to continue with his schooling. Out of frustration, Nguidjol went and bought a pair of "Puma" football shoes – he recalled the brand name almost thirty years after the event – and started to play football seriously. He later became a policeman, finishing his training second in his class, and yet – as he put it – they "put me to sell beer." His first job as a policeman was to man the canteen, that is to say, he was given no real responsibilities or possibilities for meaningful advancement. In disappointment, he decided to devote all his energies and intelligence to football. He performed the requirements of his job in a perfunctory manner, not looking for advancement, just doing enough not to lose his job, not to lose his pension, and not to be placed outside Yaoundé, as all his connections in football were there. Coach Nguidjol's interest in football was so well-known that when he was needed, his immediate superior came to look for him at the stadium, where he was training his team during working hours.

He had a long career in football, first as a player, then as a player-trainer, and finally as a coach (a common trajectory for coaches). Among his greatest accomplishments was raising a team from the Third Division to the First in four seasons, a remarkable achievement anywhere in the world.

Most teams have an official leadership consisting of, at a minimum, a president, preferably also a vice-president, general secretary, treasurer, vice treasurer, etc. These people often try to impose their wishes regarding the selection of players. This can be for a variety of reasons – one of the most common allegations made is that it is done because of "tribalism" – but as everyone considers himself an expert in football matters, there is also plenty of room for genuine disagreement.

One measure of the greatness of a coach, in the eyes of other coaches, is the extent to which he can withstand such pressures. I heard the story of the very talented coach of a "company" team repeated with great admiration. The president of the team was a high-ranking official of the company who, incidentally, also had quite a lot of power in the Federation. Apparently, when he tried to impose his choice of a player on the coach, the latter ordered him out of the stadium saying, "Mr. President, if you want me to take your position in the company, I will do so and you can be coach, but as long as I am the coach you cannot tell me what to do and you should leave the pitch." This is shocking behavior in Cameroon where respect for superiors almost always makes such open insubordination impossible. Most coaches, however, do not have the confidence and freedom to make such reckless statements. Very often, they either put up with the suggestions of the president (or other influential members) or if they find the situation truly untenable resign, or because of the tensions involved, are dismissed, or the following year choose to train another team in the hope of finding a less interfering president. In private conversations among coaches, this interference in their work is one of the most commonly cited problems.

A TEAM LIKE NO OTHER

Growing dissatisfied with being at the mercy of presidents, in 1994, Coach Nguidjol decided to create his own team. His idea was to build a team unlike any other in Cameroon. His motivations, like most people's motivations, were multiple and complex. He was hoping to make the team a "*centre de formation*," where he was to prospect for players, hone their skills, and raise them to a level at which he could transfer them to "Europe" (or failing that to local higher division teams), thereby ensuring his retirement, which despite being a policeman seemed to him less than assured. In fact, most people in the football circles of Yaoundé harbored similar dreams, as news of the transfer fees of players in Europe reach Cameroon and as there is an evident demand for African players in Europe. With the continuing economic crisis in Cameroon, both players and coaches see "Europe" as the solution to their problems. But there was more to the coach's vision than becoming rich. Unlike the presidents whom he accused of tribalism, Coach Nguidjol had a vision that he would take players from no matter what tribe, based solely on talent and would show "the world" that he could make a better team with players who had been rejected by others on account of their ethnic origin. This was what prompted his decision not to have a place-name attached to the name of the team. This was most unusual as almost all teams are identified by both a name and a place-name (*Canon de Yaoundé, Cotonsport de Garoua, Gruncam de Mindourou, Panthère de Bangante, Union de Douala*, etc.), and in fact officials and football people in general often assumed that there was a place-name to be added. The coach always answered with evident satisfaction that no, that was not the case!

The other part of his vision was a strong belief that the sport was to generate goodwill and understanding among people. In his conception, the companionship and friendship generated by the sport were among its most important attributes. He mourned the fact that he did not have the resources to invite coaches and players of other teams for a drink or a meal after a match because to him it was part of what the game was about.

In fact, such things do happen. Coach Nguidjol had great respect for one of his colleagues despite the other man training a rival team, because the two of them could sit down after their teams played a match against each other and have a dispassionate discussion of what had taken place and the relative merits of their respective players regardless of whose team had won.

I began working with the team at the beginning of the championship in February 1995. I was closely involved with its work, attending practically all their training sessions, practice matches, and championship and cup matches it took part in. My participation went so far as to be cooking for the players before matches, partly because many of the players had an inadequate diet, but at least as important was to create a sense of community among them. Better endowed teams regularly spend the night before a match together, sequestered in a hotel or at the president's house and eat together before a match, though not all Second Division teams can afford this, and there are even some First Division teams for which this becomes a hardship too.

Coach Nguidjol's ambition was to reach the Second Division, because it would have given him more exposure and enable him to have a greater choice in the players he recruited, as many players refuse the Third Division, as being beneath their dignity. He also hoped to attract more "members," who would financially support his endeavor.

The Third Division or league championship in Yaoundé is a highly competitive one, and there are enough teams (sixteen) that it takes place in two pools. The first two in each sub-pool meet in a semifinal, where the first of pool A plays against the second in pool B and vice versa (*semi-finale croisée*). The winners of the two matches meet to decide – in the so called *les barrages* – who is first and second, while the two losers play for the third and fourth place. It is only the first in the championship, who gets to play in the *interligues* competition to decide which team will accede to the Second Division.

HARDSHIPS AND SACRIFICES

In the following, I will try to give a sense of the difficulties faced by teams through the example of the team I worked with the most closely. What happened to the team exemplifies what Mbembe has to say about zombification, in that despite all of Coach Nguidjol's efforts, despite his deployment of all his resources, all his knowledge of the ins and outs of the world of football, his marshalling all his connections, ultimately the effort was unsuccessful. However, this feverish activity is fuelled by a vision, a vision of football as a world apart, where what is impossible elsewhere in Cameroon is at least imaginable; and this opening of the imaginable, or at least its illusion, is what drives people forward. It is also a vision of a better world, of clear-cut results, of unequivocal achievement, and of a certain kind of meritocracy. This is the ethos aspect of football. The worldview aspect – that which reflects reality – is what makes it impossible to achieve the ideal, but the ideal seems to escape all the trials and tribulations unscathed. I will argue at the end of the chapter that this illusion is maintained to a great extent because it represents order, and holds out the hope that it is possible to create order in the disorder, which is how people experience life in Cameroon. Some of the practices described here are strictly speaking illegal, notwithstanding the fact that to my knowledge everyone engages in them. They illustrate what Mbembe and Roitman (1995) spell out quite dramatically about the necessity to circumvent things – to work around the system. Certainly, there is no secret about this. However, as I write this, I am wondering if I am not betraying the trust of the people I worked with in describing the details of some of the maneuvers into which they are forced. Although, on more than one occasion, I was enjoined to tell the world "how we suffer in Cameroon" I am not sure that they meant for me to tell "all." In any case, I am not telling all, but even as I try to pick my words carefully, I wonder if by trying to convey some of the desperation that goes into football, I am not fixing it somehow and making it stick. Football is so important to people because it holds out the promise for individual and communal advancement, but at the same time, it also represents the possibility of the creation of a better world where order prevails, where the Cameroonian worldview (reality) is contradicted and defied. As a result, the sport gives meaning to the lives of the people involved in it.

The team was beset by all the problems characteristic of Cameroonian football (and of life in Cameroon). The expenses of affiliation, licenses, fees for using the stadium for training sessions, and fines were straining the limits of Coach Nguidjol's budget. (He had taken out a personal loan against his salary to meet the expenses.) Often he could not afford to pay taxi money to the players, and although he made promises of bonuses for matches gained, often he could meet these obligations only long after they were due. The other promise the coach made was to buy the players proper football boots, if they attained the *interligues*, but as time went on it was becoming clearer and clearer that this obligation too would be impossible for him to meet.

There was a period when the team only had one training ball, making meaningful training practically impossible. (These were plastic balls, since practically nobody could afford proper leather balls for training purposes. This of course meant that, when playing an official match, adjustments needed to be made to control the heavier weight and different bounce of the leather ball.) Every team was supposed to bring its own ball to an official match, and the referees decided whose ball would be used. Not bringing a ball resulted in a fine therefore, as Coach Nguidjol did not own a leather ball, for the purposes of matches he had to borrow a leather ball every time his team played an official match.

As the championship was progressing we kept losing players for a variety of reasons (injury, ill-health, inability to afford going to training sessions if the coach could not pay, finding a job, parents forbidding their children to play, loss of enthusiasm because of not being selected for a match or succession of matches). Coach Nguidjol countered these problems as best he could. One of the first things he did was to invite a friend of his, another coach, to co-coach the team. He was an older man and the two of them had worked together with a team during the mid-1980s. He was a gentler man than the uncompromising coach, and they formed a kind of "good-cop–bad-cop" pair vis-à-vis the players. Coach Nguidjol's combination of strategies also included recruiting new players, sometimes to posts where he already had a player; creating competition among the players and trying to flatter and cajole players into staying or coming back. He also paid bonuses when he could afford them and called upon the players' sense of honor and pride when he could not. Trying to build a sense of community among players was another tactic he used. But mostly, he attempted to retain them by pointing out that if the team made it to the Second Division, players would be rewarded by the chance of being discovered and recruited to perhaps the First Division or the national team, or even to a European team.

The continuing recruitment of new players was a strain on the coach's resources. Besides paying for the license itself, there were additional expenses, such as the photograph for the license, which if a player was wanted badly enough had to be paid by the president or the coach. According to the regulations, a medical examination also had to be made. This often (even if illegally) only meant the signature of a qualified medical practitioner, nonetheless (or perhaps exactly because of the perfunctory nature of the transaction) it required money. If a license was badly needed for a match there were ways of pre-dating it (with the complicity of a Fécafoot official) to circumvent the regulation of the federation, which required that only players who have had a license for at least two weeks could be fielded in a match, but naturally this kind of a transaction was also costly. It was also possible to play without a license in hand, if the process of acquiring it had already been put into place, but in this case, the club had to pay a fee – an official one this time – and show other proof of the identity of the player.

Added to these more or less direct expenses, there were also the more incidental ones of seeking out a player, going perhaps several times to his house to find him (very few people owned telephones in Yaoundé at the time, although by about 2002 mobile phones became ubiquitous), buying a soft drink or a meal for the player to better persuade him, etc. These expenses may seem trivial to the Western reader, but in Cameroon they constituted an enormous strain. In addition, arranging for such unforeseen necessities took time, energy, and thinking. It also required all the financial and personal resources of the coach. To carry off such irregular if expeditious maneuvers, one has to know the rules inside and out and also needs to have the personal contacts. Coach Nguidjol once told me – in practically anthropological terms – that his wealth was in his human relationships (*relations humaines*), and indeed, beyond his capabilities as a coach he only achieved what he did because of his contacts.

THE COSTS OF THE SCANDAL AT THE FÉCAFOOT: DRAINING OUR RESOURCES

The team arrived at the midway point of the championship in third place in its pool; clearly more of an effort was needed to reach the *interligues*. The coach recruited more players; we were near the cut-off point for the number of players allowed in a Third Division team. The break that was supposed to last a week between the two phases of the championship was being extended continuously. This was due to a strike instigated by the Association of Presidents of First Division Clubs, which continued even when, in response, the government suspended the Fécafoot and put a Caretaker Committee in its stead to redress the problems of football in Cameroon. The prolonged break was both good and bad news for our team.

At first, the break seemed to be to our advantage, because after all the work of recruiting and fine-tuning, the coach could start working with the players on a regular basis, as those who remained seemed to be there to stay. However, it was bad news too because it meant that special efforts were needed to continue maintaining the team's form, more taxi money, more occasional extra expenses. Nonetheless, an intense period of training and molding together the team began, and things began to come together, and the players started to work as a team, attracting more and more attention as time went on. They were winning all their friendly matches and as the team "turned" better, the players began to take pride in their game. The recruitment of several players to the same post paid off as players were vying to be selected for the team.

As the scandal at the Federation unfolded and led to a stalemate, the Third Division championship could not resume, and our team began to feel the strain. Maintaining form and motivation while there were no matches with real stakes proved to be difficult, especially as the coach's resources began to dry up. Meanwhile most of the other teams abandoned training because they could not shoulder the costs, so there were fewer sparring partners left for us. In addition, the school holidays began, which meant that a number of our players were being urged by their families to leave for the countryside, to go to their "village," where often they were also expected to play in local – unofficial – championships. An additional source of drainage on our players was that with the school holidays the *inter-quartier* championship also began all over Yaoundé, and many of our players could not resist the temptation of both making some money (such teams, which have local sponsorship, do pay) and impressing people in their neighborhoods (for an example of a more institutionalized form of such local championships in Senegal, cf. Baller 2005). It was during this period of interminable waiting that one afternoon the coach, who tended to be rather apolitical suddenly, burst out desperately, saying that "if the President [of the Republic] does not do something soon about the situation, I will become an *opposant*!" (This is the most common way to refer to people in opposition to the political regime.)

LOSING PLAYERS: FINDING SOLUTIONS

When the championship resumed about six weeks after the appointment of the Caretaker Committee, the team was playing exceedingly well, and the habitués of the Omnisports area began to take notice of it. It also received reinforcement in a rather unusual way.

A young coach, one of Coach Nguidjol's acquaintances, had built a team of children over several years. His problem was that his players were getting to be of the age- and skill-level at which they could easily be recruited by other teams. In other words, unless the team was officially affiliated with a regular team participating in an official championship organized by the Federation the players could be dispersed. He wanted to keep the team together so that the players could continue developing, besides, this was also the only way he could hope to reap some financial benefit from the transfers, and recoup some of the energy and financial resources he had expended on the players. If a player has a license with an official team, he cannot be transferred to another team without the consent of his own team, and the consent usually has a price.

Here I am talking about transfer fees owed for players by bigger and better teams to smaller teams. Transfer fees are owed in such cases, but it is often very difficult to actually receive them, as once the transfer had been made, it depends on the goodwill of the player's new team whether they pay or not. Obviously the one time the president of a team can be sure of receiving the transfer fee is prior to signing, but as is often the case in Cameroon, promises are made and not kept and there is very little recourse once there is a fait accompli. Why one would not ask for the money prior to signing the transfer form is part of the give-and-take associated with sports and the relationships between the protagonists. Partly, dictated by the sport ethic and such notions associated with it as fair-play and brotherhood of all sportsmen, sportsmen are supposed to trust each other, so when one party is promising it is unseemly to demand the bottom line. Somewhat similarly to the ambiguous paternalist relationships between club presidents and coaches or players that I described earlier, it is easy to take advantage of the trust established through sport and people waver between a sportsmanlike generalized reciprocity and a businesslike attitude. Partly, however, there is a power imbalance between a well-established First Division team and an "upstart" Third Division team. Thus, even without the desired payment forthcoming when it should, allowing the transfer of a player to go ahead has certain perceived benefits. On the one hand, there is reflected glory in having one's discovery (a talented player) go to a highly respected team, it adds to the "résumé" of either the coach or the president to have had the good eye to spot a player, to have nurtured him, to have polished his talent. A lot of the respect a coach, or even a president, expects is due to this factor, and recounting the list of these players is part of the rituals of a coach's existence. It is also a source of disappointment, as one is bound to have claim on more players than others will remember. On the other hand, not getting the money on time (or ever) constitutes a certain kind of social capital, an outstanding debt where the coach or president who provides the player without receiving an immediate payment can, in theory at least, expect some kind of a return favor some time in the future.

To return to the history of the team, juniors are players under the age of seventeen and by regulations of the Fécafoot, all teams from the Third Division up are supposed to have a junior team in order to ensure the future (*la relève*). The junior teams of all divisions of a province played a single junior championship. In practice, the junior championship never seemed to come to completion. It usually was launched but was disorganized, teams forfeited their matches, especially because they had to go to all corners of the province, and even the better endowed teams could not afford the extra expense and therefore usually a few weeks after its beginning, the junior championship floundered and was abandoned. This was so in the mid-1990s and continues to be the case ten years later (cf. F. H. 2005). The main benefit of having a junior team was thus that it afforded teams the opportunity to use them to supplement the number of players they could count among their effective lineup, because while no senior can play on a junior team, juniors can be fielded on the senior team.

As the two coaches agreed in many of their principles about coaching and football, they struck a deal that the youngsters would become our juniors, and become affiliated at the Fécafoot as such. This solved the problems of both coaches, the one could keep his team together, the other could at least maintain his team for the remainder of the season as it was becoming obvious that we continued to lose our players. Even though the championship had resumed by this time and our team was winning most of its matches, we needed the reinforcement because we had lost several key players.

One of the greatest blows was the loss of our young striker, who had attracted everybody's attention during the first half of the season by his ability to score at least one goal in every match. His disappearance had many causes: his parents were adamantly opposed to his playing, he lived far away and the expense of his transportation to training sessions and matches weighed heavily on the team's budget, causing tension among the rest of the players who received less money than he did, etc. As he was a remarkable player, apparently he was being wooed from a variety of sides to leave the team to go play elsewhere where he would be better remunerated. He presented these offers to the coaches of the team in an effort to get more support from us. As these somewhat veiled demands were not met (mostly because of lack of resources), he eventually stopped coming altogether. We later heard a rumor that he had gone to play for one of the teams in the countryside. While obviously it is not legal to play with an existing license for another team, it can be done quite easily, as the deception is unlikely to be detected unless someone who knows the player discovers it and makes a formal complaint. The computerization of the licenses which has taken place in recent years should have put an end to such practices, however, as a Fécafoot official pointed out to me in 2006, this would only be the case if the player used the same name.

Nonetheless, in the end – with the help of the newly acquired juniors – we finished the championship second in our pool, thus facing the more difficult task of playing against the first placed team of the other pool. This was a team well known to us, as they trained on the same training ground as we did, and the two teams often played against each other as sparring partners.

Lately our team had won all its matches. Nonetheless we prepared anxiously as it was the crucial match to decide whether at the *barrages* we would play for the first place, and thus have a chance to go to the *interligues,* or for the third or fourth place which would put an end to the coach's dream of attaining the Second Division that year, and would hamper the aspirations of the players. We lost the match. The disappointment was enormous and was followed by soul-searching and recriminations and self-recriminations. The players were of the opinion that the goalkeeper sold the match, to which Coach Nguidjol's reply was simply that he would not honor him by such a supposition, he was merely incompetent. In fact, our captain reported to us that he had been approached in his neighborhood by representatives of the other team who tried to persuade him to sell the match.

What weighed heavily on Coach Nguidjol's mind was that he had used his connections in the inner circles of Fécafoot to have a certain referee, whom he considered to be sympathetic to him (and who was of the same tribe as himself), appointed as the central referee of the match. As far as I know he did not have any direct dealings with the referee in question. However, the referee turned out not to favor our team at all, if anything he seemed to be favoring the other team. In any case, losing the match was a severe blow to all the people involved with the team. I'll never forget the bitterness, the sense of dejection, the feeling of hopelessness and despair that we all felt, and discussed masochistically for hours after the match in a bar.

AN UNOFFICIAL STRIKE

After this match the players began to disappear in even larger numbers. This was in fact an unofficial strike, as it was driven home to me by friends who were following the team's progress from a distance, asking me questions about what was happening, and nodding knowingly that yes, the players were disappearing. Part of the reason was the unkept promise of football boots, part of it was that Nguidjol's manipulations to create competition were backfiring. He felt obliged to call back some players for the semifinal that we were to play because he considered them to have better natural talent than some of the players who were regularly present. Naturally, this created tension among the players, and no doubt contributed to the unofficial strike. They stopped coming to training sessions, and it was clear that if it weren't for the juniors we would have little hope of even being able to present a team at the remaining match to decide whether we were to be third or fourth. These things are a matter of honor in the life of a coach. In the end, we did present a team, and won 4-0, a bittersweet victory under the circumstances.

Coach Nguidjol tried again the following year. Although the team was leading in its pool, a heavy penalty involving the deduction of 6 points was imposed on them because supposedly the captain did not have his license renewed. In light of the coach's minute knowledge of even the finest points of the Fécafoot's regulations, this charge is so unlikely as to be absurd, but of course, I was no longer there and only have his report. Be that as it may, Coach Nguidjol and the club once again lost the opportunity to try to rise to the Second Division.

The events described above could easily be seen to fit into Mbembe and Roitman's analysis of the realities of life in Cameroon. The poverty, the economic crisis, and the "new forms of rationality" are reflected in football, as are the pressures of tribalism. Minor and major forms of corruption not only reflect the larger reality, they also reproduce it, and thus reinforce it. The breakdown of the infrastructures of football could easily be one more page in their description of physical breakdown in Cameroon. The scandal at the Fécafoot could easily be seen as an example of Mbembe's zombification. The lack of proper equipment is just another instance of the economic crisis forcing Cameroonians to live under desperate circumstances. The various irregular acts Coach Nguidjol engaged in to make his dream come true were examples of the alternative modes of action people resort to in order to circumvent the impossible situations in which they find themselves. And the final futility of this feverish activity is, if nothing else, ironic. Most of all it begs the question of why people persist in the activity and brings into relief what Mbembe and Roitman have to say about the limitations of efficacious action.

A WORLD APART? HOW THINGS ARE AND HOW THEY SHOULD BE

At the same time, however, the notion that football is part of a "better, more equitable world" makes it very attractive to most of its practitioners and fans. Coach Nguidjol once told me that he loved football because "at least in football you know what the results were, no matter what happens afterwards." The "no matter what happens afterwards" is a reference to the fact that very often the result of matches, and consequently, the standing of teams in the various championships, change after the fact. Usually this is due to some supposed or real infraction on the part of a team. Obviously the team from which the Federation deducts the points always claims to be unjustly penalized, and it is hard to escape the inference that there is a certain amount of self-justification going on. However, there are enough instances of the infractions being imaginary, thinly veiled (by legalistic language), but successful attempts to influence by external forces the results achieved on the football pitch to convince me that at least some of the complaints are true. [3]

---

3 This is not uncommon in Cameroon, after all it was reported by Transparency International to be the most corrupt country in the world for two years running (1998, 1999). But it is also enough to study social realities in Cameroon to know that there are constant and recurring charges of irregularities among other things around the baccalaureate, as well as of course, the allegations of electoral fraud that have dogged the Biya government since the early 1990s (cf. Fombad 2004).

What does the coach's statement mean, why is it an affirmation of football? The coach frames what happens on the football pitch as being separate from what happens outside it, and basically claims that the result on the football pitch is more "real" than what happens in the non-football world. This is where truth is: the result was 3-2, we were first in the championship, what happened outside of the match is unreal and untrue, and, from this point of view, irrelevant. Naturally, it is very far from being irrelevant, but some of football's attraction comes from this suspension of reality, or from what could be termed as an alternative reality, where justice prevails, results are clear, either you win or you lose, or you draw, but there are eyewitnesses who saw the result. This is in stark contrast to how the change in the results came about, in the offices of the Federation, in the shadowy bowels of Yaoundé's Omnisports stadium. (Shadowy, not just as an atmospheric expression but also because for most of the duration of my fieldwork, there was no electricity at the stadium and in the offices, because the Federation's outstanding electricity bills had not been paid).

The idea that everything has a double, that things are not what they seem, is also borne out by the everyday life of football in Cameroon: from the balls which are not "real" footballs to the boots which are molded plastic or else borrowed or rented, but in any case secondhand, as are the match balls and jerseys presented at matches. One could see a double, a shadow world of football, where everything seems to unfold at least for the duration of a match, as if it were real. At the same time, of course, everybody knows that they are not.

I was once shown a large envelope full of IOUs by one of the officials of a championship. These were the IOUs of the teams that could not afford to pay the affiliation fees for the championship. As some teams did pay and others did not, there was a stalemate because the championship could not begin until all the affiliations were paid. The IOUs were the solution; they represented payment (even if they were not really payment). They allowed the championship to begin, even if the chances of actual payment were slight. (People actually do pay if they have the means, but often they don't.)

On another occasion, the leadership of the 2-0 I belonged to was discussing the team's budget and the equipment needed. I was surprised by the grandiosity of the budget – members had difficulty keeping up with their membership fees as it was, and in fact there were several members who owed or whose dues had been absorbed by some of their better-off fellows. Choosing – even if mentally – the most expensive kind of ball, the best possible equipment, two new sets of jerseys, as if money was no object seemed unrealistic to me. When I suggested that these things could be obtained for less and that cheaper solutions were also possible, my interjection was completely ignored. I knew that actually none of these pieces of equipment were going to be bought, that the team was going to continue playing with the same set of fading jerseys, that it was impossible to obtain two brand-new sets.

Thinking more about it, the idealized budget, the IOUs, the attempt at proper equipment on the pitch take on a different light. On the one hand, clearly, the "pretense" is necessary to keep up appearances; the 2-0 considered itself the most elite 2-0 of Yaoundé. In disagreements among members, frequent references were made to the "fact" that other 2-0s look up to us, and therefore we should live up to the expectations, not quarrel, not arrive late, not engage in un-sportsmanlike conduct. Such a "grand" 2-0, "naturally," had to have the best equipment. Likewise, giving the IOUs would disguise the fact that the clubs in question did not have the money to pay the affiliation fees, and also make the championship possible, having the right equipment on the pitch would create the impression of a team able to afford it, while at the same time also fulfilling the necessary requirements of the Federation. There is, however, more going on. The pretense is necessary not just to keep up appearances, to hide poverty, but by insisting on the proper form of things, a certain order, or the possibility of order, is preserved and projected. This is a source of hope, this order represents "normalcy" in a world where "things are not normal," where everything is in disorder. Football is an ideal vehicle for the expression of such order; its rules and regulations, its rituals, the need to fill in forms before the match, its whole administrative structure create a reality, a routine, a predictability which is lacking everywhere else.

CHAPTER IV

VISIONS OF THE NATION

In this chapter, I turn away from the local struggles of Cameroonian sportsmen for survival and the imagining of a better world through football to the level of international football. As discussed in Chapter I, because of its symbolic nature, football lays bare the cleavages within a society, and its polyvalent nature allows this to happen on different levels. It is, however, just as important to recognize that cleavages also delineate units of belonging. When considering Cameroon's participation in international football, the nation as a unit comes to the fore, but at times football can also give rise to pan-African sentiments. This follows more or less inevitably from the structure of the game, from what I have labeled its segmentary nature. In this chapter and in the following chapters, I examine the different meanings of the nation (as well as of such closely related concepts as nationalism, nationalist sentiment, nationalist ideology, etc.) for Cameroonians and will show that the relationship of the notion of the nation to the ethnic group rather than being antithetical is a dialectical and dynamic one.

It should be kept in mind that nations, like ethnic groups, are constituted both internally and externally. The significance attributed to the concept by members of the nation and the meanings with which they will fill it, vary depending on whether it is the internal or the external dimension that is under scrutiny or is called into action. What is important here is that given the global theater in which the World Cup takes place, its significance, of necessity, is also global, but at one and the same time, it is local too. Naturally, the two domains interact and are not sealed hermetically and in later parts of the chapter, I will outline how nationalist and ethnic sentiments can be seen to be in a dialectical relationship with each other.

CAMEROON'S WORLD CUP PARTICIPATIONS

Cameroon has so far participated in five World Cup competitions – in 1982 in Spain, 1990 in Italy, 1994 in the United States, 1998 in France, and in 2002 in Korea/Japan. This series was broken when the Cameroonian national team failed to qualify for the 2006 World Cup that took place in Germany, a shocking event that I will discuss in greater detail in Chapter VII. Qualifying for the World Cup is considered the world over to be a major accomplishment. African countries have fought a long battle within FIFA for a more proportionate representation at the World Cup, paralleling larger, better-known struggles for equal representation on the world stage. Until 1970, Africa shared one place with Asia in the final tournament of the World Cup, the winner of the play-offs staged between the continental winners gained the right to participate. African and Asian countries considered this unfair, and most of them boycotted the 1966 World Cup in England to make their protest against this injustice heard. The first time Africa had a place in its own right in the competition was in 1970 (with the qualification of the North African nation of Morocco), and from 1982, the number of representatives grew to two. The number of berths allocated to Africa once again became the subject of intense negotiation in the early 1990s, especially after Cameroon's magnificent 1990 participation in Italy. Cameroon's good showing in that competition strengthened the argument that Africans have been putting forth for since the 1960s, that the distribution of World Cup places was unfair, if not racist, and that the continent deserved more places. Issa Hayatou, the Cameroonian president of CAF and thus one of the vice-presidents of FIFA, used his influence and the relative weight of African countries in FIFA to grant three places to Africa in 1994, and an unprecedented five in 1998 (cf. Darby 2002, 2003, 2005, Sugden and Tomlinson 1998). I will refer to the significance of these struggles in the following.

In all but one of their World Cup appearances, the Indomitable Lions were eliminated after the first round, but as I will show in subsequent chapters these seemingly similar results resonated differently among Cameroonians on different occasions. The Indomitable Lions' first participation in a World Cup final was in 1982 in Spain, where they drew with all their adversaries (Peru (0-0), Poland (0-0), and Italy (1-1)), which meant that they remained unbeaten despite having been eliminated in the first round. This is a point of pride for most Cameroonians, and it is one of the themes that they often recall in connection with this World Cup. In 1982, Cameroon was only the second African team to participate in the World Cup from south of the Sahara; and the previous one, Zaire, suffered a crushing defeat from Yugoslavia (9-0) in 1974. Thus, it was very important to avoid being ridiculed in the same way, therefore, the Lions played with a rather defensive lineup. However, most Cameroonians consider the 1982 incarnation of the Lions to have been one of the strongest ever and see the defensive play of the national team differently. They blame the French head coach of the period for having had so little faith in his team that he packed it with defensive players. Kodo-Ela and Mayamba Masika (nd: 55) described it as: "an ultra-defensive formation to make sure that they don't get too many goals. With this, he [Jean Vincent, the French head coach] 'ties up' the team in a suffocating 6-3-1." The latter refers to the lineup of the team: *six* defenders, *three* midfielders, and *one* attacker, plus, naturally, the goalkeeper. The third theme that occasionally cropped up in the course of later World Cups was the denial by the referee of a goal scored by Roger Milla in the match against Peru (see Chapter VI).

But undoubtedly, the high point (until the Olympic victory of 2000) of Cameroonian football in the international arena was 1990 in Italy. What Cameroonians most often recall about it is the fact that the Lions won against Argentina, the holder of the title, while playing at a numerical disadvantage, having had two players expelled. Their subsequent arrival to the quarterfinals was a first for any African country in the history of the competition, and the achievement was a source of enormous pride for all Cameroonians, indeed for all Africans. Many Cameroonians translated it as having been "fifth in the world."

IMAGINING THE NATION THROUGH WATCHING THE WORLD CUP

When the World Cup, the sport's most important worldwide event that takes place every four years, is going on, life stops in Cameroon, and everybody is riveted by the competition. Naturally, this is especially so when Cameroon participates. With the advance of mass media into the most remote areas of the world, the simultaneous moment, about which Benedict Anderson (1983) is so eloquent, is particularly evident when the majority of the population of an entire country is able to watch or listen to a football match at the same time. Radio and television broadcast the matches in Cameroon, and as most people do not have access to television at home, the preferred method of watching an international match is in bars. In fact, even when people do watch a match at home, chances are that there will be neighbors, relatives, servants, or friends to watch the match with them, thus the event is more public than one would expect. Even those people who have TV sets at home often prefer to watch the more important matches in public because of the camaraderie and the commentary. In 1998, one bar in Yaoundé had a handwritten sign, "Come and watch the World Cup in our bar, the commentary is better than the matches." And indeed for the price of a few beers, one watches the match in the company of others and comments fly with great regularity. [1]

Those who cannot afford the beer may also choose to watch at video-screening rooms, which usually show kung fu movies or American action movies. At the time of important matches, they turn them into football viewing rooms where for a minimal fee (maybe 50-100 francs or, in remote areas, even less) people can watch the match. By comparison, the price of beer was between 300 and 450 CFA francs during the 1990s, and the price has remained essentially the same ever since. For those who could not even afford the 100 francs, in 1994, there were giant screens set up in large cities where hundreds of people could stand together closely packed like sardines to watch a match for free. Cameroon's print media also rises to the occasion and fills the pages of newspapers with World Cup reporting. In fact, the media coverage of football in Cameroon is extensive at all times, and it becomes almost exclusive during such events as the World Cup. A plethora of short-lived newspapers and magazines appear while it lasts, and the more established papers also devote a great amount of their coverage to

---

1 In Yaoundé, the majority of these comments were in French. Thus, my quotes are my translations from the French. Because French is the majority language in Cameroon, I mark especially when the comment comes from an Anglophone speaker. This may be a questionable practice, as marking always creates the marked person as the "other" and this is of course one of the main points of criticism Anglophones level against Francophones in Cameroon.

the competition. In 1994, through the medium of the call-in radio program, *Bonjour l'Amérique* and its English-language counterpart, Hi America, the national radio (CRTV) devoted five and a half hours daily to the World Cup, besides covering the matches and providing football-related news under the regular news.

For the duration of the 1998 World Cup, most offices and many stores closed early in Yaoundé. People working there had to be able to reach their homes, as it was unlikely that they would be able to find taxis to take them home during the matches. In any case, there would have been no clients to deal with, as everyone would be watching the World Cup. This was not so in 1994, when, due to the time difference between Cameroon and the United States, matches began after working hours in Cameroon. There were two or three matches a day during the first round, depending on the day of the week, so they began in the afternoon and went on late into the night. In 2000, when Cameroon was participating in the final of the Olympics in Sydney, I called a friend around 6 p.m. Cameroonian time who informed me that they were just getting ready to go to bed in order to be able to get up at 4 a.m. to watch the match broadcast live from Australia.

During international competitions, such as the World Cup, the imagined community is rejoicing and seething literally all at once, and of course, it is both real (in the immediate sense) and imagined in Anderson's sense because people in their immediate communities know that there are other immediate communities of the same kind experiencing what they are experiencing. They know this if for no other reason than because the day after the match the radio will broadcast man-on-the-street reactions to the match from all ten provinces of Cameroon (cf. Spitulnik 1994). Similarly, newspaper coverage includes all corners of the country in its reporting of the population's responses to the World Cup.

Extending Anderson's thesis on the rise of nationalism, I am arguing that football is a major force in imagining the nation. This is not only so because of imagining the nation through the communal experience of watching and rooting for the national team, but as I argued before the very structure of the national championship and the Cup of Cameroon helps make the abstraction of Cameroon as an idea, as a unit, real in the minds of people.

Talking this way about football's role in imagining the nation speaks to the internal mechanics of the emergence of national sentiments. Another facet of the internal imagining of the Cameroonian nation is mentioned briefly in Mbembe and Roitman's (1995) article. They argue that the economic crisis, which has been ravaging Cameroon since the late 1980s, has caused a substantial shift in people's self-perceptions. Similarly, Eyoh argues that social despair over the "altered conditions of material life" – [i.e. the crisis] undermined "the premises on which national identity had been conceived and the legitimacy of authoritarian rule predicated" (Eyoh 1998b: 256). Before the "crisis," Cameroon was a relatively prosperous country with one of the best "track records" in Africa (cf. Chapter II). Mbembe and Roitman (1995) state that "... this relative prosperity had been made part and parcel of official and popular representations of national identity and Cameroonian singularity" (328). A little later, seeking to elucidate how Cameroonians turn to explanations by the inexplicable to make sense of their current predicament, the authors imply that it is this sense of national identity that has been undermined by the "crisis."

> ... Cameroonian society's long-standing capacity to 'imagine' itself in a certain manner – to mentally author and, from this, institute itself – has been contradicted and seems now thrown into question. ... at the time when annual growth rates were on the order of six to seven percent, Cameroonians perceived themselves as a part of a rich nation, with infinite possibilities before them. This was, to be sure, part of a deliberate effort to imagine a national identity founded on economic attributes. Today's bankruptcy places this mode of imagining the nation in check, leaving in its wake certain forms of nostalgia. (Mbembe and Roitman 1995: 339)

Arguably, football is one of the few areas where this Cameroonian sense of singularity has survived, while it is also capable of inciting nostalgia, as the glory of 1990 and 2000 recede into the past. Bromberger (1994a) makes a similar point about football passions being strongest and most nostalgic in communities, which have lost their economic importance (176).

Mbembe and Roitman's analysis raises the question of whether misfortune, in the Cameroonian case, the "crisis," inevitably leads to the dissolution of the self, or more precisely of identity or as Mbembe and Roitman put it, of a sense of singularity. There are many examples to the contrary: Jewish identity seems to have thrived on adversity, and one could regard Eastern European national sentiments as having been primarily driven by a sense of misfortune, imposed from outside. Naturally, there are degrees of adversity. There may be a point of such societal breakdown, where no overarching sense of unity may be possible. Turnbull's (1972) controversial study of the Ik comes to mind, as well as studies of famine and warfare (Shipton 1990, Vaughan 1987). Fortunately, however, Cameroon, despite the generally drastic deterioration of the standard of living in recent years, evoked so eloquently by Mbembe and Roitman, is not at this level of overall breakdown. The point Mbembe and Roitman make is that the crisis has become so all encompassing in Cameroon as to put into question people's basic understanding of how the world works. Other authors have addressed the effects of economic hardship elsewhere in Africa in terms that indicate that the crisis has undermined people's certainties. For example, Todd Sanders (2001) argues that the rise of outrageous accusations in Tanzania, such as traffic in human skins for the production of wealth through occult means, is a reflection of people's perceptions that under the economic conditions created by structural adjustment anything is possible. He shows that through these fantastic accusations people question the legitimacy of economic liberalization, however, it is also clear that one of the effects of "unbridled liberalization" (Sanders 2001: 178) is that the changes it brings bewilder people.

In the two cases I cited above (Jewish and Eastern European identities), the misfortune is seen to derive from external sources, and this may help unite people against a common (external) enemy. In the Cameroonian case the "enemy" is not so easy to identify, or rather, there are multiple targets. Internal problems (government mismanagement, corruption, ethnic strife, etc.) may indeed lead to the dissolution of a "nationalist" sense of self, although I will argue that it is more a question of how the nation is defined than the notion of the nation that is being questioned. At the same time, it is also clear from the strong anti-French and anti-white discourses, which the various World Cups have engendered, that Cameroonians have also found an "external enemy" to blame, and against which to define themselves. In fact, it is likely that the 1998 World Cup's all encompassing anti-white and anti-French discourse is evidence of the strengthening of this line of rhetoric (see Chapter VI). But as we shall see in Chapter VII over time these attitudes are not constant.

ART VS. SCIENCE: THE BATTLE OF PLAYING STYLES

Here I would like to concentrate on the significance of the nation as an externally constituted unit. Partha Chatterjee has argued cogently that the logical outcome of Western theorizing about nationalism is to render non-Western versions of nationalism inauthentic by relegating the nationalist imagination of the Third World to a mere copying of the ready-made "modular" forms of Western nationalism. Contradicting this, he suggests that the preoccupation of third world intellectuals has rather been the opposite, to create an identity that was at the same time modern and yet non-Western. Chatterjee juxtaposes two domains: an inner and an outer, what he also calls the material and the spiritual.

> The material is the domain of the 'outside', of the economy and of statecraft, of science and technology, a domain where the West had proved its superiority, and the East had succumbed. In this domain, then, Western superiority had to be acknowledged and its accomplishments carefully studied and replicated. The spiritual, on the other hand, is an 'inner' domain bearing the 'essential' marks of cultural identity. (Chatterjee 1996: 217)

Chatterjee's bold categories of East and West, material and spiritual can be faulted for being essentialist, although from a postcolonial rather than the usual Western perspective. People in Cameroon are clearly participating in both worlds and the separation is artificial. But nonetheless Cameroonians often argue in these essentializing terms, and construct their world in equally bold contrasts of "black" and "white," European and African, etc. Chatterjee is talking about Indian intellectuals, and certainly both African and Cameroonian intellectuals have been struggling with resolving the contradictions between their yearnings for "modernity" and the equally strong need not to be simply swallowed up by the West, where they will be seen as imitators of Western paradigms and thus, as latecomers, will automatically be put at the bottom of the pile (cf. Eyoh 1998a). To counteract this, they need to assert their identity as Africans. However, this essentializing and self-assertion is not limited to intellectuals only, there are strands of this argument among ordinary Cameroonians as well.

One of the more striking examples to be heard in football is the debate that is going on about football as "art" and as "science," where Cameroonians/Africans are presented as "artists" and Europeans "robots." What people mean by these terms and their variants is part of a larger set of discourses (cf. Alegi 2004, Archetti 1996, 1997, Blain, Boyle, and O'Donnell 1993, Bromberger 1994a, 1995, Giulianotti 1999a, Hadas 1999, Leite Lopes 1997, 2000, Leite Lopes and Faguer 1994).

It is often posited by Cameroonian sportsmen and laymen, that Cameroonians (or at times Africans) are born footballers (that is to say football comes naturally to them, it is an innate quality), but more than that they are artists, creative, incalculable, and free. Juxtaposed to this are Europeans, who instead of practicing "art" practice "science." The difference is outlined in the following terms by a former player, a member of the Old Boys' Club (2-0), who had the most elaborate set of ideas on the subject.

> When we speak of Cameroonian football, we speak of African football. You see all the Africans play a bit the same way because we have the same morphology, we are ... well ... we are coordinated the same way. There is a European football, because they too ... there are things which condition them, for example nature itself and all, they will play a bit the same way, because you see the Europeans are a bit rigid, they have a way of playing and well ... they have a bit *la passion de l'école*. Well, they like to be told, well, do this, then do that.

Another informant, one of the best-known coaches of the country, and a former star himself, reflecting on the possible causes of differences in playing styles between whites and Africans (one of the supposed advantages of Europeans over Africans is that the former play a faster game) said the following:

> At the age of six they can correct (*corriger*) me, I can adopt the habit of playing fast, at the age of six, eight, ten years ... when I reach the age of twelve [he made a clicking sound to indicate finality] I am already used to playing fast, without carrying the ball, I am already used to touching [just touching] but in Africa there is no school. We have grown up like this, carrying the ball, in the street you take the ball, you dribble everyone, and you are going to score. This constitutes our strength too. Because the white, he cannot do it. The white, he plays fast, perhaps we can't play as fast as he can, but we, we dribble, he cannot dribble like we can. It is this that makes the difference, the creativity because we play ... we play with *our* genius, with our head. We learn to dribble, to do what we will (*n'importe quoi*), whereas the white, he learns to play as the master coach (*maître l'entraîneur*) tells

him ... you are going to ... you are going to play like this, from the age of six he grows up like a robot, you see, and it's different.

This is a battle of styles of playing, and what my informants assert in drawing up the dichotomy is that the pre-fabricated nature of European football diminishes the beauty and excitement of the game. Europeans tend to agree with them. In fact, the opposition is one of the tropes of global sports journalism and indeed constitutes part of the discourse of sports fans the world over. Argentinians, Brazilians, and others use similar binary oppositions to describe their style of playing, or even more commonly, to describe the styles of an earlier generation of players (Archetti 1996, 1997, Leite Lopes 1997, Leite Lopes and Faguer 1994). Hungarian sports journalism had also likened Hungarian football to "art" as opposed to the "robotized" style of Western European teams (Hadas 1999). Even Western Europeans claim with genuine nostalgia that earlier generations of football players played differently. Both sides "naturalize" the differences, while the Europeans talk about the "innate suppleness" of Africans, Cameroonians talk about the natural "rigidity" of Europeans. However, when Western journalists talk about African players along with a good dose of "noble savage," there is also a great deal of paternalism in these pronouncements. From the Cameroonian point of view, however, the tables are turned: Africans have something that Europeans are unable to attain. Africans, who are represented in almost all other respects both by the West and by themselves as inferior, "developing" nations that have not reached the finish line yet, who are always defined in terms of what they are "lacking," *possess* something that makes them superior to Europeans and to the West, and the latter are seen as lacking something instead.

This view of things, however, is often contested. Nobody doubts the artistic superiority of African footballers, and people take enormous enjoyment and pride in it. What they debate is its efficaciousness. Unimaginative, "scientific" play is more likely to yield results. Thus, if the aim of the game is to win (and it is necessary to win), then "*beaux gestes*" are not enough, results (goals) are also necessary. Especially when what is at stake is to show the world that Africans are capable of beating Europeans. On the occasion of the Chile–Cameroon match in 1998, before the whole tenor of the match was changed by an unjust referee decision (see Chapter VI), one of the viewers at the bar where I was watching said the following: "the Chileans count the goals, we, we count the goal opportunities, because," he explained, "beautiful play is good, but in the end it's the goals that count." Yet, not everybody is of this opinion. I have often heard coaches say to each other when being congratulated for a win that had been achieved in a less than spectacular manner, "Yes, we won, but how?" The above quoted former star, for example, came half way through an interview with me, mostly talking about the artistic nature of football, without once mentioning results, until I asked him specifically about it.

An unemployed university graduate talked about beautiful football in the following way:

Beautiful football in my opinion ... people could think that beautiful football is the result. For me beautiful football is when there is an aesthetic, football is beautiful when there are luminous moves (*actions d'éclats*). Football has its volunteers and the gifted footballers. When the latter make ingenious moves. When there also are results, that's the best football. Football is a noble discipline.

The former player, whom I quoted above about the natural differences between Europeans and Africans, explained the difference in the importance of art and science in football with an interesting twist:

I am convinced that football has two main elements, ... I like to speak of the scientific element first, because it is not very very very important in football, it is somewhat important, but it is not what propels football because if it were what propelled football there would not be a winning team, because everyone knows science, everyone knows technique. However, there has to be an element that overcomes this technique, this is what we call the artistic element. And it is this that a player ought to have and it is this that coaches should insist on, they should insist on this element when they choose players.

In effect, what he is proposing here is that art (creativity) is an important part of football because by virtue of not being accessible to everyone (science can be learnt by anyone), it is superior to science. Later in the interview he said the following about the question of efficacy and art:

This art, at a given moment is disorganized, but this is good disorder, because the result is good. When you have art and you don't succeed to pass ... you see it becomes embarrassing (*gênant*) and they say, but no! that's not it. And there it no longer is art. They don't speak of him [the player], the art that does not succeed is not art. Yes. Every time that you want, for example … you have an idea … or there is an immediate problem to be resolved, you find a solution that does not succeed … they won't say that you are an artist, only when it succeeds! Yes, because at a given moment it *cannot* be countered, the art, but science, you see the science of football can be countered.

This debate has its roots in colonial history and colonial discourse. Europeans were successful in colonizing Africa and the rest of the world fundamentally because of Europe's technological superiority. No wonder then that technology (science) is a permanent attribute of Europeans among Cameroonians.

People often bring up the "white man's magic" in conversation. Usually the term is used to mean technology, and though it indicates a certain amount of joking, it is also quite serious. For example, traveling in a communal taxi in Western Cameroon an old man, clearly a cultivator of little wealth and education, said to me in 1997: "The good God had given Europeans technology and to Cameroonians" – he paused for effect and concluded – "Paradise!" Technology, in this formulation, is the "God-given" realm of the European; it is not something that belongs to Cameroonians. What they have instead is Paradise, and though it is not very clear what Paradise is, it is the flip side of technology, something that is equally good, and perhaps morally superior, to have.

The perception that the imbalance of power between Africans and Europeans hinges on science/technology does not come from Cameroonians alone. Europeans were actively propagating the idea, as can be seen from the following quote cited by Mbembe (1986), from the French administrators of Cameroon from the troubled last years of the French colonial era. Following the death of Reuben Um Nyobe, the charismatic leader of the UPC rebellion for independence, the French were pre-occupied with ensuring their domination over the territory, and with "pacifying" the Bassa area where resistance was the strongest. Mbembe quotes the following from a 1958 document containing the directives of the French occupying force regarding their psychological plan of action:

[The task is] [t]o convince the Bassa that the UPC has definitely failed and it will inevitably be eliminated from the Cameroonian political scene, because European 'magic' (intellectual dynamism, technical expertise, material efficacy) unquestionably will overcome 'Bassa sorcery'. (Quoted in Mbembe 1986: 60)

What is most remarkable in this statement is that its terms, especially as relating to Europeans, keep coming back half a century later on the lips of Cameroonians. The denigration of Africans as implied by the reference to sorcery is of course an equally important component/constituent in ensuring the domination of Europeans over Africans (cf. Eboussi-Boulaga quoted in Mudimbe 1988: 51). These tactics have been successful to the extent that they continue to influence Africans' conceptions of both themselves and of Europeans/whites. Stereotypical images of European efficiency and rationalism keep cropping up among Cameroonians in discussions of comparisons of Africans to Europeans.

Actually, here lies one of the main contradictions. Cameroonians are painfully aware of the advantages Europe has over them in terms of both material well-being and power. In Cameroonian eyes, Western society is successful, certainly in the material and political sense, and they attribute this success to the "white man's way." While recognizing that the wealth of Europe (in the Cameroonian case especially of France) is largely due to the exploitation of Africans, they also attribute these differences to a different kind of rationality and organization. The combination of the hegemonic power of these stereotypes and the inadequacies of their lives (underdevelopment, poverty, mismanagement of affairs small and large) leads to the paradoxical situation that, forty-odd years after independence, many Cameroonians continue to subscribe to these notions.

The fundamental contradiction of the colonial situation was that while introducing and imposing the Western state and notions of nationalism and laying claim to universalism, the colonial state insisted on maintaining the difference of the ruling group, in other words, excluding the colonized (cf. Mamdani 1996). Of course, this exclusion continues in the global inequalities of the post-colonial world. Nevertheless, decolonization, at least on an institutional level, did take place leading to what Liisa Malkki (1995) has termed a "national order of things."

"THE NATIONAL ORDER OF THINGS"

This is Chatterjee's outer domain, where the colonized, both during colonial times and afterwards, had no choice but to choose from the "modular" forms of nationalism offered by the West. Malkki (1995) argues that the mythico-history that the Hutu refugees in Tanzania construct for themselves "is a vision of a community of distinct 'nations' entering into relationships with one another" (252). "At issue is not the denial or denaturalization of the order of nations but the attainment of a legitimate place in that order, a seat at the table" (253). The implication is that Malkki's Hutu informants' mythico-historical imaginings are validated and legitimated by reference to this system. Without it – without imagining the nation – their continued suffering, both through memory and in the continuing presence of the refugee camps they are confined to, would have little meaning. Though obviously the very refugee situation renders Malkki's case extreme, I would agree with her that the international system of nation-states makes imagining the nation in juxtaposition to other nations a compelling one.

To return to the question of the national order of things, in order to participate on an equal footing in the global world, the nation-state seems to be the only game in town. The political battle for having "a seat at the table" has been fought and independence achieved, though at a great price. At the price of having to acknowledge the superiority of the West in the outer domain and to live with the consequences, which include both the continued economic and political domination of the West and the inadequacies and contradictions of the postcolonial state.

Participation in international sports events, such as the World Cup, encapsulates this history and the concomitant contradictions, with some twists. Being part of the quintessentially Western invention, that is the World Cup, is proof of "having arrived at the table," of being an equal member of the modern, global world. This is why the struggle of African countries for a more proportionate representation in the World Cup final is of significance. The first twist is that despite the niceties of institutional equality in the global arena, Cameroon, like other Third World countries, remains unequal to the Western powers, who – not just in economic and political terms, but also in cultural ones – continue to set the rules. The other twist is more or less unique to sports participation in that, unlike in the rest of the world arena, here Cameroonians stand a real chance of being equal; sports makes it possible, not just imaginable, for them to achieve at least momentary superiority to the West. It is at this very moment of rare visible equality, of being the *same* as everybody else, that asserting *difference* becomes not just important, but possible. It is in this context that Cameroonians support the national football team unequivocally, even when they have reason to doubt whether the victory is eventually going to benefit them. I will discuss this question further in Chapter V.

NATIONALISM AND ETHNICITY: A DIALECTIC RELATIONSHIP

Though the few references to football in the literature on both Cameroon and Africa all acknowledge the sport's capacity to unite people, most authors regard the notion of the nation to be irrelevant to the concerns of the people so-united. Part of this is clearly due to the undeniable fact that as an ideology for internal consumption, the nation has lost much of its luster in Africa since the time of decolonization. (I will deal with this question in greater detail in the next chapter.) Partly, however, the disregard for the nation stems from the importance attributed to ethnicity and ethnic conflict among scholars dealing with the question. In the remainder of this chapter, I wish to turn our attention to some issues regarding the dynamics of ethnicity in football and the dialectical relationship of ethnicity and the nation in Cameroon as manifested through football.

The ethnic component has not disappeared in Cameroonian football, and in fact, on lower levels of the competition and especially outside the official system of national championships, there are many instances of ethnicity being *the* driving principle of football. Village championships organized by migrants, bringing together fellow villagers in town, are an important addition or alternative to traditional village meetings. The expressed goals are to "animate" and allow the town-born young members of the village to get acquainted with each other. Given that only descendants of members of subdivisions within the village can play on a team, people scrutinize the origins of the players. This can give rise to debates about the legality of the presence of a certain player on a team, including calling for elderly witnesses. Because the witnesses then explain how the player can be considered a member of the village, such disputes also lead to revisions and relearning of traditional ways of reckoning kinship. The village championship I observed and followed over a six months period in 1995 has meanwhile stopped functioning because of controversies over the handling of money that came in at the post-cup gala. One of the organizers remarked to me that it was a pity because the championship had become like a post office for the village: everyone knew where to go to find everybody. Very large crowds of the descendants of the village turned out for the events, and the matches constituted an informal meeting place for all.

Village championships also take place locally, when youngsters who regularly arrive "home" for the summer holidays are organized to participate in impromptu championships within or between villages all over Cameroon. This is so widespread that – as I discussed in the previous chapter – many "official" teams have difficulty holding on to their players during the summer holidays as youngsters disappear into the villages. Such local village championships are not unique to Cameroon, for example, Roman Sarro (1999) shows how these events are used in local identity negotiations and intergenerational power struggles among the Baga of Guinea (Conakry).

GOING BEYOND THE ETHNIC GROUP

However, despite the continued importance of ethnicity in football and thus its role in maintaining ethnic distinctions and boundaries, it also undoubtedly leads to a crossing of boundaries on the level of the everyday practice of the sport. Not only does football create non-traditional standards of behavior, such as a new notion of time or a turning upside down of patterns of respect (e.g. age vs. youth), but also and most importantly, it creates linkages among people who would not otherwise be linked (cf. Clignet and Stark 1974, Ntonfo 1994a and b, Onana 2004a and b).

In the course of a sporting career, football players are exposed to a great many people from different ethnic groups. As players, they often play on multiethnic teams and even when they play on a team that is ethnic – that is to say, its supporters and leadership are identified with a single ethnic group – the players themselves will come from a variety of ethnic groups. This is because despite ethnicity, teams and especially coaches, who do much of the recruiting, are often willing to seek out the best players regardless of ethnic origin (cf. Chapter III). The average football player will have played with at least three or four teams, and the ethnic mix he will have been exposed to is far broader than what he would be exposed to had he not played football. Thus, for example one of the then players on the national team, himself a Beti, in a radio interview in May 1995 recounted that he had started playing in Santos in Yaoundé (a Beti team with a Bassa coach), then he moved to a team of the Western Province (a Bamileke team) for three years, and he finally moved back to the capital to play in another Beti team. His relations with the Bassa coach were such that he had sometimes paid for the some of the coach's children's education and even bought him a set of training clothes. A former player of the national team from an earlier era, the 1960s and early 1970s, recounted a similar experience. Of Duala origin, he first played in *Oryx* and *Léopard*, both of them Duala teams. Besides these, however, he played on several Beti teams and when his work called him to Bamilekeland, he transferred into a Bamileke team in Bafoussam. (Tapa nd: 6).

In addition, teams, especially in the First Division, but even at lower levels of the competition, often play official and unofficial matches outside their regular milieu and inevitably will make contact with coaches and players from other teams and other ethnic groups. In Yaoundé, players often recruit each other and interestingly, in many cases, they will not be of the same ethnic group.

Football also creates relationships that endure beyond an active career. Much of the human structure of Cameroonian football is made up of former players, so much so that the innumerable more or less volunteer coaches, the officials of the federation, the referees, etc. for the most part have played football in their youth, and all seem to know each other as former teammates, rivals, coaches, and players. This leads to a complicated set of alliances that do not necessarily conform to the rules of ethnic exclusivity.

Then there is the "2-0," which is an institution in itself, uniting former players in recreational football. These are the "old boys'" teams, which play on weekends. The name 2-0 originates in the practice (dictated by having too many would-be players) of having two teams play, until one of them leads by two goals, at which point the losing team will yield its place to those still waiting to play.

The 2-0 of which I was an honorary member, had the representatives of at least six ethnic groups among its ranks and the friendships into which people paired off were far from being ethnically determined. The team constituted what could be seen as a voluntary association, but instead of the ethnic homogeneity characteristic of many urban African voluntary associations it consisted of a variety of ethnic groups. Members of the group used the ties thus established to seek help from each other in time of need. This could range from advice or help with banking, medical services from one of the members who was an orderly at one of the hospitals, or to help with finding jobs. One of the members, a former referee of Bassa background, upon retirement from a low-ranking job with the police returned to his village to supplement his pension through cultivation. He would only come back to Yaoundé occasionally, but, because he maintained his friendships in the 2-0, he could count on being able to sell the plantains he grew to several members of the group. In 2005, he listed one Bamileke, one Duala, and several Beti members among his regular customers. I myself have taken advantage of my membership in the team when I was in a dispute with someone. When I presented my problem to the leadership, they decided that the President (a former player of the national team from the 1960s and a well-respected coach) and Vice-President (a high-ranking military officer, also a former member of the national squad) would accompany me to settle the problem. Their presence was essential to the peaceable resolution of the dispute, mostly because it demonstrated that I had connections and backing from important people.

Beyond generalized mutual assistance certain team members had enduring friendships, often across ethnic lines. One of the noticeable interethnic friendships was that between a Bamileke and a Bassa; the two were practically inseparable. If you saw one of them, you could be sure that the other one was not far away. The former had been the coach of the latter. They even lived near each other and the two families helped each other out, thus the football relationship grew into a relationship reaching beyond the confines of sport. Another, for some time inseparable, pair was a Bamileke and a Duala. The former had his own young team and the latter for a while was its only supporter. Supporter here means turning up for training sessions, providing advice, and financial support.

Another man on the team, a former Second Division player, who is Bamileke, started his career with a team in Douala and played not on a Bamileke team in Yaoundé but on a Beti team of Sangmelima, a nearby town. He described his experience with football as something that helped him establish himself in his career as a carpenter because, instead of money, he asked the leadership of his Sangmelima team to provide him with contacts for job orders. At present, he does most of his production for a government company, which sells goods to government employees on credit. His access to the store is through a Bassa member of the old boys' team, and he faced great difficulties in getting paid for his delivery when his team member was on leave. Incidentally, this carpenter was also instrumental in organizing the village championship mentioned above. Thus, being ethnic and cooperating across ethnic lines are not necessarily contradictory.

Ethnicity is a fact of life in Cameroon. People are aware of it and, prompted in part by political rhetoric from their leaders, see "*tribalisme*" as a factor that stands in the way of national unity. They also use heavy-handed ethnic stereotypes to guide them in their daily lives and in their opinions. Yet, despite this, they trudge along in a sometimes-precarious balance with each other. In the realm of football, along with the crosscutting tendencies that bring people together across ethnic lines, there is also the constant tension caused by the centrifugal force of ethnicity. For example, the members of the 2-0 discussed above constantly bickered over what bar to go to after matches. The often unstated question related to what ethnic group the bar owner belonged to (i.e., whose group should benefit from the regular and considerable patronage the weekly revels meant), and the group often switched its allegiance to satisfy contradictory pressures from the members. The underlying "ethnic resource competition" was never mentioned publicly; instead members argued about the location of the bar, the quality of the service, the friendliness of the owners of the bar, etc. The members were aware of the "dangers" of ethnicity, and in a variety of ways consciously (albeit without openly airing the problem) tried to counteract them. This brokering of ethnic peace was obviously helped by the interethnic friendships among members of the group and by the football ethic according to which, everyone was of equal worth by virtue of being members of the team, sometimes expressed in the statement "*nous sommes des sportifs*" (we are sportsmen) to cut through some divisive debates.

Accordingly, the leadership of the team (president, vice-president, secretary, vice-secretary, treasurer, vice-treasurer, technical director, coach, head of the disciplinary committee, etc.) was carefully chosen to create ethnic balance. For example, on the occasion of the 1995 elections, when there was a "rebellion" among the membership in the course of which some younger members were nominated for some of these positions, the ethnic balance remained untouched. One of my friends, a much respected older member of the group, who was not running for office but was one of the behind-the-scenes negotiators, proudly related to me privately afterward how successful he had been in making sure that the different positions were evenly distributed between the different ethnic constituencies of the group.

Coaches often see the presence of ethnic considerations in football as detrimental to the goals of the game. On one occasion, two coaches in the stadium were discussing the performance of a Third Division team, which has been lingering in that "inferior" division for a long time. They observed that the team did not seem to be able to progress in its play because it was "too tribalist." One of them remarked, "I knew immediately that they were limited when I saw the list, all their players except for the goalkeeper belong to the same tribe." What he meant was, that choosing their players for reasons other than talent, namely ethnic belonging, the team could not possibly field the best elements. The most likely reason why the team had to settle for a non-ethnic goalkeeper is, of course, that goalkeepers have the most specialized skills of all the players, and thus are the hardest to find. When the team was unable to find a suitable one among players of the "right" ethnic group, the leadership had to compromise in signing on someone of a different ethnic background. Thus, in this view meritocracy – disregarding ethnic origins in choosing players – is the only way efficacious action is possible in football. Naturally, meritocracy contradicts and undermines one of the basic underlying principles of ethnicity.

PLAYING WITH ETHNICITY

But there are also ways in which ethnicity can be played with or its negative effects circumvented in football. On one occasion, the team I worked with in 1995 played against an ethnic team of Muslim northerners. Ethnic team here means that not only was all of the team's leadership recruited from the ranks of the Muslim community in Yaoundé, so were its players. As we saw above, a purely ethnic team can be a liability because it is not free to choose the best players. Yet, such a team can also have a plus in the commitment of the players to the team. Knowing this, Coach Nguidjol prepared a surprise. He had a former player who was a northerner and recruited him for this match. The player's appearance was a complete shock to our adversaries, and they were badly rattled by this "betrayal."

In 1998, Coach Nguidjol told me that he had had a goalkeeper who belonged to one of the autochthonous ethnic sub-groups of Yaoundé. The player was "lent" to him by his friend, the older coach, who had worked with our team in 1995. Meanwhile he had been recruited to train a team of his own ethnic sub-group in the capital; the same one from which the player hailed. When the two teams met in the Third Division championship, there was a possibility that the goalkeeper might "sell" the match, under pressure from his fellow "villagers." To circumvent this, Coach Nguidjol took the player aside and explained to him that he was going to appoint him "captain" of the team for the match. He also told him that if he sold the match, he would lose the esteem of his own people, as they would be aware of his betrayal, whereas if he delivered a great match, he would gain everybody's respect. This is actually the most common argument coaches have to dissuade players from "selling" matches, and in as much as football is about gaining or losing respect, it is a persuasive one. Needless to say, the player delivered a great match.

These examples point to the fact that while ethnicity is a factor in the everyday life of football, its effects are far from straightforward. While ethnicity can be a source of solidarity as well as of divisiveness, it can also be manipulated, turned inside out and harnessed to unexpected ends.

Both the case of the members of the Old Boys' Club brokering ethnic balance and peace and Coach Nguidjol's manipulations of ethnicity illustrate the viewpoint of sportsmen, people who are intimately involved with football. For a great number of them, at least as far as practicing the sport and achieving their goals through it, ethnicity is not an issue, except in the sense of having to overcome the complications it presents. In this sense, football people do differ from much of the rest of the population for whom very often football victories are intimately tied up with identity and prove the superiority or inferiority of "us" to "them." This of course is not limited to Cameroonians or Africans. Sports give rise to strong partisan identifications everywhere in the world. In the following discussion, I will turn to this outsider's view of football and show that rather than being antithetical to each other, nationalist and ethnic sentiments can be seen to be in a dialectical relationship, where both are part of a continuum of identity choices.

UNITING AND DIVIDING: WHO CONSTITUTES THE NATION?

On June 22, 1997, Cameroon disappointingly tied against Gabon as part of the preliminaries for gaining a berth in the upcoming African Nations Cup, which was to take place in Ouagadougou in early 1998. The Lions had done rather badly in the match. After they led by 2-0 and then 2-1, at the last minute, Gabon managed to score an equalizing goal, leaving Cameroon's qualification for the competition in doubt.

As a dispirited Cameroonian and a jubilant Gabonese team were leaving the stadium, a corpulent older man came up to me and my companion, a coach, in great agitation. He started by saying that he was very angry. He then pointedly remarked that he was angry at the First Vice President of the Fécafoot because the latter had prohibited a man, wearing a bishop's hat, a bishop's staff, and a white robe sporting the green–red–yellow of the Cameroonian flag, from circumambulating the stadium during half-time. In fact, the "bishop" is a familiar figure at all international matches taking place at the Yaoundé stadium. In excited tones, our friend exclaimed, "it's the Bamileke, always the Bamileke!" (*Ce sont les bamileke, toujours les bamileke*). He went on to explain that had the "bishop" been allowed to proceed, he would have protected the national team, and that he (our speaker) had been told that the result was going to be 2-0, and would stay that way. "It's impossible that every time there is an international match the Bamileke betray us. Because the bishop would have protected us, but

Colonel Tchatchou didn't let him." Colonel Joseph Tchatchou, who was at this time the First Vice President of the Federation, was Bamileke, and the man making the remarks was Beti. The Colonel was in charge of the stadium for the match in his capacity as a Federation official.

Much of the rather sparse literature on sports in Africa seems to deny that they have national integrative functions, although such functions have been amply illustrated elsewhere, especially in Europe (Hargreaves 1986, Holt, Mangan and Lanfranchi 1996, Mangan (ed.) 1996). Rather the emphasis has been on the divisive aspect of sports, which brings out the "ethnic" in Africans (Edensor and Koodoruth 2004, Last 2004, Monnington 1986, Stevenson 1989) even in the case of the national team. Of course, circumstances differ within Africa, and even within the same country there may be changes over time in how ethnic and national identification and sport performance are interconnected. Cameroonians tend to put aside their differences and unite behind the national team so much so that many commentators see it as the only thing uniting the country. The Cameroonian social critic, Abel Eyinga wrote the following about the national team after the elimination of the Indomitable Lions from the 2002 World Cup: "It is the only institution that brings honor to our country in the world, the only one which brings spontaneous and enthusiastic solidarity (*adhésion*) to all Cameroonians of all regions, all tribes, the only one that we all respect and love." (*Le Messager* June 12, 2002). Thus, ethnicity and nationalism are not mutually exclusive categories. In analyzing ethnicity, anthropologists have come to describe it as situational and flexible (Cohen 1978, Vincent 1974). Ronald Cohen defines ethnicity "as a *series* of nesting dichotomizations of inclusiveness and exclusiveness ... [where] ... the cultural identifiers used to assign persons to groupings ... expand or contract in inverse relation to the scale of inclusiveness and exclusiveness of the membership" (Cohen 1978: 387, emphasis in the original).

Nationalism is merely one more of these flexible and situational identities, an alternative that can be chosen at certain times from among other identities. The various alternatives need not be consonant with each other. This makes sense also because of the segmentary nature of sports competition. When lower level teams are opposed to each other, the identities that come to the fore are local identities; when higher level teams are opposed to each other, the inclusiveness and scope of the identities that are evoked are going to increase to match the level of the competition, and this allows for and even invites these "nested" identities.

Thus, at issue is not so much whether sport is promoting unity or divisiveness. It clearly does both. In Africa it even goes beyond nationalism in promoting more overarching, pan-African identifications. For example, after Cameroon's stellar showing in the 1990 World Cup, *Jeune Afrique* (No 1538, June 20-26, 1990) in a banner headline, cutting diagonally across the lower right corner on its title page, said "Africa among the great," referring to Cameroon's and Egypt's showing at the World Cup. A few weeks later, upon the conclusion of the competition – which of course had been won by Germany, – the *Jeune Afrique* (No. 1541, July 11-17, 1990) headline declared "It is Cameroon that Won!" – in handwritten block letters superimposed over the photograph of a stadium covering the entire title page.

Certainly, in 1994, after Cameroon was eliminated from the competition, Cameroonians were quick to shift their allegiance to Nigeria, the only remaining African side in the competition. Many bought the Nigerian flags being sold in Yaoundé on the night of Nigeria's match against Italy. When Nigeria lost the match, a Francophone Cameroonian friend told me the next morning that he had been so upset that he almost cried, even though Cameroonians tend to have a rather antagonistic attitude to Nigeria and in football consider them to be one of their main rivals. Interestingly enough, somebody I spoke to in 2006 recalled the same sentiments regarding that match. And in 2002, everyone rejoiced when Senegal beat France in the World Cup's opening match, which of course, had great symbolic significance for Cameroonians as well as for all the peoples of France's former colonial empire.

How easily this identification is made, and how one African country is made to stand for the whole of Africa is shown by the following statement by a woman caller to the English version of the 1994 call-in radio program on the day of the Nigeria–Italy match. She identifies Nigeria with Africa as she wishes fervently for the Nigerian team's success:

> Well, to start off the Nigerian side showed up a good game and I am sure they defended the ... *the African nation* as a whole and all I can wish them that they

should keep on and try to, at least fly *the flag of Ni … Africa.* … I hope will attend maybe even the semifinals. (July 2, 1994, emphases added)

One could object that Europeans do not automatically support the next European team when their own has lost, but shifting loyalties in such a case is a question of power relationships, and in the case of Africans such switches are facilitated by their perception of a commonality of fate vis-à-vis Europe. This is, of course, the product of their colonial history, of being dominated and exploited by Europe, and the continuing structurally weak position that African countries share in relation to Europe and the United States today.

It follows from the segmentary nature of the game's organization that football is capable of both uniting and dividing people. At the same time, we should include nationalist and pan-African (as well as ethnic) sentiments in the framework of coexisting and available identity choices, where the scope of inclusiveness will be triggered, and to a great extent, determined situationally.

To what extent it will be "determined" seems to depend on the level at which we find ourselves. That is to say, Cameroonians followed this system of increasingly widening nested identifications throughout the 1994 World Cup to the point that the majority supported Brazil against Italy in the final on the grounds that "Brazil is a Third World country, like Cameroon," and possibly, because there are blacks on the Brazilian team. I have not heard the latter explicitly stated in the case of the 1994 World Cup final, but judging by the commentary and keen interest with which Cameroonians scrutinized the racial composition of foreign teams, it is more than likely that this factor played a part in the ready identification of many Cameroonians with Brazil. To give an example of the kind of scrutiny I am talking about, there were many jocular comments on why Saudi Arabia was considered an Asian team in the World Cup, when clearly many of their players were black. I discuss the same kind of scrutiny of the ethnic/racial makeup of the French team in 1998, and the different interpretation of the same phenomenon advanced by Cameroonians in 2006, in Chapter VI and Chapter VII, respectively.

However, in the case of the 1994 final between Brazil and Italy the identification was much less binding, and a minority felt perfectly at ease supporting Italy, whereas it is unlikely that it would have been possible to openly support Italy against Nigeria, or even more pertinently, any team against Cameroon. The same trends characterized subsequent World Cups as well, albeit, with some twists at times. As we shall see, in 1998, when the competition took place in France, Cameroonians – while being adamantly opposed to France – were united behind the other African teams as well as behind all those teams that they considered to be underdogs. In 2002, Senegal's defeat of France in the opening match of the World Cup in Japan/Korea was vicariously enjoyed by most Cameroonians, expressly because people felt that by beating the former colonizer Senegal accomplished a long-awaited feat on behalf of all Africans. However, when, upon being qualified for the quarterfinals, the Senegalese boasted that they would outdo Cameroon at the World Cup by going beyond the quarterfinals, public opinion turned against them. The resentment it occasioned was remembered even four years later. Thus, when national sentiment and pride clash with pan-African sentiments, national pride wins. In 2006, the situation was more complex. As we shall see in Chapter VII, Cameroon did not qualify for the World Cup, and the significance of the event was reduced. I will also argue that the change in attitude had to do with political changes that have taken place in the country, namely with the general depoliticization of Cameroonians compared to the highly charged political climate of the 1990s. It still remained that people expressed more interest in the fate of African teams than of most other selections, but Cameroonians adamantly turned against Côte d'Ivoire, the team they considered to have "usurped" the Lions' place in Germany.

In this proposed framework of nested identities, pan-Africanism today does not make nationalist or ethnic sentiment impossible tomorrow or even the next minute, as can be seen from the contribution of the woman caller quoted earlier. Nor does the existence of nationalist sentiment exclude ethnic sentiment (and vice versa) as evidenced by our friend's statement at the stadium.

Put somewhat differently, in all the debates about ethnicity and nationalism, little attention has been paid to nationalism in areas, especially Africa, where we are not expecting to see it. In a 1996 volume on African ethnicity, Fardon, for example, devotes only one paragraph to nationalism in his conclusion to a highly imaginative analysis of the constraints imposed on "ethnic narratives" by their respective interethnic contexts. In a parenthetical aside, he mentions that nationalism should be evident in Africa, if at all, on the level of organized sports (Fardon 1996: 142).

To return to our stadium interlocutor, he was being ethnic and nationalist at the same time. His very presence at the stadium was an indication that his interest in football went beyond the purely ethnic. Someone with a purely ethnic interest in football would go to the stadium only when his ethnic team plays. This man was in fact present at every match played at the stadium, but there are many others who only turn out for the matches played by their own team, and that often happens to be an ethnic team. Our friend's fervent need to find an explanation for the result is also proof of his nationalist sentiments. Yet the exegesis he chose to present, apart from its magical undertones, was purely ethnic. He singled out an individual, who, even if the story of his constraining the "bishop" were true (about which I have no information), was only doing his duty, presiding over the peaceful unfolding of the match. And in addition to blaming the Colonel for the result, he jumped from him (an individual) to his ethnic group and generalized that the *entire* group was *always* trying to sabotage Cameroonian success in *all* international matches. The point is that in one breath our man was being both a nationalist and an ethnic chauvinist, questioning the patriotism of groups other than his own in a way that also involved questioning who exactly constituted the nation.

Many of the contributions to the radio program, *Bonjour l'Amérique*, bore witness to the fact that indeed football on the international level elicits from Cameroonians the same kind of nationalist fervor as we are used to elsewhere. In many of my interviews, the majority of interviewees predictably supported their own ethnic teams, but at the same time, they also supported the national team. Often what we find is that people go to matches only when their team plays and when the national team plays. This is no different from any European fan who will support his own team (chosen on whatever basis) and the national team, and no one sees any contradiction in this. Cameroonians act in exactly the same way and we are surprised because we supposed them to be ethnic to the exclusion of all else.

What Cameroonians debate is the definition of the nation, who is a true patriot, who is betraying "us." And this is where nationalism the "unifying force" becomes divisive, in denying other people's commitment to uphold the honor of the nation. As I tried to demonstrate earlier, football is a two-edged sword and while it can be both ethnic and nationalist, and even when it is nationalist, it can be divisive.

CHAPTER V

VISIONS OF A BETTER GOVERNMENT

This chapter continues with the issues raised about the meaning of the nation to Cameroonians, but turns to questions, which concern the internal constitution of the notion of Cameroon. Naturally, the division into internal and external aspects of the imagining of the nation is somewhat artificial, and people move smoothly back and forth between the two and often their awareness of the external aspect shapes their view of the internal.

FOOTBALL: OPIUM OF THE MASSES?

In the following, I examine articulations of national feelings inside Cameroon by scrutinizing Cameroonian responses to the 1994 World Cup. I will do this through an analysis of audience contributions to the call-in program, *Bonjour l'Amérique*, and its English language counterpart, *Hi America*, which could be heard on CRTV, the government-controlled national radio. The program became especially lively when Cameroon lost its chance to move on to the second round of the competition when it first lost to Brazil, but especially when it suffered a heavy defeat (6-1) from Russia. Before turning to the World Cup, I will briefly explore the question of whether football has been successfully used by the Cameroonian government to gain legitimacy in the eyes of the population. Based on responses to the government's efforts to usurp the Lions' quarterfinal finish at the 1990 World Cup, I will argue that their effects were at most temporary, and not only did Cameroonians tend to see through them, but they often subverted them. These attempted co-optations of football were part of what I referred to as the "unbearable discrepancy" between the government's official discourse (ideology) and the worldview of Cameroonians, their lived experience of reality. The people turned the official rhetoric against itself and, subverting the government's attempt to appropriate the game, they reappropriated it. In 1994, the population questioned vociferously the government's right to distance itself from the humiliating loss the national team suffered in the World Cup, re-appropriating football by challenging the government in the name of the nation. Here, the nation became the ethos, the ideal, which – according to many Cameroonians – was subverted by the government.

The importance of the intersection of football and the official nationalist agenda is that, unlike other aspects of the latter, which the people can dismiss cynically or with disdain, in the case of football some of the officially announced objectives and the desires of the population (winning, proving to the world that Cameroon is equal to or better than others) meet. When the national team plays, the sport's genuine popular appeal and the binary oppositions it so easily calls into action make the mobilization of nationalist sentiments much more likely than in the case of almost any other undertaking. Consequently, the opposition to the government's announced objectives becomes more ambivalent and subtle as people walk a fine line between registering their opposition to the government while maintaining their patriotism.

Cameroonians' passion in refuting their government sprang from a combination of their love of the game and love of their country. Many people thought that the government subverted football by using it for its own ends, and by extension the government also subverted the country. Both of these subversions were experienced as an affront. This is why when reeling from the humiliation that the country suffered in 1994 on the football field, people turned against the government.

One of the possible reasons why sport has been largely disregarded by anthropologists may be due to the oft-heard argument that sport is an "opiate for the masses" (just as it has been claimed for religion, yet that does not stop us from studying religion). What most authors mean by this is that sport serves to direct people's attention away from their daily problems and their causes, or that governments seem to be able to forward their agendas by taking advantage of football victories. But on closer examination, football is equally capable of mobilizing popular sentiment against governments and people are often able to see through the smokescreen of government propaganda (cf. Bromberger 1994b). It is quite likely though, that sport in itself cannot mobilize a population; rather it will act as a catalyst in situations where political discontent is already there.

1990: GOVERNMENT CO-OPTATION

Cameroon's unexpected success in 1990 helped the government, which was struggling to fend off opposition demands for greater democracy. The general euphoria and pride that the country's good showing at the World Cup unleashed provided a useful respite for the government, creating some breathing space and giving it an opportunity to try to usurp the victory, by claiming it as its own. So, for example, President Biya flew to Italy to attend the opening match, and when the team returned to the country in glory the day was made a public holiday. The Lions made a victory tour in Douala and the following day in Yaoundé. They encircled the city going from the airport to quite distant neighborhoods where, at certain points, dance groups met and greeted them. The tour included the presidential palace, various educational establishments, major markets, important traffic junctions, the Radio Broadcasting house, and finally the Yaoundé Hilton in the heart of the city (cf. Nketcha 1990/1991). All the participants, players, as well as coaches, and significantly, journalists, were decorated by the head of state.

Glorious as the event was, it did not stem the tide of dissent and, as discussed in Chapter II, public discontent continued to escalate during the months that followed. Although the government repeatedly tried to exploit the national team's 1990 success, most of the population was not taken in by these attempts. For example, as the team is called Indomitable Lions, it was not surprising that for the 1992 elections Biya's propaganda machine created an election poster divided into two panels: on one side the president, on the other side a lion and the words, in English and French, "Courage Man – President Man" (*Homme Courage – Homme Président*) overlay both images. On one of the panels it also said, "My President Paul Biya." But the poster backfired. Distorting its meaning, or rather creatively rereading it by reading the images rather than the words, people often sarcastically refer to the president as "lion man" (*homme lion*). This popular deconstruction of the poster implies that people saw through the government's attempts to usurp the Lions' victories, and by the very fact of using the term, they were denying the President's right to identify himself with the Lions. Francis

B. Nyamnjoh (2001: 35) argues in a similar vein: "In taxis, market places, bars, chicken-parlours and elsewhere, ordinary people saw Biya's message as a corruption of reality. He was a lion, no doubt. But his mission was not to save, but to devastate, for five more years, Cameroon and her people." As the Lions often symbolically stand for the nation, by challenging the poster Cameroonians also questioned the legitimacy of Biya as president of the nation. The ironic use of the term also was an expression of the contestation that was going on about who the victory rightfully belonged to, and who was to be blamed for losses. The latter theme came to the fore during the 1994 World Cup.

To mark the first anniversary of the 1992 "stolen elections," the opposition, still active in 1993, called for a general strike on the day (October 11). It fell on the day after the Lions' qualification for the 1994 World Cup, thus providing a golden opportunity for Paul Biya to declare the day a public holiday and to neutralize the commemoration. In André Ntonfo's vivid phrase this was "killing the hen of political contestation in the egg" (Ntonfo 1994a: 214).

1994: CHALLENGING THE GOVERNMENT IN THE NAME OF THE NATION

By the time the 1994 World Cup took place in the United States, people were, in general, less hopeful about the future and the continuing economic crisis, coupled with the withheld salaries and drastic decreases in the pay of civil servants, led to a somber mood. Distrust, even hate, of the government in the wake of the political upheavals of the early 1990s was still rampant. Furthermore, the 1994 devaluation of the CFA franc deepened the economic crisis, making the economic situation of a population – which felt that it was already destitute – even worse.

As we shall see, Cameroonians' love and support for the Lions was not diminished, but the general feeling was that the team had been inadequately prepared for the upcoming competition and – in light of the government's earlier attempts to co-opt international football – many secretly or not so secretly feared that were they to do well, the government would again try to take advantage of the victory. Although people were not taken in by these attempts, they constituted a keenly felt affront driving home to people, in Mbembe and Roitman's terms, the "unbearable discrepancy" between publicly announced reality and people's lived experience of that reality. It was precisely because of this that people feared that a victory would give the government an excuse to sweep things under the carpet and to pretend that there were no problems in the country and to do nothing about them.

As a young goalkeeper, who was also a university graduate, said, "When my family watches the Lions on television we no longer root for them because they will use it to their advantage, and not put anything back into the development of the sport." He hastily added, "it's not that we are not patriots ... just that the victory helps hide the problems." The young man's insistence on being a patriot despite not rooting for the Lions is interesting in that it throws light upon a fundamental split between nation and government, between popular nationalist sentiments and official nationalism, between what the government expects from the citizens and what the citizens see to be the duties of the government.

The statement illustrates rather well the ambiguity of the Lions as a symbol. In this formulation, the Lions represent both the government and the nation, and the young man is forced to turn against the government in the name of the nation. His reasons for turning against the government (as represented by the Lions) for not supporting the sport (the Lions) are peculiar to the sportsman. However, other people – as we shall see – took a wider view. They metaphorically identified the sport with the nation, and blamed the government for not living up to its obligation to protect the honor of the nation to the external world, and for using the sport to veil (and thereby disregard) internal problems. Thus, as a multivalent symbol, the Lions can serve to represent two – in this context antithetical – domains: the government and the nation.

Another person, an educated Anglophone, when watching the first match Cameroon played against Sweden in the 1994 World Cup with a group of Anglophone élites in Bamenda, wandered away from the group prior to the match. Imitating Biya he muttered in French, as if to himself, but loud enough for me and presumably others to hear, on what would happen if they won: "You see my dear compatriots with everyone pulling together we can win." The fact that he used French – an unusual act in an Anglophone milieu – highlighted his ironic intent, but the statement also voiced a general fear on the part of many Cameroonians that a victory would only hurt the people, as it would help continue the intolerable *status quo* of pretending that all was well in the country. In 2005, when Cameroon failed to qualify for the 2006 World Cup, although greatly disappointed, many people voiced the opinion that perhaps this was for the best as it might force the government at last to do something for the sport. They pointed to the fact that despite Cameroon's many victories in the international arena, no new infrastructures were in sight and local football was still suffering from a lack of proper care and attention.

In 1994, people's fear that the government would take advantage of the Lions' performance at World Cup turned out to be unfounded because Cameroon was eliminated from the competition after the first round. The national team drew with Sweden and was beaten by Brazil and Russia. The latter was a shockingly heavy loss that everyone saw as a great humiliation to Cameroon.

The match was preceded by great anticipation as there was a mathematical possibility that Cameroon could still qualify for the second round if they managed to defeat Russia by a large score. Russia had no chance of advancing, having lost all of its matches. What happened shook everyone. Russia proceeded to beat Cameroon 6-1, the most severe loss inflicted on any team in the competition. Such large scores are unusual in football and especially unusual at such a high level of competition. The lone Cameroonian goal was scored by Roger Milla, who at the age of forty-two was referred to as the Old Lion. Interestingly, in later references to the match, people often unconsciously changed the score to 6-0, as if to further emphasize the humiliation of Cameroon.

In the neighborhood bar where I saw the match people watched it with increasing dismay, although in fact the mood was one of seeming hilarity, as the rather monotonous rain of Russian goals was accompanied by premature shouts of "*but, but*!" (goal!, goal!). This communal irony was broken only when Milla scored, and the entire bar erupted in true cheer with people jumping up and down and hugging each other, dancing little dances on the side. The next day, when I went to see my newspaper vendor friend, glimpsing each other from afar, in acknowledgment of the embarrassment that befell Cameroon, both of us had rueful smiles on our faces. The defeat almost defied words. Actually, it was at this point that Cameroonians truly started to pour out their hearts on the call-in radio program, their overwhelming sentiment expressed repeatedly by one phrase, was "*ça fait mal*" ("it hurts").

BONJOUR L'AMÉRIQUE

It was after the match against Brazil that the call-in radio program *Bonjour l'Amérique* became the most listened to program of the period. It ran from 5:30 to 9:00 a.m. every morning. As Cameroon is officially a bilingual country, soon after the launching of *Bonjour l'Amérique*, an English language version, *Hi America*, also began and ran for two hours every afternoon. This was less listened to, due to its timing, but in fact there were contributions to *Bonjour l'Amérique* in English as well as in French, and the occasional French contribution also cropped up in *Hi America*.

Cameroonians responded enthusiastically to the opportunity to make themselves heard. Phone calls came in from all corners of the country although predictably the greatest number of calls came from Yaoundé and Douala, both the most urbanized areas and historically the strongholds of Cameroonian football. One might suppose that phone calls meant that responses would be limited to a narrow well-to-do layer of the society. However, calls came from phone booths as well as from offices. As one informant pointed out, household members might be coming from a variety of social backgrounds, [1] and anyone could make use of the telephone to participate in the program. In addition, there were daily sessions with the provincial stations of Cameroon, where "man-on-the-street" interview spots were commonly featured. Furthermore, people in Yaoundé could and did arrive at the Radio Broadcasting House to leave letters to be read on the program and even to participate personally, while mail arrived daily from the provinces as well. Even though the match against Russia ended about 11 p.m., by 5:30 a.m. the next morning there were some letters dropped off at the Radio Station which had been written during the night.

---

1 It is well-known that African households, especially urban ones, are hard to define clearly, as apart from family members, friends, servants, and close or more remote relatives, or even fellow villagers may be found in any given household at any given time (cf. Guyer 1981).

The focus of the program changed over time. Before the Lions were eliminated from the competition, the audience was called upon to make suggestions on the composition of the team, and in general, the program expressed the support of the nation for its team. After the defeat, the listeners were invited to analyze the causes of the fiasco and to make suggestions on how to improve Cameroonian football in the future. As Cameroon's fortunes changed for the worse, however, the program became a forum for people to pour out their hearts, air their disappointment, and try to find reasons for the poor showing. As it was a call-in program many remarked that this was the first time in Cameroon's history that people were allowed to freely express their views in the media. Actually, the openness of the program decreased over time. At first, there was very little contrary opinion expressed by the journalists to the remarks of the listeners, and the majority of the program was taken up by listener contributions. Then on July 8, Augustin Kontchou Koumegni, the State Minister of Information famous for his denial of the casualties at the University of Yaoundé in April 1991 (see Chapter II), held a press conference to account for the moneys gathered for the World Cup (see below the discussion of *Opération Coup de Cœur*). This seemed to signal the beginning of greater control over the program, as from then on there were many more prearranged interviews with experts and fewer audience interventions. Throughout the program there were some instances, however, when people got cut off, either directly or indirectly, by being told that they had spoken for too long and should finish quickly. Interpreting these instances of cutting people short is difficult, but some of the other contributors seemed to think that these were attempts at censorship. Another factor was the quality of the reception, or the phone connection, which sometimes was so bad as to render the contributions almost or totally incomprehensible, and the question arose, in my mind at least, whether this was not due to intentional interference with the reception. After a period of considerable freedom of expression censorship re-emerged quite dramatically toward the end of the World Cup, when the program was cut off by music at a point when the soon to be dismissed Minister of Youth and Sports was about to intervene and it was likely that he was going to contradict the Minister of Information (cf. Nkwi and Vidacs 1997).

The program began to gain in importance as Cameroon's situation in the World Cup worsened. As many journalists and listeners pointed out, especially after the humiliating defeat of Cameroon by Russia, it served as a safety valve. Immediately after the match, journalists started talking about the importance of remaining calm. More importantly, by allowing people to speak in an almost uncensored manner, to vent their anger, bitterness, and disappointment, more drastic action, either in the form of attacking the residences of the players and coaches or in the form of some unspecified revolutionary action was forestalled. Many Cameroonians blamed the government for the poor performance of the Lions, and their anger and humiliation may have physically turned against the government. Thus, for example, a few days after Cameroon's defeat by Russia, a Francophone caller said the following:

> ... every author of this defeat, everyone who one way or another had a hand in this, starting with the Prime Minister, Mr. Kontchou [the Minister of Information], and others should resign, because, gentlemen you are enjoying yourselves, but such a coup could smear the entire government. And it is also for this reason that we demand that the Head of State should, really, open a very important page in this story, because if not, he too will be considered an accomplice of the first order. (July 2, 1994)

No drastic action took place, perhaps partly due to this program. Callers were apparently satisfied with breaking verbal taboos. At the time, people were surprised and jubilant over the amount of freedom of speech the program afforded them, stressing how this was a first and unique occasion. Even months after the World Cup, people on the streets of Yaoundé derived a certain satisfaction from recalling the program, saying, usually as closure to the discussion, "the people spoke." That the memory of the program continues to linger in people's minds is shown by the fact that in 2005, when I interviewed a group of people about the non-qualification of the Indomitable Lions for the 2006 World Cup, one person commented with satisfaction and nostalgia halfway through the conversation, "this is just like *Bonjour l'Amérique*!"

FOOTBALL AS METAPHOR FOR CAMEROON

Talking on the program, people constantly slipped from assessing the fate of football to the fate of the country. Metaphorically identifying the sport with the country, many of their complaints no longer spoke about football, but about Cameroon. This was a reflection of both people's emotional investment in and concern for football and ultimately for the fate of the country and its people.

While dissatisfaction and disillusionment and even desperation were mounting in Cameroon, the terms for the expressions of this dissatisfaction were Cameroonian terms. People took Cameroon as an entity, and as a point of reference, for granted. It is as Cameroonians that they were disgruntled, it was as Cameroonians that they felt disappointed. Anglophones are supposed to be the least likely to buy into the ideology of national unity in Cameroon, yet the first reaction of an Anglophone intellectual, not a friend of the Biya regime by far, upon hearing from me that Cameroon's controversial goalkeeper, Joseph Antoine Bell, resigned from the national squad during the 1994 World Cup was to ask whether this meant that Bell had resigned from being Cameroonian.

Through criticizing the circumstances under which they were living, they showed visions of how the country should be. The topics they touched upon ranged widely: among others they discussed the importance of football to Cameroon, criticized the government's mismanagement of the preparations for the competition, including its inability (or unwillingness) to pay the players, the disorganization reigning in football, as well as the choice of a French coach for the Lions (I will discuss this question in Chapter VI).

An Anglophone caller who began his contribution in French then continued in English was trying to analyze the reasons why football was so important to Cameroonians:

> It is because, I guess, every imaginable aspect of our national life is therein represented to a very high degree. Consider the political dimension, the economic, the social all are clearly manifested in Cameroon football. To the extent that football has come to be the last and most respected and adored source of our national pride and hope, the greatest, and now I daresay the only incarnation of our national unity – so much has been going wrong in our football, in football, in this country and in general management of affairs of this country. (July 2, 1994)

Variations on the theme of football uniting the people and its importance to them abounded, coming from journalists and listeners alike. A Francophone woman caller said the following with great emphasis and emotional force, the tears in her eyes audible in her voice:

> Our coach should understand that even if Cameroonians are starving, even if they have problems, what remains for them is their football team. And under no circumstances should anyone take our football team lightly (*s'amuser avec*) because that is the only thing that remains for us when we have lost everything. (June 25, 1994)

The urging of the government – both from listeners and journalists – to take the matter seriously kept recurring, indicating both this concern and people's assessment that the government had been found lacking in this respect. In general, Cameroonians felt that the government did not care about their concerns, and its members were only bent on pursuing their narrow personal or ethnic interests. Francis B. Nyamnjoh, a Cameroonian political scientist, concludes bitterly: "The system is interested in nation-destruction, not nation-building, national disunity, not national unity, disintegration, not integration. It finds comfort in chaos, and makes of conviviality a subject mostly of rhetoric" (Nyamnjoh 1999: 109). Many of the responses to the 1994 World Cup echoed the despair and frustration of this statement.

When people warned and sometimes begged the government to pay attention to what was happening in football they were also begging and warning it to pay attention to what was happening in the country; and these entreaties were fuelled by frustration and anxiety that the government was allowing the country to deteriorate.[2] These statements were often contradictory because the government was clearly paying attention to football (by interfering in it, trying to control or influence public opinion about it, and by trying to usurp football victories); however, from the people's point of view, the government's attention was misdirected because instead of inter-

[2] There is a difference between the reading of Cameroonian social scientists and ordinary Cameroonians. The former are much more likely to attribute this phenomenon to conscious policy on the part of the political leadership (cf. Eyoh 2004, Kofele-Kale 1986, Nyamnjoh 1999). By contrast the latter, as evidenced in these contributions, seemed (or hoped) to believe that the government was unaware of these problems. Thus for example an Anglophone woman caller said the following: "… I think the Parliament is sitting right now. Let those parliamentarians, if they are listening to me, know that it's their duty to *talk* on behalf of the *people* to our Head of State" (June 30, 1994, emphasis in the original).

fering in ways that undercut people's efforts to achieve their desires the government should have ensured that things worked properly.

OPÉRATION COUP DE CŒUR

One of the most important failures of the government was its inability to pay the players for their participation in the World Cup. To make up for this, Simon Achidi Achu, the then Prime Minister, launched *Opération Coup de Cœur*, a fundraising drive for the national team prior to the World Cup in May 1994. It called upon people to contribute to the effort to pay the expenses of the World Cup. People understood this to mean that they were paying the Lions.

There was considerable controversy around the demand. Many considered it to be an imposition, forced upon people, and much resented in the deteriorating economic circumstances reigning in the country. However, given the ambiguous meaning of the Lions as a symbol of both the government and the people as discussed earlier, many paid, seeing that it was a necessary sacrifice to help the Lions. The collection took place all over the country. In government offices they went around with collection sheets, and people had little choice but to pay. Village associations (both inside and outside the villages themselves) also took up collections, and there were people who paid both at their workplace and in their village association.

There were frequent reports on radio and TV about the collection in various localities of the country, thus creating a competitive mood where different districts or provinces were somewhat artificially pitted against one another. The collection extended to prisons, and many who commented on the event remarked somewhat wryly that even prisoners (who by definition have nothing) paid. [3] Another recurring phrase was that "even old mothers" (*vielles mamans*) paid. People found it incongruous that the most miserable members of Cameroonian society should come to the aid of the government in meeting its obligations towards the Lions.

---

3 This was recalled even eight years later in a letter to the editor in the opposition paper, *Le Messager*, by a reader who analyzed the Lions' lack of success in the post-1990 World Cups. "They even took the money of young prisoners to – as they called it – support the Indomitable Lions" (Moukoko Priso 2002).

Humor is never buried deeply in Cameroon and given the contradictions embedded in the drive, soon there were several distorted versions of its name. *Opération Coup de Cœur* (Operation heart beat) became "*opération coup de poing*" (operation blow struck) or even simpler "*opération coup de vol*" (operation theft). Since the collection drive was seen by many as an occasion for the powers that be to embezzle the funds, these distortions stressed the forced and potentially fraudulent aspects of the collection, and thus criticized the government. Nevertheless, many people paid because they genuinely wanted to help the players as well as participate in a not uncommon display of one-upmanship.

One of the funniest, and saddest, commentaries on the campaign was when someone placed a sign saying "*Opération Coup de Cœur*" on a huge garbage heap at *Biyem Assi Carrefour*, a street junction in Yaoundé, where uncollected garbage was beginning to obstruct traffic. At the time there was no garbage collection in the capital, the company that had been collecting the garbage having folded (cf. Zoa 1995). At various points in town spontaneous garbage heaps arose, which when they threatened to take up too much space, or started smelling too badly, were burnt by the population, only to begin accumulating again the next day. Thus the sign was both commentary and subversion, in itself indicating that there were more important needs than football, and that help was needed urgently to cope with the garbage situation. It could even be said that it was a statement about where taxpayers' money should be going. The sign was pointed out to me just before the beginning of the World Cup by an Anglophone university professor, and a few months later a taxi driver friend also told me about it, amid some wry laughter, adding that the sign was later removed by the police.

THE NON-PAYMENT OF BONUSES

Despite the enormous amounts of money[4] collected through *Opération Coup de Coeur*, the players remained unpaid until after the match against Brazil (their second match in the competition). And even then they were only paid when, under the threat of a strike, Augustin Kontchou Koumegni,

[4] According to official figures, the collection amounted to 629,112,189 FCFA, which at the exchange rate prevailing at the time was a little over 1,250,000 US dollars (Messang 1995b).

the Minister of Information, was hastily dispatched as the Special Envoy of the Head of State to pay them. The non-payment (or delays in the payment) of the players' bonuses was often compared by the listeners of the radio program to the delays in the salary payments of civil servants. This created a public debate on whether the players should put their patriotism first (and play even without pay), or whether they were justified in putting their self-interest before the national interest. A Francophone woman argued that "the players should first defend the colors of the country" (June 30, 1994), contrasting their behavior to that of civil servants whose salaries were withheld and who, according to her, continued performing their jobs anyway. There were two responses to this, one from an Anglophone woman, the other from a CRTV journalist from Ebolowa. The woman said the following:

> "... whatever happened to our Lions, we all are crying today to the economic crisis. We say we are not paid, we trek on foot to work, and that kind of stuff. These guys are professional players, I mean they have to be *paid* for *what* they *do* ... " (June 30, 1994, emphasis in the original)

She followed up by arguing that the players have for years been giving a good name to the country, therefore they deserved to be paid. The journalist responded:

> Some Cameroonians would say why is it that the Lions have demanded their dues before playing? Because there are doctors ... there are civil servants who, who work without salary. I say to these Cameroonians that it is not right (*c'est pas normal*) that Cameroonians work without salary, may be it is becoming habitual (*habitude*), but it is *not* right (*c'est pas normal*) that Cameroonians, the Lions included, should work without salary. (July 1, 1994, emphasis in the original)

This statement takes us back to what I argued about Cameroonian perceptions of the proper way of doing things in Chapter III. Claiming that what happens in the country is not right (or not normal) posits that while working without proper payment is a common practice, it is unacceptable, that no matter what the realities are there exists a set of standards to which people should hold themselves. Thus implicitly these statements are invoking universal standards which are seen to be lacking in Cameroon.[5] In this case,

5 Eastern Europeanist scholarship has also noticed this tendency of people living in unfa-

the journalist was reminding the listeners that what they put up with on an everyday basis was not how things should be.

It is worth bearing in mind that journalists even in the government-controlled medium of the CRTV do not fall into a monolithic category. They often express views contrary to government directives and, not surprisingly, when they go "too far" they are suspended or transferred to less desirable posts. For example, after the 1994 World Cup, two journalists were suspended for having cut short the broadcast of the Chadian president's departure from Cameroon in favor of broadcasting an interview with Joseph Antoine Bell, Cameroon's iconoclastic goalkeeper, upon his return from the World Cup (cf. Nkwi and Vidacs 1997).

DISORDER AND CHAOS

In the same vein, listeners talked bitterly about the disorder and chaos reigning in Cameroonian institutions. Referring to the otherwise much disparaged French head coach, some listeners pointed out that the many problems Cameroonian football faces had rendered his task well well nigh im possible. One caller put it this way: "no matter who the coach is, no matter what his competence, it's not three months before the event that a country like Cameroon, which moreover has great ambitions in football, should have looked for a coach ... " (July 1, 1994).

A woman caller went further, condemning the disarray in Cameroon's football and sports organizations:

> ... we blame the ... the ... the coach, He ... Henri Michel. Henri Michel finds a situation which is already rotten, he cannot work with a federation which does not exist; with a Ministry of Education [she corrected herself] ... of Youth and Sports which does not exist ... (July 1, 1994).

Another caller, this time from the town of Ebolowa in the south, placed the problems of football into the wider context of the problems the country was facing and stressed the responsibility of all Cameroonians.

---

vorable circumstances to postulate a normalcy whose model is the "West" to which they aspire and in the name of which they label "abnormal" what is happening around them (cf. Fehérváry 2002, Rausing 2002).

Let's take stock of what is happening to us today, because the problem with which we are faced [...] it is the management, the management ... of public goods, the management of people, the management even of structures ... because I put it to you to show me any department, any service where ... where we don't find Henri Michels, ... Joseph-Antoine Bells. The problem is at every level. Look at the state of our stadiums, look at the national education system ... that is to say everywhere, in every domain. (July 3, 1994).

Many listeners made critical comments on the general disorder in the midst of the official delegation of Cameroon at the 1994 World Cup. There was indeed considerable confusion around the organization of Cameroon's participation. Soon after qualifying in 1993, several bodies were created to manage the Lions' preparation. The spheres of authority of these groups were unclear. Usually, the Ministry of Youth and Sports and the Federation share these responsibilities. In 1994, however, both of these organizations were crippled. The Federation was in disarray due to infighting which led to the deposition of its government-appointed president and elected a new president, whose legitimacy, however, the government did not want to acknowledge. The Ministry was also in chaos because of jostling for power within the government (cf. Ntonfo 1994a: 120-122).

Yet other callers drew attention to the resulting sense of confusion about who was in charge and who was responsible, and complained vocally of the disorder and uncertainty this entailed. This debate, too, pointed to larger issues concerning not just football but people's daily lives, leading one listener to address himself to the journalists:

You, journalists, ... we are going to the World Cup, none of our special correspondents speak of either the Minister of Youth and Sports, or of the President of the Cameroonian Football Federation. That means at bottom (*au fond*), we have political problems, that they have mixed with football ... it cannot work like that. .... Well, we have spoken a lot of Bell, of Nkono, of Songo'o [Cameroon's three goalkeepers] I think the problem was much more with politics being mixed in with football. The president of the CTO, we don't speak of him any more, so that one no longer knows who effectively directs (*dirige*) the Indomitable Lions who are in the United States. (July 1, 1994)

Speaking of disagreements among players another listener went even further, exclaiming "... it is terrible. You cannot live in a country, ... you cannot live in a country where everything is in disorder!" (July 1, 1994). Again, these statements were ambiguous. While on the one hand people resented government interference in football, by demanding clear-cut spheres of authority they also criticized the weakness of the government, in effect demanding greater interference.

It is worth noting that in decrying the confusion and mismanagement, people were often longing for greater order, and these wishes bordered on demands for a more autocratic treatment, in the hopes of a more predictable life. Nyamnjoh, writing about the 1996 constitution of Cameroon, which, as we saw in Chapter II, is viewed by many as deeply flawed, arguing that the best constitution is worthless if disregarded, wryly remarks: "I dare conjecture that if Cameroon were to be confided to a self-professed dictator, one with a vision and one ready to take Cameroon forward without a constitution – the worst-case scenario – such a person would endear himself to ordinary Cameroonians much more than have most smoke-screen democrats in high office today" (Nyamnjoh 1999: 113).

Several authors have noted that African governments have used the rhetoric of order and chaos to muzzle the political opposition (Odhiambo 1987, Bayart 1985, Haugerud 1995, Schatzberg 1993). In Cameroon's case this was so with the UPC rebellion, the adherents of which, after the movement's defeat, were criminalized by the Ahidjo government, and a similar rhetoric was used after 1990. During the early 1990s, especially "*villes mortes*" did cause considerable disorder. Therefore, it is conceivable that some of the speakers were supporters of the regime, or that they had internalized the regime's language of order and disorder, and that is why they found disorder so abhorrent. However, many other contributors made their anti-government stance quite clear. My impressions of personal encounters and conversations in Cameroon also convince me that quite a few people, possibly influenced by government and even colonial rhetoric, genuinely believe that order was necessary – not for silencing the opposition – but for living a livable life. It is as if they were protesting against what Patrick Chabal and Jean-Pascal Daloz (1999) identify as the "instrumentalization of disorder," by which they mean that the disorder that reigns in Africa, although opposed on the level of rhetoric by African leaders, is in fact fomented by them for their own benefit. In their disappointment over the performance of the Lions and general frustration caused by the many daily affronts of the inadequacies of the system, some people called for quite drastic measures. Referring to Henri Michel, a Francophone woman called attention to larger problems:

> ... it does not serve any purpose to speak of Henri Michel, because Henri Michel has been used by the government to cover itself. The problem is that we the Cameroonians should not continue to close our eyes to our ... our situation, our problem, we are in a country that we ought to direct and we should make all efforts so that things work here because we are all united in the same fate. So, what I am saying is that the government and the whole government resign, because it is not the fault of Henri Michel. ... So, all those who are concerned in this defeat should resign because it cannot continue like this. The country has run aground and we are in the process of dishonoring ourselves in front of the whole world, we could somehow continue to exist with our shame here in the country, but if it ... goes beyond the borders, we can't tolerate that. So, I myself, I demand the resignation of the government. Thank you. (July 5, 1994)

She touched on several important issues. Unlike many of her compatriots, she chose to see the issue of Henri Michel (external forces) as a red herring. Instead, she concentrated on the internal problems of the country, first affirming the unity of Cameroon by insisting that all were united in the same fate, and then called for the resignation of the government because "the country has run aground," the government had failed in its stewardship of the country. It is striking that while she attributes the problems of the country to internal factors, what she seems to find the most unacceptable about the situation is that the country is being dishonored in the eyes of outsiders. Her concern with the outside world takes us back to the impossibility of separating the external and the internal aspects of conceptualizing the nation, and to the tremendous importance attributed to the external view of their country for Cameroonians. She was not the only one to ask for the resignation of the government. What seems to be the most important in these demands is that they spring from a deep concern for the people, for the nation, and in effect, they juxtapose the nation and the government, blaming it for the humiliation of the nation and disregarding the plight of the people.

POPULAR VS. OFFICIAL NATIONALISM

In a 1998 overview of social science writing by Africans about the prospects of democracy on the continent, Dickson Eyoh, a Cameroonian political scientist, frames the debate as being that of nationalism. He argues that:

> Much of modern African social and political thought articulates a nationalist discourse motivated by the desire for technology-driven modes of economic organization and by the wish to transform national territories inherited from colonialism into viable political communities. Nationalist discourse has taken for granted institutions that universalize (Western) modernity as the foundation for contemporary society, but this discourse has always resisted the 'truth claims' of paradigms that insist on the universality of the Western model of development. ... Thus, the central point of contention in African nationalist discourse has been the extent to which the institutional and normative frameworks for nation formation and economic development required an uncritical emulation of the Western paradigm. (Eyoh 1998a: 281)

As is well-known, the match between nation and state in Africa is less than complete (cf. Mamdani 1996), although one could easily make a similar case for Europe. The idea of homogeneity even in the core European countries is proving to be more of an ideal than actuality (due to incomplete homogenization in the first place, ethnic revivals among hitherto "homogenized" populations, and the influx of immigrants) (Verdery 1996). However, this has been one of the cornerstones of the argument that nationalism is not applicable to Africa, because the arbitrariness of boundaries and the multiethnic character of the populations contained within them make ethnic sentiments more pertinent than nationalist ones. In the previous chapter, I questioned the validity of this argument, suggesting that nationalist and ethnic sentiments along with pan-African ones are likely to coexist and do not necessarily seem contradictory to those who express them. However, part of the argument against Western-style nationalism taking hold of the continent stems from considerations of the nature of political relations in Africa. Bruce Berman, in a thorough analysis of the historical roots and the present workings of ethnic relations in Africa, contrasts "moral ethnicity" with "uncivil nationalism," saying:

> ... internal processes of moral ethnicity, groping towards defining communities of cultural identity and social responsibility, contrast with an external realm of competitive tribalism defined by purely materialistic and opportunistic relationships to the state through the control of patronage. What is missing is the development of a trans-ethnic arena grounded in universalistic norms and the essential relations of social trust in the disinterested competence and probity of millions of others that are the foundation of the day to day transactions of both capitalism and the nation-state. (Berman 1998: 339)

Most Western scholars and many Africans would agree with much of Berman's pessimistic view. In essence what Berman argues is that continuing the trajectory of the colonial state the postcolonial state has not succeeded in creating either capitalism or the nation-state, and this is what explains the "lack" of universalistic standards in Africa. In contrast to this, Eyoh's overview, while not minimizing at all the problems faced by the continent, [6] suggests a different outcome. He asserts that regardless of what side the African scholars he discusses take in the debate on the prospects for democracy and the reasons for underdevelopment, they are committed to imagining a better future for the continent. [7] As he puts it:

> What is striking about the democracy debate is the determination of African intellectuals not to succumb to the despair that suffuses commentary on the continent's current predicament. The debate proclaims, in many ways, faith in the desirability, indeed the moral obligation, of articulating collective social visions. (Eyoh 1998a: 297)

It might be argued that being an African social scientist himself, Eyoh and the colleagues he writes about, are part of the very institutional barriers that Berman points to as the reason for the incomplete achievement of the

6 In fact, in another article Eyoh (1998b: 249) argues for the "incipiency of African nation-states, that is, that these are as yet in an unrealized state of becoming."

7 Eyoh identifies three schools, amidst disclaimers of difficulties of categorizations: universalist, popular democratic, and nativist. According to him, the first, roughly speaking, posits a straightforward extension of the need for universal democratic rights to Africans, the second argues that this extension of rights would reinforce the exploitation of Africans by completing the domination of the elite, which remained incomplete under colonialism, and the third rejects the applicability of liberal democracy to African societies, while at the same time affirming the ability of Africans to create democracy on their own terms by mining their own communal "African" traditions.

nation-state or capitalism in Africa. Eyoh actually grapples with this problem both in this article – the title of which significantly is "African Perspectives on Democracy and Dilemmas of Postcolonial Intellectuals" – and in a 1996 article in which he bitterly recognizes the likelihood of the co-optation by African regimes of intellectuals. "The result is the not unfounded popular cynicism in African societies of the political ambitions of intellectuals; as they say in Cameroon, Nigeria and other places, they protest until they get posts" (Eyoh 1996: 73, cf. also Bayart 1986). Here Eyoh argues that while the aspirations of African intellectuals express a strong commitment to Western modernism by virtue of their very positions in their societies, they are situated within reach of power even when in an opposition position and therefore easily co-opted.

However, that these yearnings for democracy are not limited to intellectuals could be seen from the response I got from a Fécafoot official when I asked him who had been the best president of the Federation. He answered without hesitation that it was Issa Hayatou, because in his time "the law applied equally to everyone." (The official in question is Bamileke, while Hayatou is from the North.) Based on Cameroonians' articulations of their profound disappointment with their government and their very palpable yearnings for a better world presented here, I do not think we should deny or dismiss the existence and significance of these ideas.

Nationalism may not be the right term to describe the popular rhetoric international football gives rise to in Cameroon. At the very least, we need to differentiate between official and popular nationalism. It may be useful to adopt the distinction Neil Lazarus (1994) makes via Frantz Fanon (and Anouar Abdel-Malek) between nationalism as an ideology of the ruling classes aimed at wrestling power for themselves away from the colonizers and nationalitarianism as an expression of genuine popular sentiments. The latter would lead to much greater social revolution, in fact to "the reconquest of the power of decision in all domains of national life" (Abdel-Malek, quoted in Lazarus 1994: 198). Lazarus is referring to the anti-colonial struggle and the aspirations of a revolutionary vanguard. Eyoh (1998a) talks in a similar vein about official and unofficial discourses of contemporary nationalism in Africa, and applies the latter term to intellectuals only. This view seems to me to be too restrictive. Ordinary Cameroonians, not just the educated élite, also protest the government's attempts to usurp the nationalist agenda, and through negating it, articulate an alternative vision of the nation.

Because of the continued saliency of ethnicity in many contexts, and the obvious emptiness of much of the official nationalist rhetoric, Africans, and among them Cameroonians, tend to be distrustful or, at the very least, doubtful about the possibilities of national integration, and do not easily accept the exhortations of their governments for national unity, which are seen to be empty, even cynical, rhetoric. In as much as nationalism is an ideology of the modern (nation-)state, it is largely rejected by Africans (cf. Eriksen 1993). One of the questions this chapter raises is whether this also means that nationalist sentiments are non-existent.

Merely using the term nationalism hides as much as it reveals. The meaning of these sentiments depends on the circumstances. The 1994 discourses on the Lions' humiliation throw light upon how the people conceive of the state and the nation, and what they hold the duties of the government to be. People were challenging and calling to task the government in the name of the nation, accusing it of disregarding the problems the people were faced with, humiliating them in the eyes of the world, and generally just not caring enough about their fate.

In his 1996 article, Eyoh states that it is a mistake to take for granted "that the nation-state has passed from being a contested referent for political community in Africa" (66). A little later in the text, however, he suggests that the dismissal of the notion of nationalism for Africa may be premature, raising the question "whether there exist in African societies today social agents to write alternative scripts for the ongoing task of inventing nations that depart significantly from the statist–developmentalist versions of nationalist ideology" (Eyoh 1996: 67). He argues that in viewing nationalism as a ruling class ideology, the North American political sociology literature "grossly underestimates the ubiquity of the yearnings of African nationalism ... " (Eyoh 1996: 67).

The discourses that emerged in *Bonjour l'Amérique* and *Hi America* can also be seen to express these "yearnings of African nationalism," but they come from a larger cross-section of the population than the circle of intellectuals Eyoh is talking about. This yearning is in part connected to the external aspects of nationalism I discussed in the previous chapter, based on Malkki's notion of the "national order of things," in which nationhood serves to legitimate African countries as equal members of the global world, but in part, springs from internal factors as well.

CHAPTER VI

VISIONS OF FRANCE/VISIONS OF WHITES

In this chapter I return to the external dimension of identity formation and nationalist sentiments in Cameroon. I will concentrate on how Cameroonians saw their relationship to France and the wider world – to whites as an essentialized general category – as articulated through football during the 1990s. I will discuss how these attitudes changed by 2006 in the next chapter. Here, I will argue that football provided a way for Cameroonians to define themselves in opposition to France, define who they were not. Talking about this relationship, they recalled their colonial history and reaffirmed their anti(neo)-colonial sentiments, and created a framework to talk about the external constraints that the country's continuing relationship to France imposes on their lives. These constraints reflect more accurately than does the Cameroonian government's and France's official rhetoric the self-interested nature of France's dealings with Africa. These anti-colonial sentiments were neither rooted exclusively in the past nor in an opposition to the neo-colonial constellation of things in Cameroon in the abstract, but rather constituted responses to the events of the present, in this case, to what took place at the World Cup. At the same time, World Cup football also allows Cameroonians to envision symbolic revenge for the indignities of colonization. I will argue that in situating themselves as a part of Africa and the Third World, and reacting to what they saw as unfair treatment, Cameroonians called attention to the hypocrisy of the West and claimed for themselves the application of the universal standards supposedly so dear to Westerners. While in the previous chapter I concentrated on how people saw the local constraints on their lives, in this chapter I will show how Cameroonians viewed the external constraints. What is striking is that, paralleling the turn against the government in the name of the nation as an ethos in 1994 and interpreting what took place as "white injustice," people turned against whites in the name of the ethos of sports which whites did not seem to live up to. By insisting on the ethos aspect of football Cameroonians called the white man's "bluff" of equality and universal standards.

CAMEROON'S RELATIONSHIP TO FRANCE

We should recall that Cameroon gained its independence in 1960, along with the majority of African countries, but in fact, Cameroonians waged a bloody struggle against the French in the late 1950s, which was ultimately unsuccessful. The fact that independence came about on French, rather than on Cameroonian, terms and therefore with many compromises made in France's favor, has created a sense that independence is less than complete and has undermined the legitimacy of subsequent governments in the eyes of many Cameroonians (cf. Bayart 1985, Mbembe 1986). Opposition to France is thus never far from people's minds, all the more so as Cameroon's largely unpopular governments are seen to be propped up by the French. On the surface, however, France is projected by the official propaganda of the Cameroonian government, and by the French themselves, as the beneficent "mother country" of Cameroon (and of its other former colonies).

In part, this closeness between France and its former colonies is due to what is usually referred to as the colonizing style of "direct rule" employed by the French as opposed to "indirect rule" exercised by the British; the former were much more committed to imparting their cultural values to the peoples they colonized than the latter. [1] In the present, this is also a question of France's wish to maintain the primacy of the French language, "*la francophonie*" (a hegemonic quest if there ever was one), to counterbalance the spread of the influence of the English language and American culture. Jean-François Bayart (1993) puts forth the argument that this closeness, or as he calls it "intercontinental cultural sociability" (197), plays an important role in the creation of "postcolonial historic blocs," which successfully dominate African politics. This may well be true on the level of elites, [2]

---

1 It is worth noting, however, that this opposition of "direct" and "indirect" rule is something of a simplification, in as much as the French were quite willing to resort to indirect rule when circumstances and their interests required (cf. Berman 1998, Shimada 1984).

2 An example of this closeness with France of Cameroon's ruling elite could also be heard in 1998 from Gervais Mendo Zé, the director of CRTV. In the course of the opening cer-

and apart from a very real sense of cultural connections it may also bear the stamp of realism and pragmatism. However, on the level of the "little people," as Bayart refers to them, the relationship to France is at best ambiguous and opposition to the French is never far from the surface. Football appears to be one of the areas where these ambiguities and otherwise submerged dislike can come to the surface.

Most of what has been written by social scientists about the relationship of the colonized and colonizer in relation to sport naturally concentrates on the colonial period (Fair 1997, 2001, 2004, Martin 1991, 1995, Ranger 1987, Stoddart 1988, Stuart 1996) and does not usually examine the lingering impact of the colonial relationship on how sport is imagined and talked about on the continent. These authors, by and large, see sport as an area where Africans could challenge the *status quo* of the colonial order by appropriating the imported organizational forms and by aspiring to beat the colonizers at their own game, while at the same time, forging new identities for themselves. Due to the pervasive effects of colonization and the continuing neo-colonial ties that still bind former colonized peoples to their erstwhile masters in the "post-colonial" period, the socio-economic relationships of inequality continue. Africa is more than ever dependent economically on the West, and the cultural and psychological effects of colonization persist. People in Cameroon are not blind to this and, as I argued in Chapter IV, in this context of continuing inequality on a global scale, football takes on a special significance as a possible means of – at least symbolically – redressing the balance.

FOREIGN OR LOCAL COACHES: HENRI MICHEL, THE "SPECIAL AGENT" (1994)

One of the ways in which the legacy of colonialism manifests itself in Cameroonian and African football is in the choice of the head coach of the national team. A quick survey of African national teams will show that

emony of the World Cup broadcast on Cameroonian TV, in a quasi-religious ceremony where French- and English-speaking priests prayed for the success of the Lions, he also asked that France, as the organizing country, be especially blessed. When he also declared on national radio that he supported France and Cameroon in equal measure, the comment upset quite a few people.

very often they tend to employ foreign coaches.[3] Of the five African teams participating in the 2006 World Cup in Germany, only one, the Angolan national selection, had a local coach; the rest (Côte d'Ivoire, Ghana, Togo, and Tunisia) had foreigners as their head coach. What is more, these coaches are not only foreign, but also white, and often come from the ranks of the former colonizers of the country. This raises the specter of colonialism and reminds people of the continuing ties to the ex-colonial powers, thus forcing them to rethink these issues and their relationship to the former colonizer. Needless to say, football is not the only crucial field in Africa that is dominated by foreigners in general and the former colonial masters in particular. As a result, frequently, when they talk about foreign coaches, people are metaphorically talking about Cameroon, just as they did when they used football as a metaphor to talk about the internal affairs of their country. However, in the case of foreign coaches the fate of the country is considered with regard to the outside world, and especially to the former colonial power, France. In the 1994 radio program, besides blaming local circumstances, much of the blame for the Lions' poor performance was put on Henri Michel, the French head coach. Thus, employing metonymy, Henri Michel also stood for the French, and even for whites; and the ques-

---

3 Cameroon has had a succession of expatriate coaches over the years. Some were French, some German, but there were also some Yugoslav coaches in the 1980s, and in 1990 the victorious "Italia" squad was led by a Soviet. More recently, there have been two Germans, one Belgian, and a Portuguese as well as a Dutch coach. Often the pattern in Cameroon has been for national/local coaches to qualify the national team for international competitions only to have to relinquish their powers to the incoming foreign coaches, who then take the team to the next, international level. This was the case in 1994, when Henri Michel was engaged to lead the Indomitable Lions to the World Cup in the United States, just a few months before the beginning of that competition. Things have not changed much since, although at the 2000 Olympics the national team had a Cameroonian head coach, Jean-Paul Akono. The foreign head coach was reinstituted after the Lions' return, however. (See also Bissohong 1998 for an analysis of the Cameroonian reception of Claude LeRoy just in time for the 1998 World Cup, and what he characterizes as Cameroonians' fascination with "heroes coming from elsewhere.") Many of these coaches are only hired a few months before an international competition, and people rightly complain that they are unfamiliar with Cameroon and with the players. For example, Otto Pfister, a German coach was only hired on October 26, 2007, to take the Indomitable Lions to the African Nations Cup, which was to begin on January 20, 2008.

tion of the relationship of Cameroonians to Henri Michel also became the question of the relationship of Cameroonians to France, and when blaming Henri Michel for the poor showing of Cameroon they were also blaming France.

We have to keep in mind that in the political climate of Cameroon of the early 1990s, in the eyes of many Cameroonians opposed to President Biya's regime, France was maintaining him in power against the will of the people. Therefore, criticism of Henri Michel, and by extension of France, also reflected indirect criticism of the regime. The fact that Henri Michel was French also contributed to the chagrin of the people, because it served as a reminder of the colonial past and the neocolonial present, the incompleteness of the ending of colonialism. At the same time, however, the reverse was also seen. Reminiscent of the anti-government discourses I discussed in the previous chapter, some contributors to the program regarded Henri Michel as a red herring and pointed to the Head of State for the failure of the Lions in the United States. Several of these callers drew attention to the fact that Henri Michel was taking orders from the Cameroonian president.

One listener was satisfied with merely raising the rhetorical question: "We are looking at Henri Michel, but at the end of the day who gave the orders to Henri Michel?" (June 29, 1994) Others went further and firmly, if sarcastically, pointed out the connection:

> Everyone complained that Henri Michel is a dictator … Let us remember that the President of the Republic asked him in France … told him in France that he had a green light. Well, when it is the President of the Republic who gives a green light to someone, then this gentleman has no longer to be accountable to anyone. (July 5, 1994)

Another caller went further in irony, expressing the same sentiment in a tongue-in-cheek statement.

> I would like to call to the attention of Cameroonians that when they reject (*désavouent*) Henri Michel today that they should nonetheless know … that the President of the Republic, as First Sportsman (*Premier sportif*[4]) had given full powers to Henri Michel in Paris by even giving him a grant of a hundred million to

4 According to Nketcha (1990/1991), "*Premier sportif*" is one of the official (honorific) designations of President Biya. Golf is his preferred sport. The term is often used ironically (cf. Bikoun 2003, Kom 2007).

distribute to the players. That they pay attention! that they don't hide behind this story to reject the Cameroonian First Sportsman. (June 30, 1994)

These statements indirectly criticized the untouchability and unaccountability of the President, their humor barely disguising the bitterness. The implication of the powerlessness and frustration of the people in the face of such powerful forces is hard to escape, yet the ironic undertone of the statements also undermines the government's message.

Many of the callers to *Bonjour l'Amérique* demanded a local Cameroonian coach to head the national team. They pointed out that there were Cameroonian coaches equally well qualified as the foreign coaches.[5] Contributors also reminded their fellow listeners that the national team had been qualified by local coaches, and Henri Michel only took over after the qualification had been achieved. An Anglophone woman caller for example said:

... the ... the national team qualified with people like Manga Onguéné and Jules Nyongha [the actual assistant coaches of Henri Michel]. I don't see why Henri Michel is there. He has not done anything at all and if I *were* the Cameroonian authority ... I would ask that he resign or we ... we dismiss him! (June 25, 1994)

A little later, she continued:

---

[5] Apart from the felt need to assert sovereignty, one of the main reasons why expatriate coaches are resented by many, and especially by sportsmen, is that the resources to which expatriate coaches have access are far superior to those at the disposal of local coaches. The salary of the foreign head coach is several magnitudes higher than that of the local head coach. The latter is a civil servant, and being appointed to be coach to the national team does not bring any immediate financial benefit, although in the case of a good performance by the Indomitable Lions, the coaches receive generous bonuses and decorations. Furthermore, it is widely known in Cameroon that expatriate coaches work under infinitely better conditions than local ones. For example, they have a car with a government-provided petrol allowance to go prospecting for players, which, according to Cameroonian coaches, would never be the case for Cameroonians. The inequity of these practices does not escape anyone's notice, and Cameroonian coaches, as well as the general public, are quick to draw attention to this. Like so many other things, it drives home to them that even in their own country they cannot have the respect that is their due. After 1998, this problem became obsolete in that the players of the national team are chosen almost exclusively from the ranks of players who play abroad.

… I believe this … this is time we have to overcome our complex and trot out … our nationals … our nationals. When they were qualifying, was Henri Michel there? He wasn't there. Why is it that when … when we qualify … they … they have to go and bring an expatriate to come and spoil our team?! (June 25, 1994)

Similar comments abounded, sometimes stressing the need for Cameroonians to take charge of their affairs, as for example in the comments made by a man in Maroua, in the course of a "man-on-the-street" interview:

I say, when we are speaking about Cameroonian football, Cameroonians should be in charge of our … our football. Because what I see actually is that the … the expatriates whom they bring here to Cameroon cannot really control things. When we speak … when we speak on the national level, really it is still our coaches who can at least achieve something. When they bring the expatriate coaches we do not get to the outcome that we want. So, let us really, us Cameroonians, do our thing so that, so that we can see what may arrive. (July 1, 1994)

Another Francophone speaker made the connection between nationalism and foreign coaches even clearer: "We have seen what Jules Nyongha was capable of doing … […] because if they bring a Westerner here … that is something …, that is somebody who has no patriotism" (June 29, 1994).

There were two counter-arguments to the demand for national coaches. One was employed primarily by journalists and sports professionals but it was also echoed in some contributions by listeners. This was that foreign coaches were necessary because if the results were unsatisfactory and the coach was local, the population would attack the coach and his family. The second one could mostly be found in listener contributions. This was the question of tribalism, where the argument ran that expatriate coaches were necessary because, not being Cameroonian, they could stay above the problems caused by tribalism. Here, for example, is what a Francophone woman caller from Yaoundé said:

Henri Michel here and there and everywhere! No, we are all tribalists and really we practice tribalism in Cameroon. If it had been Manga Onguéné or Jules Nyongha we would have said he had taken more Bamilekes than Ewondos. No, we shall always need an expatriate because we are *too* tribalist in Cameroon. Too much. So, we are shooting at Henri Michel, we need such a person to come … to settle our quarrels. Let's try … amongst ourselves to stop this tribalism, that way we would be able to go further. Thank you. Goodbye. (June 29, 1994)

Others acknowledged the force of this argument but argued against having of all whites, a French head coach. Another Maroua speaker said the following in a man-on-the-street interview:

> Because … to bring a French coach here to Cameroon, we want that to stop. Henri Michel is the last French coach who came here to Cameroon. … We know that Cameroonians will always be Cameroonians. … That they bring other coaches, because the Cameroonians will always do their tribalism. So, I myself, I propose that they bring a coach other than a Frenchman. This is what I wanted to say. (July 1, 1994).

There was more to these vehement rejections of Henri Michel than the assertion of national autonomy. Several contributions to *Bonjour l'Amérique* represented an undercurrent of strong anti-colonial sentiments. As another caller put it succinctly "… already the choice of Henri Michel, it's as if it was a form of *re-colonizing*, well, *Africa*," (June 29, 1994, emphasis added). These sentiments gained their fullest expression in a discourse that was fully anti-colonial. In effect, they articulated the strongest anti-French perspective, basically suggesting that since the French had not been able to qualify for the World Cup themselves, it was foolhardy for Cameroonians to think that a Frenchman would lead Cameroon to success.

A woman who had submitted a letter set the stage for her contribution by stating that "since 1960, and even before, these French did not want to give us our independence, but we got it at the price of blood." Rejecting Henri Michel, she continued later, "we want that our affairs return into our own hands" (July 2, 1994).

Others went further in their statements, outlining a veritable conspiracy theory. The following statement is from the Francophone man I quoted above, who suggested that foreign coaches cannot have the necessary patriotism to lead a national team. He continued, saying:

> Let's look at the case of Henri Michel, this is a Frenchman. We know that France was eliminated by Bulgaria. I don't know how Henri Michel could find it in his heart of hearts to want to do something for … for [… the line is bad] from his heart. The white man says to himself that the Negroes, the Negroes cannot ever advance … (June 29, 1994)

Another caller, placing the question into the context of international politics, went even further and described the expatriate French coach of Cameroon during the crucial and humiliating Cameroon–Russia match as someone who was on a special mission to undermine Cameroon. He said:

> … I would like to call the attention of Cameroonians to what happens on the international scene. We have seen the great powers that put everything into destabilizing other rising powers … . I think that from the moment when Cameroon was, wasn't it, considered to be one of the great football nations of the world … well, we must not forget about these little games. So, I see clearly that if we observe carefully Henri Michel's comportment throughout this competition, his intrigues have shown that he was, wasn't he, a special agent (*envoyé spécial*) who came to destabilize our team in this World Cup. So, really if we look back at the Cameroon–Russia match, you will see his outbursts, you will see his outbursts of satisfaction, his eye movements, his attitude which was, wasn't it, one of a … of a man who was satisfied with having accomplished a certain mission. (July 3, 1994)

In the very fact of their construction these narratives transcend the question of the actualities of football and become metaphors for the relationship of the colony/post-colony and the colonial/neocolonial power. Naturally, there is no way of knowing whether there is any factual basis to them; in fact, they seem rather far-fetched to me, but that is not the point. Taken as symbolic statements, they talk about a different layer of truth, that of colonial past and neocolonial present, where the intentions of the erstwhile masters have not changed and cannot change, because they are based on self-interest and pride. It is in the sense of this deeper historical truth about the French, that the significance of these remarks about the French head coach should be understood. It is clear to everyone that independence has not delivered to Africa the prosperity or the social and economic justice, in short, the promise it held. The root causes of this failure are very often to be sought in the past, in colonial history, and in the exploitative neocolonial present. France, as well as other Western powers, continues to safeguard its own interests, and despite rhetoric to the contrary, its interests are often served by upholding a *status quo* that may serve the local elites, but to the majority of Africans, seems to be against the interests of the people. Thus victory on the football pitch against the former colonizers would take on dimensions well beyond the scope of the match itself, demonstrating the "revenge" of the underdog.

As André Ntonfo (1994a: 230-235) has shown, this is the case even at a remove, for example, when Bulgaria beat France and thus eliminated it from qualifying for the 1994 World Cup, Cameroonians, despite their usual interest in and support for French football, were dancing on the street celebrating the discomfiture of France. In 2002 when Senegal beat France, the reigning world champion, in the opening match of the competition Cameroonians openly rejoiced.

In 1994, when the Lions were defeated, Cameroonians symbolically evoked history by blaming the French coach and saw the shortcomings of the national team and of the nation itself as the result of this history. Fantastic and hyperbolic as these narratives may seem, they were not so different from those explanations of the defeat discussed in Chapter V, which took stock of the less than ideal circumstances in which Cameroonian football found itself. These anti-colonial narratives saw the same situation but took a wider view, and contextualized the problem differently.

1998: DRACULA DEVOURS THE LIONS

In light of the reactions to the French head coach in 1994, it should not be surprising that the fact that the 1998 World Cup took place in France was especially significant to Cameroonians even before the event. A Francophone university professor told me in 1995 that for him it was essential that Cameroon should qualify for the 1998 World Cup because it was going to be a unique historical moment for the country to play against France. As it happened, Cameroon never got a chance to play against France, and in fact was eliminated after the first round of the tournament under circumstances that were highly irregular.

The match that seemingly decided Cameroon's fate was that between Cameroon and Chile. It was a dramatic match with dramatic consequences. It took place on June 23 in the afternoon. In order to advance to the second round, Cameroon absolutely had to win, whereas for Chile even a draw was enough to advance. Chile opened the score around the thirtieth minute. Toward the end of the first half a Cameroonian goal was refused because of being offside. In the second half, one of the Cameroonian defenders got a red card, and Cameroon continued the game at a numerical disadvantage. Despite this, with beautiful and determined play, the Cameroonians started to dominate and eventually managed to equalize. Then François Omam Biyick, the captain of the team, positioned a little behind two Chileans, scored a goal, which was refused by the Hungarian referee for no reason that anyone could see.

I watched the match in a bar in Yaoundé, and there was palpable shock in the room. People could not believe their eyes. They shouted scandal, someone yelled, "it's impossible, whites don't want blacks to win!" A woman behind me asked in disbelief, "so, whites do such tricks?" They kept repeating "it was a good clear goal!" Meanwhile another Cameroonian player was expelled, and eventually the match ended on the score of 1-1, and thus the Indomitable Lions were eliminated.

Immediately following the match, there were riots in Yaoundé and Douala, where the public – for the most part the young and disenfranchised of these two cities – attacked all whites who happened to be around. Spontaneously, from some of the popular areas of town, young people carrying placards saying things like, "enough is enough," "whites go home," and chanting anti-white and anti-FIFA slogans had filed down to some central areas of the city, trying to find whites to beat up, and in several instances managed to do so. Ironically, many of these whites happened to be people who were completely unaware of what had happened. The rioters surrounded one of Yaoundé's supermarkets where many whites are known to shop and had a face-off with the police who were protecting it. Elsewhere in town, some whites were pulled out of their cars and roughed up, while some windshields got broken. The police dispersed the crowd with tear gas, and by evening the hostilities were over. According to an Anglophone news report:

> The pandemonium was brought to a halt when the delegate general for National Security, Bell Luc René, suddenly appeared. He called his boys to order then moved towards the demonstrators who were already constituting groups and pleaded. "Your cause is genuine and your point has been made". (*The Herald* No. 624, June 24-25, 1998: 2)

Apparently, elsewhere too, the police mostly pleaded with the population to stop. One can imagine how difficult it was for the police themselves to contain their own emotions.

Being Hungarian, like the referee, I had an additional reason to be concerned for my safety, but in fact, I saw nothing of the riots, as after the match, I took refuge first in a restaurant and later at a friend's house. Until this match, I took pleasure in telling people that I was Hungarian. Following it, I found it prudent to say that I came from the United States when asked (an equally true statement). My personal friends, aware of my nationality, could easily make the distinction between me and the referee, and if anything, they were amused by the irony of the situation I found myself in, while at the same time remaining sympathetic. All of them expressed concern, one going so far as to come and visit me two days later, saying that he had been worried about me as he had not seen me the previous day.

All the headlines in Cameroon's newspapers the following day dealt with the match and the racism involved. To quote some of the titles: "The cretin," "Dracula devours the Lions" ("Two goals cynically refused, and two red cards. Dracula has freed himself to drink the blood of the Lions." *La Nouvelle Expression*, 380: 6, June 24, 1998). Regardless of political leaning, they were unanimous that what had happened was a blatant example of racism. This confirmed what had all along been the opinion of many people: whites were in cahoots to frustrate Africans. Even prior to this match, throughout the World Cup the distribution of red cards as well as other decisions of the referees seemed to people to be biased against Third World peoples in general, and against Africans in particular. Although, as I indicated in Chapter IV, Cameroonians are apt to identify Brazil as a Third World country, in discussions of this aspect of the competition, Brazil was identified as one of the "great football countries," and thus assimilated to the powers that be. In this context the riots seemed justified, and there was practically no condemnation in the newspapers of the violence unleashed on the capital and on Douala, as it was seen by everyone as a natural response of frustration to what was seen as inadmissible partiality on the part of the referee.

This perception of bias was further reinforced by the fact that the same evening there were two other matches, one between Morocco and Scotland

and another one between Brazil and Norway. They were played simultaneously to avoid fixing the results to benefit one of the teams in passing to the second round. Brazil was already qualified, but if Norway managed to beat Brazil, it would advance instead of Morocco. Morocco beat its opponents 3-0, but at the last minute, the referee of the Norway–Brazil match awarded a penalty kick to Norway, which the Norwegians translated into a winning goal. The penalty did not seem justified, raising charges that it was awarded in order to ensure that Morocco would not advance to the second round [6]. This event coupled with Cameroon's questionable elimination made the suspicion of racism perfectly plausible to everyone.

The following day I spent most of the morning in a "*téléboutique.*" [7] As I entered the shop, the first sentence I heard from the young woman running the store was, "we are going to kill whites here!" At almost the same moment, a young man who was setting up his CD-stand which was also inside the boutique, said to me, "Don't be afraid, Madame." Amidst these contradictory statements, I sat down to wait my turn to make a long-distance phone call to Douala. I spent more than an hour waiting, and heard a wide array of commentary on the match, and people's interpretations of what had happened. During most of the discussion I was ignored (perhaps studiously), but some people (people kept coming and going during the whole time) even engaged me in conversation.

Primarily the discussion consisted of reliving the match and the disbelief and hurt that everybody experienced during and after. A lot of what was going on was venting, in general against whites and the injustice that

---

6 Morocco's coach in this competition was none other than Henri Michel. After Morocco was eliminated under these dramatic circumstances, the black sheep of Cameroon's 1994 participation was welcomed back in Morocco as a national hero, and according to the Cameroonian media was given honorary citizenship. Interestingly, while other aspects of the 1994 competition kept cropping up, in 1998, there was practically no reference to Henri Michel's role in the performance of the Lions in the 1994 World Cup.

7 These were little stores with a couple of telephone booths and often one could also find a photocopying machine, or a computer, where someone did word processing. It was an ingenious way of overcoming the lack of infrastructure. People could make phone calls, receive messages and keep "phone dates." Because cell phones became widely available by the early 2000s, *téléboutiques* became obsolete in Cameroon. Cyber cafés have taken their place to some extent.

had befallen Cameroon. The young woman kept repeating that whites were going to be killed. Another young woman added, "It is not even the referee, but FIFA. But what is FIFA? Is God white? The whites cheat. They are afraid of us, so they resort to such tricks." The young CD vendor said that if he were the government he would declare the return of the Lions a holiday. Behind this statement was a sentiment that kept being repeated for the next few days, and which was actually how the match got etched into Cameroonian memories: in the eyes of Cameroonians, the Lions had won the match. The return of the Lions is usually declared a holiday when they win or do extremely well, as for example in 1990, or when they qualified for the participation in the 1994 World Cup, thus, making the day a holiday would symbolically "correct" the result on the football pitch.

During the next couple of days, the pure hate that emanated from people against whites was quite amazing to experience. The day after the match, I was in a restaurant with my research assistant where two men kept watching us for a long time. When they left, they addressed him in Ewondo (one of the Beti languages). He later recounted that they warned him that because he was "guarding" me, they would get him too. However, the most striking example of this sudden surge of hatred was that strangers on the street who normally referred to me and addressed me as "*la blanche*" (white female) when they wanted to call my attention to themselves, suddenly were looking at me appraisingly and said with considerable disgust "*le blanc*" (generic white [male]). This "de-gendering" and essentializing indicated more eloquently than anything else the depth of people's bitterness over what happened in the Cameroon–Chile match. It also demonstrated how such discourses were constructed. I, along with all whites, became the enemy, reduced to one aspect of my identity, the color of my skin. Race and gender are two of the most obvious markers of any person's biological identity; taking away one of these, as these people were doing, meant that the battle lines could be drawn more sharply, white against black, black against white, just as people perceived it to have happened on the football pitch. Since women are not considered to be seriously concerned with football, identifying me as a female would have given an opportunity to sidestep the issue and see me as negligible from the point of view of the "war" that was being declared.

Within a few days the sentiment got translated into jokes, some of them also indicating that recognition or non-recognition of my gender status constituted an important dividing line in deciding whether I was perceived as the enemy or not. Two days after the match I was in one of Yaoundé's textile markets with a friend, and we overheard two teenagers making the following exchange: "is this the white who killed us?" "No, this is a woman!"

The discourse to which the Cameroon–Chile match gave rise in Cameroon was remarkable for its consistency and centeredness. It was an essentializing discourse, which as shown in the above example, removed all possibility of ambiguity and alternative interpretation. To a great extent, the government set the stage for it. Thus, it was the Minister for Youth and Sports who first started to talk about the injustice and racism of whites already in the case of Cameroon's second match against Italy, where the defender, Raymond Kalla, had received a red card. The day after the match, in an interview on CRTV, the Minister recalled the 1982 World Cup in Spain where Roger Milla's goal against Peru was refused, and attributed the refusal to the racism of the referee (*La Nouvelle Expression*, June 24, 1998). Interestingly, nobody had ever mentioned this event during my earlier stays in Cameroon, and the few written accounts of the match did not speak of racism in this regard either. CRTV later proceeded to re-broadcast that segment of the match. The riots were a spontaneous expression of people's frustrations. The newspaper coverage produced a seamless totalizing discourse on white racism, and a conspiracy theory according to which FIFA wished to eliminate all Third World teams from the competition. This theory was buttressed by evidence from earlier matches of the World Cup.

Dissent within this discourse was almost impossible, which is surprising in the sense that, as I showed in the previous chapter, Cameroonians on other occasions were quick to lay the blame on the government or on other factors within Cameroonian society, even if we accept Mbembe's thesis that ultimately there is a certain kind of collusion in these expressions of dissent. In this case, however, in finding an external enemy, the government and the people could find a common ground, and in the totalizing anti-FIFA, anti-white, and anti-European discourse the fragmentation of the postcolonial was temporarily hidden, and the wink (which Werbner (1996: 2), paraphrasing Clifford Geertz, called the par excellence gesture of the postcolony) was lost. Mbembe's collusion was there, in that everybody forgot what they knew about the insufficiencies of the preparation for the competition and the pervasive ills of Cameroonian football. It should also be noted that an important feature of this essentializing and totalizing discourse is to be found in a decontextualization of the match in different ways. Cameroon's 1998 World Cup participation was reduced to this one match; the other matches the Lions played were of no relevance, and the effects of the local (insufficient preparation, lackluster performance in the African Nations Cup, late appointment of the head coach) on the performance of the team were forgotten. At the same time, the match was also recontextualized within the historical framework of earlier World Cup injustices and of global power relationships (which also are historically conditioned).

"LET'S KILL JOSEPH-ANTOINE BELL"

There were some attempts to frame the match differently, but they were drowned out. The following discussion of the grounds on which some people tried to put this particular match into a larger context in a certain way falsifies the tenor of the debate because by devoting equal time to it I will give an exaggerated sense of its impact. Nonetheless, it merits our attention because it highlights the nature of the postcolonial condition both in and out of football in Cameroon. The main voice of criticism was that of Joseph-Antoine Bell, the outspoken former goalkeeper of the Lions, who tried to frame the debate within the context of Cameroonian football.

Bell's main point was a flat denial that there was a conspiracy against Third World peoples. He claimed that Cameroonian players were just not as good as their opponents, and that crying racism was a way to hide the inefficiency and corruption of the Cameroonian football establishment and of Cameroon in general. He also called attention to the fact that if Cameroon had won its first match against Austria, the "misjudgment" of the referee would not have mattered against Chile. Partly, however, he criticized Claude LeRoy, the French head coach, for having made a wrong tactical decision once Marc Vivien Foé was prevented from participating in the competition because of a broken leg. LeRoy put Patrick Mboma, who normally was an attacker, in the midfield to replace the midfielder Foé. Bell's argument was that all teams went to the World Cup with twenty-two players precisely to have two people for every position. Therefore, instead of making Mboma take on a new position, LeRoy should have maintained him as an attacker and put whoever was the regular replacement for Foé into Foé's position (Bell 1998). I heard the same argument explained in great length in a taxi, without any reference to Bell, put forth in answer to someone's remark that "you have to admit that Claude LeRoy did the best he could in so short a time."

This statement was made just before the final of the World Cup, ten or so days after Cameroon was eliminated from the competition. However, there was an even earlier manifestation of the same argument, the day of the Cameroon–Chile match. LeRoy changed his lineup for this match, and for the first time lined Mboma up in his proper position. Mboma, finding himself in his element, delivered a good game, so much so that he scored Cameroon's lone goal that was admitted by the referee, and the second disallowed goal, which caused all the furor, scored by Omam Biyick, came from a pass by Mboma. Seeing Mboma so useful in his accustomed position, one of the spectators at the bar where I was watching the match said, "Oh, so Claude LeRoy did kill us (*nous a tue*) when he didn't align Mboma as an attacker!"

Many Cameroonians were of the opinion that Bell was being unpatriotic and an apologist for FIFA. One opposition paper dubbed him a "spokesperson of FIFA," primarily trying to safeguard his position as commentator to *Radio France Internationale* (RFI), and accused him of being bitter since he had made an unsuccessful bid for the position of president of the Cameroonian Football Federation, in 1996. Others accused him simply of unpatriotic conduct. Among my friends, there were people who simply stated that they could not agree with Bell even though many of them had supported him in earlier times.

Some letters to the editor in the opposition paper, *Le Messager*, tried to defend Bell. One letter writer started with the provocative and ironic title, "Let's kill Joseph-Antoine Bell." Among others, he wrote:

> For some, the majority of Cameroonians only the results count; for others, above all for Joseph-Antoine Bell, the way in which they are achieved is just as important. ... He goes against the tide. Here in Cameroon a market share obtained by corruption, an election won by the stuffing of the urns, a profit realized by the exploitation of the people (*les salariés*) are proof of patriotism. It is sad, really sad to see the journalist who takes "*gombo*" (bribe), the policeman who sells the road,

the teacher who sells exam papers, the minister who gives away an enterprise for a symbolic franc after having received a tip, to declare that Joseph-Antoine Bell is not a patriot." He concludes saying "Henceforth it is clear that Bell is our bad conscience. While the entire Republic is praising the Indomitable Lions he is still pointing accusatory fingers. ... Let's kill Joseph-Antoine Bell, so that we can finally have peace in carrying out our dirty little affairs. (*Le Messager*, July 19, 1998)

This impassioned defense of Bell showed that there were some Cameroonians who saw the problem of football in the larger context of the country's problems. His bitterness about problems that were largely internal to Cameroon was unmistakable and by extension so was his patriotism. There were a few other such voices too. Primarily, Pius Njawe, the then imprisoned journalist and owner of *Le Messager*, also called attention to the lack of preparation and other problems in an editorial, but in the same issue there were also two scathing articles decrying the racism of the World Cup. Mongo Beti, one of Cameroon's most famous writers, also raised similar objections. Unlike Bell, these commentators agreed with the popular interpretation that these events were part of white racism, but contextualized the problem similarly to Bell. However, on the whole, these voices were drowned out, and the average Cameroonian could only see the issue in the totalizing framework described earlier.

ROOTING AGAINST FRANCE

After the Indomitable Lions' questionable elimination, the interest of Cameroonians turned to the matches of France. The wish that France be defeated by any opponent was oft-repeated throughout the event, and in what follows I will examine the ways in which Cameroonian anti-(neo)colonial attitudes were played out and how Cameroonians, at least on a symbolic and rhetorical level, managed to wrest the victory from France.

France's performance at the World Cup was perceived and also conditioned by what happened to other African and "Third World" countries in the competition. These impressions were also influenced by the commentary of *Canal+*, the French cable television company, which broadcast the matches to Africa. Beyond the immediacy of the World Cup as an event, but closely related to it, was what Cameroonians perceived about France under contemporary conditions; in particular, the way immigrants were treated and the influence of France's extreme right-wing politician Jean-Marie Le Pen. Beyond these spheres of reference lay the history of Cameroonian–French relationships, which led Cameroonians to see France as ungrateful towards the people whose exploitation led to her greatness.

The general impression of most people in Cameroon was that there was a bias against Third World teams in general and African teams in particular, and this set the tone for the World Cup. This view was reinforced by what seemed to be an overwhelming number of red cards given to Third World teams for less than obvious infractions. Among these, naturally, the highly controversial refereeing decisions made in the Cameroon–Chile match had a special significance for Cameroonians. These decisions were seen to have had the effect that only one (Nigeria) of the five participating African countries[8] made it to the second round. As in the case of Cameroon, this perceived bias was largely explained as fear of the "outsiders" among the powers that be of world football, which forced them to resort to "dirty tricks" to protect *their* interest in maintaining the footballing *status quo*, i.e. the domination of European and a few (select) Latin American teams.

In seeking to find explanations for this bias, Cameroonians drew upon two further issues that had to do with FIFA and saw them as subtexts of the referee decisions. One was the change in the leadership of FIFA just prior to the beginning of the competition, and the other, closely related to it, was the issue of the number of places allotted to Africa in the competition (cf. Chapter IV). In early June 1998, Joseph S. (Sepp) Blatter was elected the new President of FIFA, replacing João Havelange who had dominated the world football body for twenty-four years. This surprised many commentators because Lennart Johansson, the head of the *Union of European Football Associations* (UEFA), seemed to be the favorite candidate prior to the elections. In fact, John Sugden and Alan Tomlinson (1998), British sport sociologists who had studied FIFA, as good as predicted Johansson's election. As they demonstrated African countries and *Confédération Africaine de Football* (CAF) represent an important voting bloc in FIFA, therefore whomever they support has a good chance of winning such an election. One of the cornerstones of their argument for their prediction was that Jo-

8 The others, besides Cameroon, were Morocco, South Africa, and Tunisia.

hansson had been supportive of Issa Hayatou (the Cameroonian president of CAF) who waged a long battle within FIFA to secure more places in the final phase of the competition for African countries. In the event, however, Blatter persuaded some African countries to support him against Johansson, so in the end a number of African delegations voted for Blatter and that was enough to elect him. In 2002, Hayatou presented his own candidacy for the position of FIFA President against Blatter, but was defeated because the African countries did not unite behind him (cf. Darby 2002, 2003, 2005).

With this situation in mind, extrapolating from their experience of politics in their own country – as they were watching the unfolding of the 1998 World Cup – Cameroonians wondered aloud whether the distribution of red cards and the favoritism shown toward European teams was not a reflection of Sepp Blatter's "revenge" against those countries whose delegates did not vote for him in the elections. Alternately, they wondered whether the early elimination of African countries did not have to do with a wish on the part of FIFA/Blatter to revert to having fewer African teams in the final phase of the competition, thus maintaining a European monopoly on the game. This is a recurring fear, which I heard repeated during the 2006 World Cup. At that time, in the context of the rather poor performance of the African teams, people asked themselves whether it would not have the effect of reducing the number of berths Africa would have in future World Cup finals.

WATCHING THE 1998 WORLD CUP ... THROUGH FRENCH LENSES

I saw most of the matches of the 1998 World Cup in one of two bars. One was a large popular place, attracting an audience consisting predominantly of poor people, the majority of whom were men. The other was more upscale and expensive in the administrative center of town. Here the audience was largely made up of civil servants, often dressed in suit and tie. In both places commentary flew freely on all aspects of the game, including the broadcasting. We may add to the list of injustices the nature of the commentary on *Canal+*, the French chain broadcasting the matches to Africa. Cameroonian TV had its own broadcast of the World Cup with bilingual

French and English commentary, but most people preferred to watch the French broadcast. [9]

Watching the World Cup on *Canal+* in Cameroon was an unsettling experience. The French commentators wholeheartedly and unashamedly praised their own team, even at the beginning of the competition when the "*Bleus*" (as the French team is familiarly called) faced teams that were rather weak. It should be said that this kind of unbridled nationalism is nothing new in sports broadcasting, and certainly not limited to the French. But what was discomforting about it was the fact that they were broadcasting to an international audience which was likely to have loyalties elsewhere (cf. Blain, Boyle and O'Donnell 1993), and there did not seem to be any acknowledgement of this in the coverage. It was as if the commentators expected everyone to share in their admiration of the French team.

There were instances when the surrounding programming was in bad taste, if not downright racist, as for example in a pair of supposedly humorous sketches broadcast before one of the matches as light entertainment. In both versions, we saw two Cameroonian players lying in bed, asleep when the alarm rang. In the first sketch, entitled "wake up call *à la française*," upon hearing the alarm the two players jumped up immediately and ran to wash and get ready, whereas in the second, which bore the title "wake up call *à la camerounaise*," they turned over and continued to sleep!

The not so latent racism of the commentators was also evident during matches. For example, when Nigeria defeated Bulgaria the French commentators explained Nigerian superiority by arguing that it was very hot in Paris, and the heat favored the Africans. Most of the players on the Nigerian team play in Europe and thus are as used to or unused to the heat as the Bulgarians. An older man, sitting a few places away from me, also noted the partiality of the statement, and using me as a reference point exclaimed with feeling: "The heat! They are only looking for excuses, always excuses, they can't accept it that Africans can beat them. During the summer it's hot there too, isn't it, Madame, in Greece it is 40 degrees, hotter than in Africa!" This sweeping attempt to cast the World Cup in a hegemonic light where seem-

9 One reason given was that there were technical hitches on CRTV at least at the beginning of the World Cup, for example, there was considerable delay between sound and picture. Some people explained to me that they preferred the French broadcasts because of the quality of the commentary.

ingly everything was justified about the refereeing, the rules were applied evenhandedly, and the *Bleus* were just one team among many, but clearly the best and playing the most beautiful game, sent a message of French hegemony.

WATCHING THE 1998 WORLD CUP ... THROUGH CAMEROONIAN LENSES

The overwhelming majority of Cameroonians wanted France to be beaten. After the wish that Cameroon should meet France, the second choice expressed by many was that Nigeria, standing as proxy for the whole of Africa, should encounter and beat France. Beyond that, the majority of the population supported whoever was France's adversary. Naturally, this opposition to France became most evident in the reactions during the matches of the French team. Apart from rooting against France, the tenor of these comments also spoke of the larger concerns of Cameroonians, such as their perception of inconsistency in referee decisions, and showed how these perceptions fitted into a broader discourse about the relationship of Cameroon and France.

SAUDI ARABIA – FRANCE

A case in point is the Saudi Arabia–France match. This took place the day after Cameroon played Italy and lost, and one of its defenders (Raymond Kalla) received a red card, which many Cameroonians considered terribly harsh. This perceived injustice influenced Cameroonian's reactions to what happened in the Saudi Arabia–France match. After about twenty minutes of play, the referee expelled a Saudi player for an infraction that was less than clear – supposedly for tackling from behind. My companion, Coach Nguidjol who is something of a free thinker and an upholder of the rules, said to me in great disgust that "this World Cup is no good. It's not worth it." Obviously, others were of the same opinion because following the expulsion of the Saudi player, every time there was an action where the Saudis took the ball away from the French, people started to mockingly shout "Red! Red!" sarcastically urging the referee to sideline more Saudi players. Furthermore, the spectators in the bar expressed their general sentiment by clapping ferociously when the French failed to score. The impression of biased refereeing was not even dispelled by the expulsion, toward the end of the match, of the French team's star player and playmaker, Zinedine Zidane. Despite the French broadcasters' boasts to the contrary, generally people also insisted that France was in a rather weak group for the first round, some going so far as to suggest that the draw for determining these groups had been rigged to favor France.

FRANCE – ITALY

The first really serious opponent the French team faced was Italy in the quarterfinals. The match was one of the tensest ones of the World Cup. The bar where I watched it (the more popular of the two) was full to capacity with about eighty people, which was double the regular crowd. Everyone seemed to support Italy. Although people around me kept affirming that the Italians would beat France, after ninety minutes the game ended in a goalless draw. The match went to extra-time and eventually was decided by penalty kicks. As we were waiting intently for the penalty kicks to begin and I sat nervously tapping with my hand on the table, one of my fellow viewers said to me encouragingly: "don't worry, Madame, we are going to beat them!" The impersonal "*on*" is used to mean "we," and in this case Italy became the "we." But it was not to be. France won the penalty shoot-out.

People left quietly after the match, and I too left the bar, somewhat bleary-eyed, and very disappointed. On the street, I crossed paths with a young stranger, who asked me whom I had supported. When I answered "Italy," he replied with great feeling, "we were together!" This sense of *communitas* (cf. Turner 1967, 1974) that emerged through opposition to the French, speaks volumes to how football unites people; and how easily anti-French sentiment, despite or perhaps because of the close ties with France, could come to the surface at the smallest of provocations.

FRANCE – CROATIA

In the semifinal match France faced Croatia. The latter were the surprise team of the World Cup, having beaten Germany in a dramatic encounter. I saw this match in the smaller, upscale bar, but even here, where some of the lower echelons of the bureaucracy congregated, the mood was decidedly anti-French, with exclamations like "Croatia is going to give at least five [goals] to the French. We are going to win, France can't do it! Croatia!" flying freely.

When the French made fouls and were not penalized there were comments calling attention to the arbitrariness of the distribution of cards by the referee: "there are no more cards?!" or "give the card!" Seconds into the second half, Croatia scored and everyone jumped up and cheered in jubilation. Half a minute later when the French equalized, only three people cheered. One of those cheering was a man who exclaimed that "now there is match!" His remark indicated that to him it was the spectacle rather than the anti-colonial political agenda that counted, and the equalization promised a more exciting game.

When Laurent Blanc, one of the French players, received a red card, there was some jubilation. Suddenly the French were in complete disarray. One viewer exclaimed, "Come on, you are not the first ones [to play at a numerical disadvantage]! We have played eight against fifteen!" Amid general laughter he explained, "against eleven Chileans and the center judge, and the [two] linesmen and even against the fourth referee who is now there!" [10] This was of course a reference to Cameroon's match against Chile discussed earlier. The speaker actually made a "mistake," because Cameroon played with nine and not eight players, but the hyperbole only heightened the effect.

When France won 2-1, people were subdued. One person said, "Brazil is going to cure that." Another exclaimed, "Brazil is going to correct the French!" This was in anticipation of France's next and last match in the finals of the World Cup against Brazil, the acknowledged best team in the world.

SCRUTINIZING THE ETHNIC COMPOSITION OF THE FRENCH TEAM

During the match against Croatia, a portly gentleman in suit and tie remarked that "France's best goalkeeper is on the bench because he is black." He was talking about Bernard Lama. Scrutinizing the ethnic composition

[10] The fourth referee has the role of keeping time during the match, and his presence was one of the innovations of the 1998 World Cup.

of the French team seemed to be a favorite pastime for Cameroonians. I have heard remarks on other occasions as well, asking what kind of French team this was on which all the players were foreigners. Indeed many of France's players bore the stamp of France's colonial past: Lilian Thuram from Guadeloupe, Christian Karembeu, who is a Kanak from New Caledonia, and Zinedine Zidane, the star of the French team, of Algerian Kabyle origin.[11] During this particular match, someone remarked that there were no French players on the team, to which somebody else replied that, no, there were some, and started enumerating them. The portly gentleman interrupted and said, "Oh, they are Germans, as they are bordering on Germany, the people of Strasbourg!" By hyperbolically denying the presence of any "French" players in the ranks of the French national team he was playing with the notion of divisions within France, which have nothing to do with race. When France won the match with two goals by Lilian Thuram, a player of color, this fact did not go unnoticed, and was cause for jubilation. Even though people wanted France to loose, if that was not to be, at least France should win through a representative of the very people whom the French wished to eliminate from the competition, and, according to the French far right propaganda, from France itself.

Cameroonians took vicarious pleasure in the fact that "foreigners" (naturally they have to be nationals of France in order to qualify for the team) played such a prominent role in France's performance at the World Cup. Some of this was the triumph felt by the underdogs who were aware that France, through stringent immigration laws, was forever trying to prevent them from migrating there, and that there was widespread racism and discrimination against blacks. Nobody in Cameroon is ignorant of the progress of the extreme right in France, and Jean-Marie Le Pen's career is watched with care. This scrutiny was not exclusive to ordinary people. It was reflected in Cameroonian newspapers as well. *La Nouvelle Expression* (No. 387, July 10, 1998), one of the two most important opposition newspapers in the country at the time, carried Thuram's photo with the caption "Lilian Thuram, the Guadeloupean who qualified France." In the same issue,

[11] Thirteen out of the twenty-two players were more or less directly originating from elsewhere than France, their places of origin including Algeria, Armenia, Ghana, Guadeloupe, Guyana, Italy, New Caledonia, Spain, etc. (cf. Marks 1999: 52-53).

two articles discussed the paradox between the composition of the French team and French racism. One was entitled "The Black Heroes of a Racist France," the other "Blues, Whites and Blacks," which was a pun on the name of the team, *Bleus*, and the French tricolor (blue, white, red). In addition, an article about immigrants in Paris was published, the title quoting one of the interviewees: "God has chosen Thuram to speak to the French," while the subtitle was "Ingratitude." Another typical response was the headline of *Le Messager* (No. 787, July 13, 1998), which read, "Africa saves France" after the final when France had won the World Cup. The subtitle again played with the nickname of the French team and the French tricolor, referring to them as the Blues–Whites–Blacks. The article drew a parallel between African participation in the liberation of France during the Second World War and the role of Africans in this victory. Underlying this emphasis on the presence of players of color on the French team is the sentiment that France would be nowhere without the very people who are otherwise looked at with disdain in France. These are concretized instances of a much broader argument that the wealth of France in the present is due to its colonial past.

The ethnic composition of their team also raised eyebrows in France. Previously, during the 1996 European Championship, Jean-Marie Le Pen objected to the number of "foreigners" on the national team (Marks 1999: 50). When Thuram's play helped France to victory against Croatia, his ethnic and racial background did not escape French notice either, and it was reported to me that according to the press review of Radio France Internationale, one French journal carried the headline: "France–Croatia 2-1, France–Le Pen 2-0." [12] From what I saw of the eventual celebration of victory in the World Cup, notwithstanding the less than sensitive coverage that *Canal+* provided, the French media did present the event as a cause for celebrating multiculturalism.

It is evident from French reports of the World Cup that the French themselves were not at all certain of their victory; and that it came as not only a great surprise but also as a source of great relief to them. The uncertainty in fact may explain in part the boasting that went on in the commentary of *Canal+*, rather than a sign of strength, it could be seen as an attempt to

[12] I am indebted to André Ntonfo for calling my attention to this.

bolster French self-confidence. However, this aspect of their commentary was not evident when watching the broadcasts in Cameroon.

It is also clear from Western coverage of the 1998 World Cup that some of the French public as well as commentators considered the victory to be of tremendous importance in combating the National Front (Dauncey and Hare 1999a, 1999b). As Patrick Mignon (1999) commented, "The celebrations of 12 July were indeed a symbol of a call for unity precisely because that unity is far from real. The multiracial nature of the French national team exemplified a diversity which is not accepted by everyone, in particular not by those for whom the experience of life is not one of successful integration, but the experience of the difficulties young people have, whether 'white', 'black' or *beurs*, in integrating themselves in society" (96). A similar appreciation of the unusual nature and importance of the effects of a victory by a multiracial team on French consciousness is expressed by Lucy McKeever in the same volume: "It is hard to conceive the following eulogy to multiracial France appearing in *Le Figaro* [which she characterized earlier as a right-wing paper] before or since: "What would we be without our ethnic communities? Thank you to our overseas territories, thank you Africa, and thank you Kabylia" (McKeever 1999: 163).

It is an interesting question how and why this aspect of the French discourse about the World Cup did not make it to Cameroon. On the one hand, the Cameroonians were turning Le Pen's arguments upside-down by calling attention to the multiracial and multiethnic nature of the team; they also insisted that the French should both be grateful for and acknowledge the contributions of "foreigners." Yet, when Le Pen's French enemies celebrated the victory as a coup for greater inclusiveness in France, for the most part this was ignored. I can only make a tentative suggestion as to why this should be so. Grant Farred (2003), in an insightful paper about South African township football, argues that the working-class colored community of Cape Town could overlook the racism evident in English football when identifying with English clubs because these details are "lost in the process of cultural translation" (135). In the same way, some of what was significant in the World Cup victory for France was also lost in translation to Cameroonians and the details that filled in the gaps left by the loss reflected their own concerns. Partly, disregarding the French anti-racist block meant that the contrast and sense of injustice were heightened, and partly, the denial by omission of the possibility of the existence of opposition to racism in France reinforced anti-white sentiments and made them seem even more justified.

GIVE US THE HONOR AND WE'LL GIVE YOU THE MONEY

The final of the World Cup produced a discourse, which again highlighted the anti-French sentiments of Cameroonians, but at the same time also exhibited a certain kind of accommodation to the realities of life. Within a day of the French semifinal victory against Croatia, people in taxis, bars, and alongside football pitches were convinced that a French victory was a foregone conclusion.

I heard one of the fullest expositions of this view in a taxi. The argument was that France had bought the match from Brazil. The French had gone to the Brazilians and said, "You have had the honor four times, give us the honor and we'll give you the money." When I hazarded that the Brazilians might not wish to relinquish the honor, the answer was immediate: they are a Third World country, they are poor, they cannot but accept the money. I tested this view on as many people as I could. Most were convinced that this was the case, among them one of Cameroon's foremost intellectuals. He went so far as to call me the day after the final to explain that he had been right, that you only had to look at the "purposeful" misses of the Brazilian team, the bad positioning of the players, etc. to realize that they had sold the match. He even suggested that the fact that all was ready in Paris for the celebration of France's victory, including signs, fireworks, and the like, clearly indicated that the French knew in advance that they were going to win the World Cup. [13]

[13] In fact, the host country often wins the competition. Whether this is due to some kind of favoritism or to the well-known advantage that home teams have on all levels of competition is open to debate. However, suspicions of partiality among referees in World Cup competitions are not limited to Cameroonians. François Thébaud (1998), a veteran French sports journalist, analyzing the decisions of referees throughout the history of the World Cup, suggests that the results of past World Cups were often dictated by politics with the collusion of referees.

In any case, most people I spoke with or listened to were convinced that France had bought the match. There were some exceptions to this view. One of them was my friend, Coach Nguidjol, who found it impossible to credit that any team in the world, and especially the Brazilians, would do such a thing. He also added that there were enormous financial interests behind the Brazilian team, and they did not need France's money to benefit financially from the World Cup. Another person said that he could not believe it because the Brazilians could not do such a thing to all the poor people in Brazil who had been putting aside their money for four years (since the last World Cup) in order to go and see their team win the World Cup in France. One of Cameroon's eminent opposition figures and intellectuals found fault with the argument, not on the merits of whether Brazil would or would not sell the match – he is one of the few people I know in Cameroon who professes to have no interest whatsoever in the game – but rather with the framing of the whole issue. Upon hearing the rumor, he wondered aloud whether this meant that Cameroonians thought their own team would do so in a similar position, and then queried the notion that Brazil should even be considered a Third World country in the same way as Cameroon.

There is a certain kind of logic to this assumption of corruption. In part, it follows from the observation made throughout the competition that the World Cup seemed to be going against Third World peoples. Therefore, the idea that whites in general and the French in particular, would do anything to win the competition was already well-rooted. As in match after match, people's wish that France should be beaten and drop out of competition failed to materialize, the only possible (or rather acceptable) explanation that remained was that France would win by cheating, and thus not really win. Also, as was suggested by the noted opposition figure above, this particular explanation would be readily comprehensible in a country from which Jean-François Bayart could borrow the expression "politics of the belly," to characterize the entire continent. Money will get most Cameroonians out of trouble, and their identification of Brazil as a Third World country made the assumption perfectly plausible while at the same time achieving the desired end of denying France the very glory that it was striving for.

The final match of the World Cup between France and Brazil did nothing to allay these suspicions. Not only did France win, but also it looked as if the Brazilian team was not even there. The result was 3-0, and Brazil did not seem to present a credible opposition, let alone threaten France's victory, thus confirming what everybody already knew in Cameroon. When it was disclosed that Ronaldo, Brazil's star player, who had not played too well throughout the competition, and was unrecognizable in this match, had had a seizure in the hours preceding the game, this "rational" explanation came too late to change the conviction shared by so many Cameroonians that France had "taken," but not "won" this World Cup.

As metaphor, football serves in part to explain social reality but, like folktales, it also improves on that reality, symbolically setting the world right. Faced with the seeming inevitability of a French victory, Cameroonians were quick to work out an explanatory framework, which, although it acknowledged the French victory, at the same time denied its legitimacy and strengthened the general view that France deserved the disdain of Cameroonians.

The perception of the level playing field – which as I argued in Chapter I, lies at the heart of the game – was the one that was upset in the 1998 World Cup. The whole edifice of the notion that the better team of the moment wins collapsed, thus upsetting a certainty that is one of the few that still hold in the otherwise uncertain lives of Cameroonians. This is connected to the positive aspects of the ambiguous stereotypes held of whites, in the sense that it could be argued that lacking in local certainties, Cameroonians, like other Africans, ambiguously turn to (or rather create) outside models (of the "great nations") to make some kind of sense of their own lives. Francis Nyamnjoh and Ben Page (2002: 632) also argue that for Cameroonian youths "[t]he image of the West provides an alternative to the existing system of social and political organization in Cameroon, which they disdain." The ideals that are attributed to football do not quite function in Cameroon. However, they are very important as a reference point, and by positing the level playing field, people also posited that somewhere, if not at home then outside Cameroon, there is fairness and justice. The "ideal" world of football has shown itself to be lacking in fairness. Reality (the socio-economic power structure on a global scale) reasserted itself with a vengeance, and I would argue that this smashing of the illusion of the level playing field (and the concomitant postponement of the revenge of the underdog) was what created the bitterness, disbelief, and despair.

As we have seen, when talking about football and allocating blame for losses, Cameroonians could go either in the direction of blaming internal factors or external ones. Their response varied partly according to the actualities of the event, but partly it also depended on how the issue was framed. Some might call the various conspiracy theories paranoia. Fredric Jameson has this to offer on the question:

> Fully as striking on another level is the omnipresence of the theme of paranoia as it expresses itself in a seemingly inexhaustible production of conspiracy plots of the most elaborate kinds. Conspiracy, one is tempted to say, is the poor person's cognitive mapping in the postmodern age; it is a degraded figure of the total logic of late capital, a desperate attempt to represent the latter's system, whose failure is marked by its slippage into sheer theme and content. (Jameson 1988: 356)

Though this explanation is tempting, I am not so sure it is correct. While it is true that the deft conspiracy theories produced by Cameroonians to explain losses on the football field can sound far-fetched if they are taken literally, I would suggest that they should rather be taken as metaphoric statements, which in such a reading do indeed address the "logic of ... capital." The point I am arguing for is two-fold. On the one hand, any oppressed group of people is likely to know far more about the world of its oppressors than the other way round, therefore to suppose that they do not understand the "logic" of what is happening to them seems to me to be questionable. On the other hand, most of the conspiracy theories discussed in this chapter have to do with the perceived racism of whites. Apart from the historical record of whites on this score, which would already go at least half-way to justify the conspiracy theories, in fact racism, in and out of football, continues to exist. Thus, while conspiracy theories can be seen to be paranoid, and, as some have argued in Cameroon, can lead to avoiding an objective assessment of what went wrong; at the same time, they bespeak of a reality that is undeniably true, if not in its concrete details, then as commentary on the world as it is.

CHAPTER VII

DISILLUSIONMENT AND IRONY: ARE THE VISIONS GONE?

In the preceding chapters I described Cameroonian reactions to football on the national and international level during the 1990s, and interpreted them as challenges to the postcolonial condition, as well as to the postcolonial state, and to the continuing domination of the erstwhile colonizer. In the aftermath of the political upheavals of the first few years of the decade, the democratizing spirit still lingered in people's minds, and what was suppressed in public discourses found expression in many of the interpretations and exegeses of World Cup football.

By the time the 2006 World Cup came around, the Biya regime had consolidated its position through neutralizing the opposition, as well as through fomenting factionalism and encouraging the "politics of belonging." As a result, the focus on national political interests, so prominent in the early 1990s, for most people has disappeared, political activism decreased, and the sense of outrage that was still prevalent in the mid-1990s began to die down. The worst manifestations of the economic crisis have abated even if this has not meant appreciable improvement for the bulk of the population of the country. Coupled with the cynical ostentations of power and wealth among the mighty and their seeming impunity, these developments have led to widespread disillusionment and political apathy among Cameroonians (cf. Gupta 1995, Fombad 2004).[1] The government's and especially

[1] In February 2006 the government launched an anti-corruption campaign, entitled *Opération épervier* (cf. www.postnewsline.com/2006/02/anticorruption.html), in the course of which several high-ranking officials close to the highest circles of power were accused of corruption, removed from office and arrested, some even ended up in prison. Despite this, people I spoke with in 2006 remained skeptical and maintained that not much (or even nothing) has changed. They pointed to the fact that the campaign stopped

Paul Biya's staying power and evident recovery of their strength also contributed to a general loss of faith and hope for meaningful change any time soon. Naturally, this kind of apathy cannot be said to extend to everyone but the majority turned away from open political activity.

The extent of the disillusionment of the people can be captured in the reactions to the 2006 World Cup which was held in Germany. No doubt, the fact that Cameroon did not qualify for the competition contributed to the changed attitudes of the spectators that I experienced while watching matches with them. However, I will suggest that the changes in people's reactions were also related to the depoliticization that Cameroon has undergone in recent years. In stark contrast to earlier occasions, Cameroonians were not following the World Cup avidly and were not using it as a forum for political discussion. Rather, those people who were still watching were taking seemingly random contradictory positions about the various teams. The tenor of the commentary of the spectators was ironic but the irony was no longer directed at the powers that be. It was as if politics had been drained out of football, and what remained were technical and aesthetic preferences as well as a collectively self-deprecating dialogic ironic discourse.

2006: THE NON-QUALIFICATION OF THE LIONS

The situation in 2006 was substantially different from the World Cups discussed in earlier chapters in that, for the first time since 1990, the Indomitable Lions did not qualify for the finals. During the continental qualifying phase of the competition the Elephants of *Côte d'Ivoire* (as the national selection is known) were in the same pool as Cameroon. In the early phases, the Indomitable Lions had not done well, and it was only when they managed to beat Côte d'Ivoire in September 2005 that people began to hope that Cameroon might after all qualify for the World Cup. Given the Lions' earlier poor results – even though they beat Côte d'Ivoire *aller-retour* (i.e. in both the home and away legs of the qualifying phase) – their qualification depended on their last match, which took place at the *Omnisports*

too early and did not go far enough. What was remarked upon particularly was that some of the imprisoned officials continued to conduct their business affairs from prison and, most importantly, they did not have to return the money they had embezzled.

Stadium of Yaoundé on October 8, 2005, against Egypt. Egypt was already eliminated but Cameroon needed a victory in order to qualify; a draw would have meant that Côte d'Ivoire would be the country to go to Germany 2006. In the event, the Cameroonian selection could not rise to the occasion and the match ended in a draw. However, the circumstances under which this result came about were dramatic. At the 94th minute, Cameroon was awarded a penalty, which Pierre Wome executed and failed to translate into a goal. If a penalty is kicked well, the goalkeeper is not expected to save it, so much so that people in Cameroon usually start dancing and ululating the minute a penalty is awarded because it almost certainly is a goal. Thus, failing to score a penalty calls for an explanation. [2]

THE CURSED STADIUM: WHY THE LIONS FAILED?

I was in Cameroon just a few weeks after the match, in November 2005. At the time, the general consensus was that the failure of the Lions was due to the curse (*malédiction*) of the "elders" (in some accounts the "ancestors") of the autochthonous population of the Omnisports neighborhood of Yaoundé. They were supposedly taking their revenge for the lack of sufficient compensation for the appropriation of their land on which the Omnisports Stadium, which was constructed to host the 1972 African Nations Cup, had been built.

The 1972 Nations Cup was, to the Cameroonians, scandalous from more than one point of view. On the one hand, Cameroon was unexpectedly eliminated in the semifinal by Congo, a team considered weaker than Cameroon. On the other hand, following the event, it also transpired that large sums of money had been embezzled by several people in high as well as low places. Ahmadou Ahidjo, the head of state, reacted vigorously by imprisoning the culprits. At least this is how people recount the events in Cameroon. Although Charles Nguini (1996) argues that this was not the case and in fact, most of the high-ranking officials were released rather quickly, this story of swift retribution has become one of the nostalgic nar-

2 The international press reported that Wome's younger brother was beaten and his house attacked after the match, but this was denied in Cameroon even though it was acknowledged that there were some cases of vandalism after the match (cf. Nsigué 2005). Wome himself said in some interviews that he had been afraid for the safety of his family and himself.

ratives retold about the Ahidjo regime (cf. Chapter II). In any case, in 2005, immediately after the Lions lost their chance to go to Germany, people came up with an exegesis that referred back to 1972 and constituted a narrative that combined magical overtones with elements of social justice.

The Omnisports stadium of Yaoundé, a large stadium with natural turf and a capacity of 40,000 fit to hold international encounters, had to be constructed specifically for the occasion of the 1972 African Nations Cup.[3] The area was to be turned into a sports complex and the population on whose land it was built needed to be compensated for the loss of their lands and, according to one account, for the fact that the bones of their ancestors had been disturbed by the construction (Ndogkoti 2007). In my friends' and informants' accounts of the event in 2005, however, although compensation had been given at the time of the construction, the amount paid was derisory and did not satisfy the displaced autochthons of the area. Thus, according to the majority of Cameroonians I spoke to, in their dissatisfaction, the elders cursed the stadium so that the Lions could not win in it. To forestall the effects of the curse on the match against Egypt, the Minister for Sports and Physical Education took "five head of cattle" along with other gifts as well as cash to the elders to placate them prior to the match. Several people told me the story and apparently the presenting of the gifts prior to the match was reported in the media (cf. Nsigué 2005, Nana and Mbunwe 2006, Binyam 2005, Ndogkoti 2007).[4] However, as they did not reach the "right" people, the gifts did not diminish the anger of the elders and, in any case, their value was deemed insufficient. Other accounts claimed that the elders could not agree on how to divide up the gifts, and it was those who felt shortchanged who had cursed the stadium. In some of the accounts I heard the *malédiction* was also justified by the fact that a new neighborhood of villas rose up in the place of the long-promised but never realized

3 In addition, two smaller stadia, with no turf and without any seating were also built at the time. These became the two *Stade Annexe*-s where Second and Third Division clubs train and Third Division matches were held. This was the training ground of Coach Nguidjol's team with which I worked during my 1994-1995 fieldwork.

4 I could only find retrospective accounts of the presenting of the gifts in the Cameroonian media. Since I was not in Cameroon at the time it was supposed to have happened it is not impossible that such accounts existed and I simply could not locate them through internet searches. However, I think it is also possible that these accounts were post-facto explanations for the failure of the national team to win the match against Egypt.

sports complex, while the autochthons remained "homeless." In November 2005 the story circulated widely in Cameroon, for instance, when I visited a small village in the West Province, the villagers were already aware of it.

Although I had never heard this story before, in its retelling, people tended to claim that the Lions had in fact never won in this stadium, starting with the elimination of the Cameroonian national squad by the Congo in the 1972 Nations Cup. Nobody seemed to question the justness of the elders' action. Rather, despite Cameroonians' disappointment over the non-qualification of the Lions for the World Cup, there seemed to be a consensus that the elders were justified in acting the way they (supposedly) did because of the failure of the government (past and present) to adequately compensate them. Akhil Gupta (1995) argues that discourses about corruption are about the state's accountability. No doubt, the way these stories combined juxtapositions of the Ahidjo and the Biya regimes' reactions to corruption – along with the implications of corruption in the use to which the Omnisports area had been put – are suggestive in this regard. Interestingly, this discourse had died down by the time of the World Cup some nine months later (I only heard one specific reference to it during the entire event), but the smarting over Cameroon's absence in Germany did not.

THE 2006 WORLD CUP

Given that the competition was taking place in Europe there was no substantial time difference, so the matches were broadcast in the afternoon and evenings. During earlier World Cups even matches that did not involve Cameroon were very well watched, especially in the evenings, but matches of great significance to Cameroonians (such as those featuring other African teams, France, or such acknowledged masters of the game as Brazil or Italy) would attract large crowds from all social backgrounds, albeit, often at different venues, no matter what time of the day.

In 2006 I followed my earlier strategy of watching matches at different venues to try to get a variety of responses. Although the two bars where I primarily watched the World Cup were side by side in one of the popular neighborhoods of Yaoundé, one of them was more genteel than the other. In the former, interspersed with symbolic representations of France – for example a neon replica of the Eiffel tower at the entrance and several photographs – there were pious quotes on the wall, and the owner had made obvious efforts to create a welcoming atmosphere. The tables had tablecloths, and he prepared reasonably priced and tasty dishes on demand. The other bar was a partially covered, bare verandah with no decorations, just rickety metal chairs and tables. The situation was no better inside. While many of the patrons in the first bar wore suit and tie, the customers of the second seemed mostly to be poorer people, primarily un- or underemployed youths but also some laborers and petty traders. Despite the differences in clientele and style, I found people's reactions to the matches of the World Cup in the two places to be remarkably uniform. Not only was the attendance at broadcasts of matches lower than usual, but for the first time, some bars could be practically empty during matches, and even when matches were watched in a bar, almost never was the entire clientele involved. Some people – usually couples or larger groups of friends – would be there ostentatiously not watching, literally or figuratively turning their backs on the screen. They would be eating, drinking and holding animated conversations.

This lack of sustained interest in the World Cup was also evident in other parts of town. For example, I saw the first match of Tunisia against Saudi Arabia (classified as a representative of Asia) on June 14, in a restaurant/bar in the central part of Yaoundé. The establishment had printed its own score card for the World Cup, which naturally also served as advertising. In this somewhat upscale establishment the television set was placed on the terrace. Although there were some customers during the first-half, none stayed for the entire match. They had their drink or dinner and then left. In one instance a middle-aged man was watching the match for a while but when his partner arrived he became engrossed in conversation with her and forgot about the match. Eventually, besides the two waiters, the cook and myself, the only spectators remaining were the two night watchmen of the neighboring building, watching from outside the actual premises. The same situation on the occasion of several early afternoon matches may seem understandable, but this match was shown at 5 p.m. after office hours and nevertheless failed to attract an audience.

Predictably the greatest interest surrounded the matches played by African teams. With the exception of Tunisia, they were all newcomers to the World Cup: Angola, Côte d'Ivoire, Ghana, and Togo. Cameroonians did not have a clear favorite, but they *did* have a clear *bête noire* and that was Côte d'Ivoire. As we have seen in earlier chapters, on other occasions Cameroonians overwhelmingly tended to support African teams when Cameroon was no longer present in the competition. In 2006, however, there was a conspicuous lack of interest even in the African teams, although attendance was still higher for their matches than for almost any others. For the most part, there was only lukewarm support for the teams from sub-Saharan Africa, and because of the common Cameroonian perception of North Africans as racist towards black Africans, Tunisia garnered even less support and interest. But as we shall see the greatest disdain was reserved for Côte d'Ivoire.

The commentary centered on some recurring themes. I will examine the following in some detail: the absence of Cameroon from the competition often combined with some comparisons to earlier World Cups in which Cameroon did participate; the weakness of Côte d'Ivoire, Cameroon's archrival for the qualification, as well as the conduct of its players and supporters. I will discuss these discourses first and then will turn to analyzing Cameroonian attitudes to France, which showed considerable change from earlier World Cups. What was striking in all the commentary was that even though many of them, on the face of it, reinforced the self-affirming discourses with a nationalist bent familiar from earlier World Cups, this time around there would always be someone to challenge and put into question the statements being made.

CAMEROON'S ABSENCE: "IT HURTS"

It was during the first round of the World Cup, when all the African teams were still in competition, that the spectators especially commented on the absence of Cameroon – often paying more attention to the discussion than to the match at hand. They were repeatedly reminding themselves of it, almost compulsively returning to the subject. The television viewers compared the African teams competing at the World Cup unfavorably with the Indomitable Lions, asserting that they would have played better than the African teams actually taking part in the competition. Most often they commented on the supposed lack of self-confidence or purposefulness of the team in question and made some version of the claim that, unlike their rivals, Cameroon had to be reckoned with until the last minute of a match or that the moment the Lions stepped on the football field they knew that they had come to accomplish something. Such boasts, however, were regularly challenged by other members of the audience who would point out that in fact Cameroon was not there to show how much better it was. For example, during the Côte d'Ivoire–Netherlands match on June 16, two young men commented on these assertions of putative Cameroonian superiority by calling out "But are they there?" The fact of course is that Cameroon had not really been successful in its World Cup appearances since 1990, although it had stellar results at the 2000 Olympics and won the African Nations Cup on two occasions in the recent past.

Another recurring theme within this discourse – pouncing on some of the commentary of *Canal+* – was that "the whites" would also prefer Cameroon to be there because the Lions were sure to deliver engaged and spectacular play. People usually made some kind of triumphant comment upon hearing this, rejoicing that the Lions' absence was being noted in Germany. Some of this was most likely pure bravado to cover up the sense of loss many Cameroonians felt over the non-qualification of the Lions. On the occasion of the United States' match against the Czech Republic, I was alone with the shopkeeper-cum-barman of a little establishment which had a television set and two benches with room for about 8-10 people to watch a match. Upon hearing one of these comments from the television commentator, the barman remarked with a rueful smile: "it hurts when you hear that!" However, delight and pride were much more common responses to these remarks, but there was always someone to poke fun at the person rejoicing and to point out realistically that the Lions were not there and it was no use fantasizing about how much better they would do than those present at the World Cup.

THE MEMORY OF EARLIER WORLD CUP PARTICIPATIONS

Another way people found to feel better about Cameroon's absence at the World Cup was to recall the Indomitable Lions' earlier glories. When Côte d'Ivoire played its first match against Argentina, Cameroonians were reminded of their own spectacular victory against that country in 1990, with nine players against eleven. So even though people cheered when Didier Drogba, Côte d'Ivoire's greatest star, scored against Italy, when the Elephants eventually lost the match Cameroonians could also feel relieved that the Lions had not been outdone. At other times the comparison had less of a negative tone. For instance, when toward the end of Angola's match against Mexico the Angolan side got a red card and thus had to finish the match with ten men against eleven someone remarked in excited tones that it was just like Cameroon in 1990.

References to Cameroon's 1982 World Cup participations also kept cropping up. The fact that the Indomitable Lions remained unbeaten in their first ever participation in the World Cup was probably recalled so many times because there were four African novices in the competition and also because that achievement still remains something to be proud of. Despite the positive self-image projected by such statements, there were people who questioned the appropriateness of bringing up the events of 1982, half-ruefully and half-ironically pointing out that those results were in the past and, at present, Cameroon was not even at the World Cup. Thus, during the same match of Angola against Mexico, at the less "elegant" of the two bars a drunken member of a group that was not really watching the match unexpectedly launched into a rambling discourse on the significance of 1982 addressed to a youngish, heavyset, bespectacled man. The latter after putting up with the loud comments for a good fifteen minutes eventually told him dismissively: "leave us alone with 1982, it was too long ago!" However, on another occasion I overheard a young man at the more upscale bar explaining in earnest tones to his companion, a young woman, what a great achievement it was that Cameroon had remained unbeaten at the 1982 World Cup.

A THORN IN THE SIDE OF CAMEROON

Côte d'Ivoire's presence at the World Cup was a thorn in the side for many Cameroonians, and people kept commenting on it throughout the competition. Some people were especially outraged that Côte d'Ivoire qualified for the World Cup when in fact Cameroon had beaten them twice in the qualifying phases. Naturally, qualification is a question of the aggregate results of all the matches a national selection plays against the members of its pool. It is unlikely that the people who questioned the rightfulness of Côte d'Ivoire's presence in the competition were unaware of this fact. It was rather that by recalling Cameroon's superiority vis-à-vis Côte d'Ivoire they were consoling themselves and softening the blow of not having made it to the World Cup. However, whenever such a discussion arose there would always be somebody to point out that the results against Côte d'Ivoire were not enough if the other results were not up to par.

It is also likely that some of the negative commentary on the African teams in general and on Côte d'Ivoire in particular was due to their rather weak performance.[5] Thus, in the more downscale bar, while watching Côte d'Ivoire's match against the Netherlands, people were supporting Côte d'Ivoire animatedly crying out encouragements *(il n'y a rien!, lève-toi!, marque!)* as long as the Elephants seemed to be on an equal footing with their adversaries. The mood changed dramatically when the Netherlands scored two goals in quick succession. At this point popular opinion turned against the Côte d'Ivoire team and the same people who were until then urging the Elephants on, became completely dismissive of their efforts. The change in tone was noticed by a youngster who sarcastically asked, "a minute ago you supported Côte d'Ivoire and now you support Holland?" Somebody added "it is not Côte d'Ivoire that eliminated Cameroon, so why are you so upset?" The response to this was the familiar one of "but how, a team that we've beaten coming and going?"

THEY ARE LOUD-MOUTHS ...

The other objection people had to Côte d'Ivoire's Elephants was that the Ivoirian players were "too cocky" in pre-competition proclamations about how they were going to surpass Cameroon's record quarterfinal finish at the World Cup. This was taken as a lack of respect and cheeky, and many people summed up their dislike of Côte d'Ivoire by stating that they did not like the Ivoirians because they were loud-mouths (*gueulards*). This was a similar reaction to what happened in 2002 with regard to Senegal. Cameroonians supported Senegal in the World Cup and were overjoyed when the Senegalese team brought off the exploit of beating France in the opening match of that competition. However, they turned against them when upon reaching the quarterfinals (thus arriving to the same elevated level of competition as had Cameroon in 1990), El Hadj Diouf, the star player of Senegal, announced that they were going to do better than Cameroon had done

[5] Of the five African participants, only one, Ghana went on to the second round. Out of fifteen matches played by the African teams there were four wins (Ghana 2, Angola 1, Côte d'Ivoire 1), eight losses, and three draws (Angola 2, Tunisia 1).

in Italy (i.e. they would be victorious in their quarterfinal match and thus surpass the Lions). People in Cameroon took offence at these statements and from then on most of the Cameroonian public rooted against Senegal (cf. Abou 2002, Anonymous 2002, Toukas 2002). Côte d'Ivoire's similar boasts elicited comparable but even stronger reactions in Cameroon in 2006 because, as we saw above, many Cameroonians felt that Côte d'Ivoire in essence had usurped "their" place at the World Cup. Yet, in the less "elegant" bar, upon hearing some of their fellow spectators fuming against the boasts of the Ivoirians, two young men pointed out to each other with evident amusement that the bragging of the Ivoirians constituted a compliment since it showed that Cameroon was still the standard to which other African teams held themselves. As they put it: "they can't compare themselves to Equatorial Guinea!"

MERCI WOME!

It did not make things better when, during Côte d'Ivoire's first match on June 10, against Argentina, a Côte d'Ivoire supporter was shown on TV in the stadium in Hamburg with a T-shirt that was a mock-replica of the Indomitable Lions' jersey, bearing the legend "*Wome – Merci*." (Although photographs of the match show the legend thus, Cameroonians reversed the words and spoke about it as "*Merci Wome*.") As shown in the photographs of the article that appeared in the newspaper *Mutations* (Samnick 2006, see also Moadougou 2006), there were other jerseys mocking other players of the Cameroonian national team too. Pierre Wome, of course, was the Cameroonian player who had missed the penalty that was awarded to the Lions at the last minute in the October 8, 2005 match against Egypt, with the consequence that Côte d'Ivoire went to the World Cup instead of Cameroon. The gesture was not a friendly one and Cameroonians were not amused. For days after the match, people from all walks of life brought up the T-shirt disapprovingly, decrying the unsportsmanlike attitude evident in it and protesting the intended insult. The incident was not only seen on TV, it was also written up in newspaper columns, and confirmed people's negative feelings about Côte d'Ivoire. Everyone, no matter how cynical they were about the World Cup, felt outraged at this T-shirt.

In the event Ghana went farthest among the African teams. The Ghanaian selection was beaten by Italy in its first match, the strongest team of their pool (and eventual winner of the competition) but defeated both the Czech Republic and the United States and thus qualified for the second round of the competition as the lone representative of Africa. It is characteristic of people's state of mind in Cameroon that after Ghana defeated the Czech Republic someone (echoing the T-shirt incident) at the bar where I was watching remarked "Merci Ghana!" and the newspaper *Mutations* used the same phrase as the title of its article about the match (Samnick 2006). But even this match was not watched by everyone in the bar.

As it became obvious that Côte d'Ivoire was in fact unlikely to go very far in the competition, men and women alike kept remarking gleefully that the World Cup proved to be too difficult for them. On one occasion a young man exclaimed "the World Cup was too much for the Ivoirians!" ("*la Coupe de Monde a dépassé les Ivoiriens*!"). Many others made similar statements. A middle-aged woman who owns a boutique selling beauty products said to me and a friend from the 2-0 (the Old Boys' Club) after Côte d'Ivoire was beaten by Argentina: "Your Côte d'Ivoire couldn't do it, what did they go to the World Cup for?" My friend recounted that everybody was saying the same thing and not only about Côte d'Ivoire, but about the other African teams as well. It was also my experience that spectators stopped supporting the African teams as soon as they saw that they did not do well. The allegiances of supporters – especially with regard to teams to which they do not need to have too much loyalty – tend to change rather quickly and are extremely adaptable all over the world. I don't think it would have been impossible for Cameroonians to support Côte d'Ivoire wholeheartedly had they gone farther in the competition. This is because people also wanted Africa to make a good showing.

CHANGES IN ATTITUDES TO FRANCE

Perhaps the most significant change of 2006, especially compared to 1998, was that the anti-French consensus that was so noticeable on that occasion disappeared, and along with those rooting against France, there was also a vocal group who supported the former colonizer. Some people openly announced that they were going to support France while some others just as openly declared that they would not do so under any circumstances. The situation was the same in both of the bars where I watched the matches regularly. In both places the spectators of the World Cup were divided over the question of whether to support France or not. Unlike in 1998 when rooting against France seemed deadly serious and in earnest, this time people were taking an oppositional stance toward each other and mocking one another for their choices. It seemed that neither party took their position very seriously. Thus, immediately upon the completion of the match between France and Togo (discussed below) a man in suit and tie at the more "elegant" of the bars turned to someone who had supported France, shook his hand and congratulated him: "Your team has won!" (*ton équipe a gagné*). On another occasion, just before the beginning of France's semifinal match against Portugal two people got into a debate over the question of whom to support. A thin young man in suit and tie was vocally supporting France while another in military garb objected to this, reminding him of all that the French did not accomplish in Cameroon as opposed to the Germans (cf. Chapter II). However, as the match was about to begin somebody sitting next to me called out to them in mockery: "But you are going to miss your match!" During the same semifinal match, at the more upscale of the two bars, one of the patrons who was rooting against France called out to the owner pointing to one of the other customers: "Give the supporter of France a beer!"

A few tables away a group of people was vocally supporting Portugal, creating a somewhat tenuous link between themselves and the Portuguese side by making reference to the fact that Cameroon got its name from the Portuguese word "*camarões*."[6] In fact, this slight connection to justify support for Portugal was invoked at both bars every time Portugal played. There was a certain kind of almost farcical hyperbole to many of these exchanges, and it seemed to me that, rather than signaling a sincere difference in opinion, the challenge and the verbal sparring involved was more important than the actual positions being disputed. The juxtaposition of these differing opinions had a humorous effect that seemed to have come into existence through the medium of the dialogue itself.

It was my impression that people took opposing positions almost arbitrarily throughout the competition. This was especially noticeable in the case of France, if only because on earlier occasions Cameroonians' com-

6 Prawns, because of the multitude of crayfish in the Wouri River (cf. LeVine 1971: 2).

mitment against the former colonizer had been so complete as to practically exclude the possibility of supporting it.

TOGO VA OÙ?

The contrast in Cameroonian attitudes to the French national team's performance in 2006 as compared to 1998, was especially striking on the occasion of France's match against Togo. The Sparrowhawks (*Eperviers*) of Togo, the least well-known African team, had an inauspicious beginning at the World Cup.[7] Having lost their first two matches they had no chance of advancing when in their final match of the first round the Togolese were to face the – at that point rather lackluster – French national team.

France had drawn its first two matches and in order to advance to the next round needed a victory badly, otherwise it would have had to bow out of the competition after the first round, as it did shockingly in 2002. This was an important match from the point of view of Cameroonians since both participants held an intrinsic interest for them (a fellow-African country and the former colonizer pitted against each other). And indeed, there were quite a few people watching this match and unlike other occasions, the clientele even in the shabbier of the two bars did not consist mostly of youths but had some middle-aged people among its numbers. The chances of Togo winning were practically nil. In the first half of the match Togo's Sparrowhawks actually turned out their best game: they held out valiantly against the national team of the former Metropole, and at the break the result was a goalless draw. Therefore, it was even more remarkable when after half-time Togo's defense collapsed, and they were easily beaten by the French team by two goals to zero.

Judging by prior experiences in Cameroon one could expect such a sudden change in the course of the match against the former colonizer of both Togo and Cameroon to cause a major uproar and to give rise to a whole plethora of explanations charging that France had bought – or Togo had

---

[7] Even before the event properly began there were rumors and then news that the players were on strike, demanding to be paid. Otto Pfister, Togo's German coach, resigned in support of the players, but was persuaded to come back. Thus, Togo presented a not unfamiliar image of mismanagement and problems – nevertheless it was the first African team to score a goal in the 2006 World Cup – against South Korea. However, in the end it was beaten 2-1. It lost its next match against Switzerland (0-2).

sold – the match. We saw that in 1998 a similar explanation with regard to Brazil was used by Cameroonians to discredit the French. In keeping with the ambivalence of the 2006 World Cup, this both did and did not happen. Many people commented on the sudden change in Togo's performance and there were some quite biting remarks about its swiftness but the tone and purpose was very different from 1998. Suggestions did fly that the French asked, or sometimes ordered, Togo to desist and let them pass, all the more so as Togo had nothing (but prestige) to gain by beating France as it had no chance of going on to the next round. However, unlike 1998, the supposed "selling" of the match did not discredit France in the eyes of Cameroonians. Rather it was presented as a reasonable move. The ground was prepared for this already on the eve of the match, when some people were actually debating the question whether Togo should or should not let France win the match. One person expressed this by the rhetorical question "*Togo va où*?" literally, "where is Togo going?" but meaning something like "what is it to Togo?" (to let France win, since they were already eliminated, i.e. going nowhere anyway.) Some of these speculations were repeated a few times even after the match – and by some people negatively – but the great difference from earlier World Cups was that these suggestions did not take root. They were floated and then went nowhere.

AFRICA IS IN THE FINAL!

Echoing one of the main elements of criticism of the French team in 1998, discussed in the previous chapter, there were some people who remarked upon the presence of players of African descent on the French team. However, instead of using the fact to deny France's claim to football glory as they did on the earlier occasion, they were co-opting France's prominence in a tongue-in-cheek, mocking way. During the second half of the semifinal match, when it was already clear that France had qualified for the final someone exclaimed in mock excitement: "Africa is in the final!" On another occasion, a young man explained in mock seriousness that Africa had *six* teams at the World Cup: Angola, Côte d'Ivoire, Ghana, Togo, Tunisia, and *France*!

Yet others were objecting to such identification with France, reminding their companions of the racism prevalent in that country. For example, when someone at the shabbier bar called out during the second half of the semifinal match "we, the French are leading," another person confronted him, pointing to his skin and asking him why he would support the people who do not accept him. Arguably the original statement itself was ironic, so it could be thought that the person challenging it was not "getting" the joke. Ambiguously, some of these remarks may have been heartfelt and sincere just as on earlier occasions, but in the middle of all the other comments that were purposely frivolous they not only got drowned out but the context made them almost a mockery of themselves.

Disillusionment and Depoliticization: Irony and Resistance

What are the reasons for these transformations in Cameroonians' attitudes to World Cup football as evidenced in the discourses surrounding the 2006 World Cup? Clearly, one of the possible explanations is that Cameroon's absence from the event made it significantly less important to most Cameroonians than on earlier occasions. There may well be merit to this view but it is contradicted by the fact that at other times Cameroonians continued to express interest in the competition (by avidly watching and attributing political meaning to it) even after the Lions had been eliminated. This explanation is also made insufficient by reports from other parts of Africa according to which, even in countries that have no stake in the competition the World Cup garners enormous interest. So much so that an inopportune cut in electricity during the broadcast of a World Cup match almost triggered a riot in Guinea Conakry (Goerg 2002). It is also possible that the rather poor performance of the African teams could also have led to the loss of interest, distancing and generally ironic tone surrounding the World Cup.

However, I think that another contributing factor behind the transformation in people's attitudes during this World Cup is to be found in the changes that have taken place in the political climate of Cameroon in recent years. In the highly charged and politicized atmosphere of the 1990s, football too was a politicized aspect of Cameroonian public life. As we have seen in earlier chapters, people used it as a metaphor to talk about the country and about politics, and through talking about the sport they also expressed their aspirations for a more just and better life (both personally and communally). It was also a vehicle for veiled and sometimes open defiance of the government. When demands for democratization in Cameroon turned out to be unsuccessful, under the circumstances of what one author has labeled "stalled democratization" (Mbaku 2002) and another "cosmetic democracy" (Nyamnjoh 2002 b, but cf. also Takougang 2003, Fonchingong 2004), people became disillusioned and consequently depoliticized as the possibility of a real democratic transition any time soon became less and less likely. People can only go so far in actively resisting a political system, and no doubt ordinary Cameroonians have become just as disillusioned and jaded as the academic commentators. In the midst of the hardships of the lingering economic crisis and with the likelihood of meaningful change receding, reality – the need to survive – reasserts itself and resistance – without realistic hope for its success – begins to look foolhardy. This does not necessarily mean that people forget about their aspirations, rather they put them aside and go on with their lives. As Arjun Appadurai (2004: 65) has aptly put it "[t]he poor are neither simple dupes nor secret revolutionaries. They are survivors."

IRONY

Irony has been presented as one of the ways the poor and the oppressed survive. It is often described as one of the typical "weapons of the weak," and as a somewhat slippery but nonetheless real form of resistance (cf. Scott, 1985, 1990). Thus irony is often seen in the anthropological literature as a "natural accompaniment" to resistance. While acknowledging the importance of James Scott's ideas on resistance several authors have questioned some of his assumptions. Indeed, much of the literature on irony questions whether recourse to irony is effective, whether as a form of resistance it can lead to any kind of change (Fernandez and Huber 2001: 14-18). Is it merely a safety valve that allows people to feel better about themselves and continue putting up with oppression (Torres 1997), or does irony actually contribute to the perpetuation of oppression? (Herzfeld 2001: 75-78). Other authors have stressed the subtleties of the dynamic between resistance and accommodation evident in ironic commentaries by the oppressed (Abu-Lughod 1990, Gal 1995, Ortner 1995).

Irony is notoriously slippery and multifaceted, which – as many authors have pointed out – is what makes it difficult to define as well as to interpret, and even recognize. Michael Herzfeld (2001) calls it "as elusive as the sense of smell" (65). This elusiveness is part of irony's essence as is its ambiguity, and the impossibility of pinning it down. [8] As Fernandez and Huber as well as many others point out, while irony relieves the speaker of responsibility through its ambiguity by the very same token it also is capable of opening up alternative ways of looking at things. What is just as important, however, is that "most frequently the ambiguity inherent in irony (does the speaker mean to be ironic or not?) allows ironists to accept or condone contradictory intentions and ambivalence about where they stand" (2001: 5).

The preceding chapters have shown that during the 1990s Cameroonians had a fairly unequivocal utopian vision and often articulated it when talking about football at times resorting to irony and humor against the powers-that-be as a form of open or veiled criticism and opposition. However, the changed attitudes I have described in this chapter point in a different direction. People's opinions were never completely uniform but the direction in which emphases have changed reflects and enacts changed circumstances. It is not so much accommodation that we see here but rather a withdrawal from politics into an ironic, playful, and absurdist mode, which, however, leaves the door open (even if ambiguously) for resistance as well as for accommodation.

DISCURSIVE COMMUNITY AND THE DIALOGIC NATURE OF IRONY: BUILDING ON THE PAST – TALKING TO THE PRESENT

According to Linda Hutcheon (1994), irony comes into being not so much as a result of the intentions of the ironist or the understanding of the interpreter, but in a dialectical process, which rather than creating a community presupposes one, what she refers to as a *discursive community*. As she puts it: "irony happens because what could be called 'discursive communities'

8 It follows from the above that the recognition and attribution of meaning to irony very much depend on how it is interpreted by those who hear an utterance, and the fact that it is *meant* to be elusive renders the task of any interpreter difficult and that of the anthropologist, who is an outsider, even more so.

already cxist and provide the context for both the deployment and attribution of irony" (Hutcheon 1994: 18). In her view, a discursive community is a necessary prerequisite for irony to "happen" because a common font of cultural knowledge or context is needed for people to draw upon to create irony. Hutcheon argues that irony is dialogic in the Bakhtinian sense. She quotes Bakhtin as follows:

> [e]very utterance must be regarded primarily as a *response* to preceding utterances of the given sphere. Each utterance refutes, affirms, supplements, and relies on the others, presupposes them to be known, and somehow takes them into account." (Hutcheon 1994: 100-101)

Although she is building her argument based on examples from contemporary Western art, Hutcheon's notion of discursive community can be usefully applied to the Cameroonian situation I have been describing in this chapter. The repartee between the participants in these exchanges built on each other's utterances in the dialogic way described by Bakhtin, and the participants' responses and even the positions they were taking were predicated on certain common understandings and common historical and cultural knowledge. Among the themes discussed earlier in this chapter, the evocations of earlier World Cups (especially of 1982 and 1990), the negative evaluations of the French in comparison to the Germans, the scrutiny of the composition of the French team, and the playful references to Portugal all belong to this common font of knowledge.

But even more strikingly, in the commentary on the matches of the 2006 World Cup the dialogism (and humor) was heightened by the fact that much of it was taking place in response to the absent discourses of the past. It seemed to me that the changes in attitude also pointed to an awareness of earlier attitudes, and the exchanges gained their (ironic) meaning from the implicit juxtaposition with those earlier views. Thus, the support for France or the co-optation of the French team as "African" had a double and consequently even more ironic meaning not just because the pro-French and anti-French sides were mocking each other but also because of people's awareness of the earlier generalized anti-French attitude of the Cameroonian public. As a result when the themes discussed in earlier chapters reappeared in 2006 they were doubly in quotation marks, as it were. By echoing the earlier standpoints in these exchanges and simultaneously challenging both the old and the new attitudes and calling attention to the self-contradictions, people were in effect putting all of it into quotation marks, making all of it ironic and thus ambiguous. The dialogism was not only manifest in the conversations that were taking place between different people but also between – often well known – themes toward which some people expressed significantly different attitudes from those they professed on earlier occasions. The fact that there were always some people who provided some meta-commentary on what was going on by immediately questioning the others' point view only amplified and multiplied the juxtaposition and multivocality of the discussions as well as their humor and irony.

Chapter VIII

Concluding Thoughts

I started this work with the description of the mural in Douala in which tears flow down the "face" of a football. Can I answer in the conclusion what those teardrops mean? Are they tears of frustration or of hope? Are they tears of joy or defeat? Tears of defiance or desperation? They are all of those things and more. In other words football in Cameroon, just as the lives of the Cameroonian people, is fraught with contradictions and paradoxes.

The book covers a twelve-year period in which Cameroonian social realities have changed from an extraordinary moment of revolutionary fervor to complete disillusionment and depoliticization. The early 1990s saw the first major challenge to the postcolonial state, but by 2006 the regime regained and strengthened its position, and the opposition became completely neutralized. These political changes can be captured in the transformations of people's attitudes to football. In the aftermath of the pro-democracy movement of the early 1990s, in 1994 and even in 1998, Cameroonians held up football as a model (or ethos) that had the potential to transform their lives (both individually and collectively), but at the same time, the life they aimed to escape caught up with them, and they reproduced the very conditions which they wanted to escape.

During the 1990s, on both the local and the international level, people viewed the sport as if it were possible to divorce it from the everyday power relations of the "outside world." It was as if they were taking an earlier page out of sports sociological writings, which John Hargreaves justly criticized in the following terms in 1982: [sport is] "treated as a separate, quasi-sacred realm where values, difficult if not impossible to realise in the normal course of existence are indeed capable of realisation" (Hargreaves, John 1982: 33).

Unacceptable as such an attitude may be from social scientists analyzing social life, for the majority of Cameroonians this was precisely how football appeared. I suggested that this was so in great part because of the desperation of poverty and a continuing history of being downtrodden. As I explained in the Introduction, football's very structure encourages such a sealing off. I would also argue that this is one of the main reasons why football players and sportsmen in general tend to be apolitical. In order to be allowed to play (a sporting career is limited in time), most sportsmen and women often refrain from expressing political views, making Joseph-Antoine Bell of Cameroon and the Black power salute of the Mexico Olympics such rare occurrences.

This idealized aspect of sport makes both fans and sports commentators decry the interference of politics in it. It is one of the paradoxes of sport that the very people who reject this interference are the ones who imbue sport with the symbolic meanings that make the interference possible, even inevitable. This is so everywhere, not just in Cameroon, but the meanings attributed to football in Cameroon are conditioned by the social, economic, political, and historical realities particular to the country. It is also the polysemy (and therefore inherent multivocality) of the symbolic meanings attributed to it, which lend much of the tension to the sport, and which make it a worthwhile subject of social inquiry, and let's not forget it, make it exciting to watch.

I examined three areas where Cameroonians expressed such visions of a better world through drawing on the ethos aspect of sport. The first was the daily struggle of football people to make football happen in Cameroon and to try to transform their lives in the face of the constraints placed upon them by the everyday realities of life in the postcolony. I mostly used the example of one team and showed that, to some extent exemplifying Mbembe's notion of zombification, the efforts of the owner/coach of the team ultimately failed. These efforts were driven by football's perceived transformative potential (its ethos), while, at the same time, they also expressed people's yearnings for a better world, where values such as meritocracy and fairness prevailed and where – in contrast with what seemed to be the rule in Cameroon – results were clear-cut and proportionate to the effort. Some of this was illusory because being part of the social realities of Cameroon, these efforts got regularly derailed, yet insisting on the proper way of doing things, people also upheld the ethos they had constructed for themselves.

The second area I concentrated on was the vision of a better government through examining the kind of grievances people expressed toward their government in the commentary surrounding the 1994 World Cup. What transpired from this examination was that people – reeling from what they saw as a humiliation that their country suffered on the football field – turned against the government and challenged it in the name of the nation. They rejected the government's nationalist ideology and instead presented their own version of an idealized nation. Such views were expressed in Cameroonians' notions of how things should be; in the very negation of their actual circumstances, they articulated their yearnings for an orderly and more equitable life.

The third area I examined was how Cameroonians envisioned their place in the world as Cameroonians and as Africans through analyzing Cameroonian views about the French and about whites in general. Through talking about football, people articulated their attitudes to their history, as well as their view of their place in the world and the forces they saw to be constraining them. While in the previous chapter I concentrated on how people perceived the local constraints on their lives, in Chapter VI I showed how Cameroonians viewed the external constraints by concentrating on commentary relating to whites in general and especially the French in the course of the 1994 and 1998 World Cups. What was striking was that, paralleling the turn against the government in the name of the nation as an ethos, and interpreting what took place as "white injustice," people turned against whites in the name of the ethos of sports that whites did not seem to live up to. By insisting on the ethos aspect of football Cameroonians called the white man's "bluff" of equality and universal standards. The commentary also served as a vehicle for Cameroonians' expression of their disapproval and dislike of the French.

Although irony had never been lacking in the comments of Cameroonians with regard to World Cup football, what I witnessed in 2006 was significantly different from earlier times. Metaphor was replaced by irony. Metaphor points to a direct relationship between two realities – irony hides one reality behind another and renders its own meaning ambiguous. The most noticeable change in the commentary described in Chapter VII was that in 2006 much less direct (or even indirect) political criticism was addressed to those in power than on earlier occasions. This in part reflected the depoliticization of football and in part signaled a significant change in the direction of the commentary.

In earlier World Cups, the irony was often directed at some absent but powerful "Other" (the government, politicians, FIFA, referees, whites, and the French). However, by 2006 what had been a fairly unified (though not completely uniform) politically partisan discourse of resistance became seemingly apolitical. People were still taking some political stances but in the apparent arbitrariness of their choices, in the exaggerations, in what seemed to be joyous opposition for opposition's sake these standpoints cancelled each other out and were emptied of political meaning. Another way that this arbitrariness became evident was that instead of positions being taken on some kind of principle, personal preferences regarding football stars, styles, or countries gained prominence, also signaling the depoliticization of football.

But there still was irony. The most prevalent became a distinctive form of self-mockery in which, by almost randomly taking opposing stances on matters footballistic, by the juxtaposition and the quick turning around of opinion, the spectators were on a metalevel making fun not only of each other, but also of themselves. The target of irony in this case was the group itself, and by extension Cameroonians.

Lawrence J. Taylor (2001), in discussing self-deprecating Irish stories/discourses (what he refers to as self-irony), makes two interrelated points. On the one hand, he argues that this form of humor is a preemptive strike, a challenge to outsiders. Through criticizing themselves, the Irish gain the upper hand over outsiders who would criticize them. (It seems to me that this point is less applicable to the Cameroonian discourses surrounding the 2006 World Cup, although in football people often resort to a similar kind of preemptive tactic, when seemingly rooting against their own team.) Taylor's second point is that self-irony also "is a recognition of the performer's condition in effect acted out in the performance itself" (Taylor 2001: 185). It is the latter point that is of great importance in the Cameroonian case. In the ironic exchanges of 2006 Cameroonians spoke about their own condition. In part, they mitigated the sense of loss felt over Cameroon's non-qualification to the World Cup, but in part, and I think more importantly, the humorous exchanges indirectly commented on the situation of Cameroon: on the long-standing political stalemate and on the outrageousness of nothing ever changing, and also on people no longer holding on to their convictions. This "anything goes" attitude which questioned and ridiculed every position at the same time undermined and destabilized all positions thus re-creating the very thing it was ridiculing.

Karin Barber's characterization of the "shifting self-subverting quality" of Yoruba popular theater comes to mind. Talking about the ideology Yoruba popular theater represents, she says: "... almost every position taken up is shadowed by its own opposite, and no single coherent dogma has the last word" (Barber 1986: 26).[1] This seems to me to be a strikingly apt characterization of the Cameroonian commentaries on the 2006 World Cup. I would put the emphasis on the ambiguity arising out of the ironic exchanges and the resultant destabilization. In the juxtaposition of often diametrically opposing (past and present) positions, it seems that all is put into question, and if, as Hutcheon argues, irony is transideological (i.e. wavers ambiguously between conservatism and resistance) this holds the possibility for both. Under the circumstances of the disappearance of realistic hope for political change any time soon in Cameroon, this overarching self-deprecating irony and the willingness to maintain collective ambiguity may freeze the picture, but still holds out the possibility of hope.

[1] I thank Dr. Eckhard Breitlinger for making Barber's article available to me.

BIBLIOGRAPHY

Abou

2002 Les Sénégalais en haut, les Camerounais en bas: Le mondial 2002 a entamé sa phase déterminante hier. *La Nouvelle Expression*, June 12, p. 5.

Abu-Lughod, Lila

1990 The Romance of Resistance: Tracing Transformations of Power through Bedouin Women. *American Ethnologist* 17(1): 41-55.

Afrika Spectrum

2006 The Other Game: The Politics of Football in Africa. *Afrika Spectrum* 41(3): 325-478 (Special Issue).

Alegi, Peter C.

2004 *Laduma! Soccer, politics and society in South Africa*. Pietermaritzburg: University of KwaZulu-Natal Press.

Anderson, Benedict

1983 *Imagined Communities*. London: Verso.

Anonymous

1998 La gouvernance du Cameroun: le pouvoir ethnico-tribal de Biya mis à nu. *Le Messager*, 6 July.

2002 Wata Foot Foot and Héros. *Mamy Wata*. July 1, p. 9.

Appadurai, Arjun

2004 The Capacity to Aspire: Culture and the Terms of Recognition. In *Culture and Public Action: A Cross-Disciplinary Dialogue on Development Policy*, V. Rao and M. Watson, eds. Stanford: Stanford University Press, pp. 59-84.

Archetti, Eduardo P.

1996 In Search of National Identity: Argentinian Football and Europe. In *Tribal Identities: Nationalism, Europe, Sport*, J. A. Mangan, ed. London: Frank Cass, pp. 201-219.

1997 The Moralities of Argentinian Football. In *The Ethnography of Moralities*, S. Howell, ed. London: Routledge, pp. 98-123.

Ardener, Edwin

1996 *Kingdom on Mount Cameroon: Studies in the History of the Cameroon Coast, 1500-1970*. Oxford and Providence: Berghahn Books.

Armstrong, Gary

2002 Talking up the Game: Football and the Reconstruction of Liberia, West Africa. *Identities* 9(4): 471-495.

2004a Life, Death, and the Biscuit: Football and the Embodiment of Society in Liberia, West Africa. In *Football in Africa: Conflict, Conciliation and Community*, G. Armstrong and R. Giulianotti, eds. Houndmills and New York: Palgrave MacMillan, pp. 183-209.

2004b The Lords of Misrule: Football and the Rights of the Child in Liberia, West Africa. *Sport in Society* 7(3): 473-502.

Armstrong, Gary and Richard Giulianotti (eds.)

2004 *Football in Africa: Conflict, Conciliation and Community*. Houndmills and New York: Palgrave MacMillan.

Austen, Ralph A. and Jonathan Derrick

1999 *Middlemen of the Cameroon Rivers: The Duala and Their Hinterland, c. 1600–c. 1960*. New York: Cambridge University Press.

Azarya, Victor

1978 *Aristocrats Facing Change: The Fulbe in Guinea, Nigeria, and Cameroon*. Chicago: University of Chicago Press.

Azeyeh, Albert

1994 Syncrétisme culturel et surdétermination de l'ethnie. In *Ethnies et développement national*: Actes du Colloque de Yaoundé 1993. Collectif Changer le Cameroun, ed. Yaoundé: Editions C3, Fondation Friedrich Ebert, and Editions du CRAC, pp. 58-65.

Baker, William J. and J. A. Mangan

1987 *Sport in Africa: Essays in Social History*. New York: Africana Publishing Company.

Baker, William J.

1987 Political Games: the Meaning of International Sport for Independent Africa. In *Sport in Africa*, W. J. Baker and J. A. Mangan, eds. New York: Africana Publishing Company, pp. 272-292.

Bale, John

2004 Three Geographies of African Footballer Migration: Patterns, Problems and Postcoloniality. In *Football in Africa: Conflict, Conciliation and Community*, G. Armstrong and R. Giulianotti, eds. Houndmills and New York: Palgrave MacMillan, pp. 229-246.

Bali, János

2001 Ferencváros, Hungary and the European Champions League: The Symbolic Construction of Marginality and Exclusion. In *Fear and Loathing in World Football*, G. Armstrong and R. Giulianotti, eds. Cambridge: Berg, pp. 251-265.

Baller, Susann

2005 Creating the Postcolonial City: Urban Youth Clubs in Senegal. In *Urbanization and African Cultures*, S. Salm and T. Falola, eds. Durham: Carolina Academic Press, pp. 139-154.

Barber, Karin

1986 Radical Conservatism in Yoruba Popular Plays, *Bayreuth African Studies Series* 7 Drama and Theatre in Africa. E. Breitinger and R. Sander, eds. 5-33.

Barnes, Sandra T.

1986 *Patrons and Power: Creating a Political Community in Metropolitan Lagos*. Bloomington: Indiana University Press.

Bashkow, Ira

2000 "Whitemen" are Good to Think with: How Orokaiva Morality is Reflected on Whitemen's Skin. *Identities* 7(3): 281-332.

Bayart, Jean-François

1973 One-party Government and Political Development in Cameroun. *African Affairs* 72(287): 125-144.

1978 The Birth of the Ahidjo Regime. In *Gaullist Africa: Cameroon under Ahmadu Ahidjo*. R. Joseph, ed. Enugu, Nigeria: Fourth Dimension, pp. 45-65.

1985 *L'état au Cameroun*. Paris: Presses de la Fondation Nationale des Sciences Politiques.

1986 Civil Society in Africa. In *Political Domination in Africa, Reflections on the Limits of Power*, Patrick Chabal, ed. Cambridge: Cambridge University Press, pp. 109-125.

1989 Cameroon. In *Contemporary West African States*, D. B. Cruise O'Brien, J. Dunn, and R. Rathbone, ed. African Studies Series 65. Cambridge: Cambridge University Press, pp. 31-48.

1993 *The State in Africa: The Politics of the Belly*. London: Longman.

Bell, Joseph Antoine

1998 A qui la faute? *Le Messager*, July 3, 1998. Downloaded from http://www.cybernum.com/messager/030798/f.htm (accessed April 25, 1999).

Berman, Bruce

1998 Ethnicity, Patronage and the African State: The Politics of Uncivil Nationalism. *African Affairs*, 97: 305-341.

Bikoun, Bertille M.

2003 Cameroun: Lions indomptables: La sélection controversée de Schäfer. *Le Quotidien Mutations*, November 7, 2003. Downloaded from http://fr.allafrica.com/stories/200311070501.html (accessed January 10, 2007).

Binyam, Junior

2005 Cameroun: Emotions: la Nation dans une cuvette, *Le Quotidien Mutations*, November 21, 2005. Downloaded from http://fr.allafrica.com/stories/200411211249.html (accessed January 10, 2007).

Bissohong, Théophile

1998 Football et imaginaire au Cameroun: des héros de l'ailleurs. *Mots Pluriels*, 6. www.arts.uwa.edu.au/MotsPluriels/MP698tb.html (accessed January 3, 1999).

Black, David R. and John Nauright

1998 *Rugby and the South African Nation*. Manchester: Manchester University Press.

Blain, N., R. Boyle, and H. O'Donnell

1993 *Sport and National Identity in the European Media*. Leicester: Leicester University Press.

Bourdieu, Pierre

1978 Sport and Social Class. *Social Science Information* 17(6): 819-840.

Bowen, Elenore Smith [Laura Bohannan]

1964 *Return to Laughter*. New York: Doubleday.

Bromberger, Christian

1994a Foreign Footballers, Cultural Dreams and Community Identity in Some North-western Mediterranean Cities. In *The Global Sports Arena: Athletic Talent Migration in an Interdependent World*, J. Bale and J. Maguire, eds. London: Frank Cass, pp. 171-182.

1994b Football Passion and the World Cup: Why So Much Sound and Fury? In *Hosts and Champions: Soccer Cultures, National Identities and the USA World Cup*, J. Sugden and A. Tomlinson, eds. Aldershot: Arena, pp. 281-290.

1995 Football as World-View and as Ritual. *French Cultural Studies*, 6(18): 293-311.

Bromberger, Christian, Alain Hayot, and Jean-Marc Mariottini

1995 *Le match de football: Ethnologie d'une passion partisane à Marseille, Naples et Turin*. Paris: Editions de la Maison des sciences de l'homme.

Burnham, Philip

1972 Racial Classification and Ideology in the Meiganga Region: North Cameroon. In *Race and Social Difference*, P. Baxter and B. Sansom, eds. London: Penguin, pp. 301-318.

1996 *The Politics of Cultural Difference in Northern Cameroon*. Edinburgh: Edinburgh University Press.

Castoriadis, Cornelius

1987 *The Imaginary Institution of Society*. Cambridge: Polity Press.

Ceuppens, Bambi and Peter Geschiere

2005 Autochthony: Local or Global? New Modes in the Struggle over Citizenship and Belonging in Africa and Europe. *Annual Review of Anthropology* 34: 385-407.

Chabal, Patrick

1996 The African Crisis: Context and Interpretation. In *Postcolonial Identities in Africa*, R. Werbner and T. Ranger, eds. London: Zed Books, pp. 29-54.

Chabal, Patrick and Jean-Pascal Daloz

1999 *Africa Works: Disorder as Political Instrument*. Oxford and Bloomington: The International African Institute, Indiana University Press and James Currey.

Chatterjee, Partha

1996 Whose Imagined Community? In *Mapping the Nation*, G. Balakrishnan, ed. London: Verso, pp. 214-225.

Clignet, Remi and Maureen Stark

1974 Modernisation and Football in Cameroun. *The Journal of Modern African Studies*. 12(3): 409-421.

Cohen, Ronald

1978 Ethnicity: Problem and Focus in Anthropology. *Annual Review of Anthropology*, 7: 379-403.

Crapanzano, Vincent

2004 *Imaginative Horizons: An Essay in Literary–Philosophical Anthropology*. Chicago, IL: University of Chicago Press.

Csaplovics, János

1822 *Ethnographiai értekezés Magyarországról*. Tudományos Gyűjtemény, pp. 3-4.

Collectif Changer le Cameroun

1992 *Le Cameroun éclaté? Anthologie commentée des revendications ethniques*. Yaoundé: Editions C3.

1994 *Ethnies et développement national*: Actes du Colloque de Yaoundé 1993, Yaoundé: Editions C3, Fondation Friedrich Ebert, and Editions du CRAC.

Coquery-Vidrovitch, Catherine
2002 Book review. Achille Mbembe, De la postcolonie. Essai sur l'imagination politique dans l'Afrique contemporaine. Paris: Karthala, 2000. From H-Africa (H-Africa@h-net.msu.edu), March 22, 2002 (accessed June 17, 2007).

Coronil, Fernando
1992 Can Postcoloniality Be Decolonized? Imperial Banality and Postcolonial Power. *Public Culture* 5(1): 89-108.

Darby, Paul
2002 *Africa, Football and FIFA: Politics, Colonialism and Resistance*. London: Frank Cass.
2003 Africa, the FIFA Presidency and the Governance of World Football: 1974, 1998, and 2002. *Africa Today* 50(1): 3-24.
2005 Africa and the 'World' Cup: FIFA Politics, Eurocentrism and Resistance. *International Journal of the History of Sport* 22(5): 881-903.

Dauncey, Hugh and Geoff Hare
1999a "33 jours de fête": A Diary of France 98. In *France and the 1998 World Cup: The National Impact of a World Sporting Event*, H. Dauncey and G. Hare, eds. London: Frank Cass, pp. 184-204.

Dauncey, Hugh and Geoff Hare (eds.)
1999b *France and the 1998 World Cup: The National Impact of a World Sporting Event.* London: Frank Cass

DeBoeck, Filip
1996 Postcolonialism, Power and Identity: Local and Global Perspectives from Zaire. In *Postcolonial Identities in Africa*, R. Werbner and T. Ranger, eds. London: Zed Books, pp. 75-106.

DeLancey, Mark W.
1989 *Cameroon: Dependence and Independence*. Boulder, CO: Westview Press.

DeLancey, Mark W. and H. Mbella Mokeba
1990 *Historical Dictionary of the Republic of Cameroon.* Metuchen, NJ: The Scarecrow Press.

Derrick, Jonathan
1992 One Party, Many Parties and the State. *Africa Insight* 22(3): 165-178.

Deville-Danthu, Bernadette
1998 Le développement des activités sportives en Afrique occidentale française: un bras de fer entre sportifs et administration coloniale (1920-1956). *Revue Française d'Histoire d'Outre-mer* 85(318): 105-118.

Dossier
2005 Ahidjo – Biya: bilans comparés de 23 ans de pouvoir suprême. *Le Messager*, November 7, 2005, pp. 5-8.

Duke, Vic and Liz Crolley
1996 *Football, Nationality and the State*. Harlow, Essex: Longman.

Eboussi Boulaga, Fabien
1993 *Les conférences nationales en Afrique noire: Une affaire à suivre*. Paris: Karthala.

Edensor, Tim and Ibrahim Koodoruth
2004 Football and Ethnicity in Mauritius: (Re)Producing Communal Allegiances. In *Football in Africa: Conflict, Conciliation and Community*, G. Armstrong and R. Giulianotti, eds. Houndmills and New York: Palgrave and MacMillan, pp. 135-149.

Eko, Lyombe
2003 The English-Language Press and the "Anglophone Problem" in Cameroon: Group Identity, Culture, and the Politics of Nostalgia. *Journal of Third World Studies* 20(1): 79-102.

Eriksen, Thomas Hylland
1993 *Ethnicity and Nationalism: Anthropological Perspectives*. London: Pluto Press.

Essono, L. M. Onguene
1996 La démocratie en chansons: les bikut-si du Cameroun. *Politique Africaine* 64: 52-61.

Eyinga, Abel
2002 Les Lions Indomptables et les institutions. *Le Messager*, June 12, 2002, p. 13.

Eyoh, Dickson
1996 From Economic Crisis to Political Liberalization: Pitfalls of the New Political Sociology for Africa. *African Studies Review* 39(3): 43-80.
1998a African Perspectives on Democracy and the Dilemmas of Postcolonial Intellectuals. *Africa Today* 45(3-4): 281-306.
1998b Conflicting Narratives of Anglophone Protest and the Politics of Identity in Cameroon. *Journal of Contemporary African Studies* 16(2): 249-276.

1998c Through the Prism of a Local Tragedy: Political Liberalisation, Regionalism and Elite Struggles for Power in Cameroon. *Africa* 68(3): 338-359.

2004 Contesting Local Citizenship: Liberalization and the Politics of Difference in Cameroon. In *Ethnicity and Democracy in Africa*, B. Berman, D. Eyoh and W. Kymlicka, eds. Oxford and Athens: James Currey and Ohio University Press, pp. 96-112.

Fabian, Johannes

1998 *Moments of Freedom: Anthropology and Popular Culture*. Charlottesville, VA: University Press of Virginia.

Fair, Laura

1997 Kickin' it: Leisure, Politics and Football in Colonial Zanzibar, 1900s–1950s. *Africa* 67(2): 224-251.

2001 *Pastimes and Politics: Culture, Community, and Identity in Post-Abolition Urban Zanzibar, 1890-1945*. Athens: Ohio University Press and Oxford: James Currey.

2004 Ngoma Reverberations: Swahili Music Culture and the Making of Football Aesthetics in Early Twentieth Century Zanzibar. In *Football in Africa: Conflict, Conciliation and Community*, G. Armstrong and R. Giulianotti, eds. Houndmills and New York: Palgrave MacMillan, pp. 103-113.

Fandio, Pierre

2004 Nouvelles voix et voies nouvelles de la littérature orale camerounaise. *Semen*, 18, De la culture orale à la production écrite: Littératures africaines, 2004. Internet edition April 29, 2007. From http://semen.revues.org/document2298.html (accessed January 25, 2008).

Fardon, Richard

1988 *Raiders and Refugees: Trends of Chamba Political Development 1750-1950*. Smithsonian Series in Ethnographic Enquiry. Washington, DC: Smithsonian Institution Press.

1996 'Crossed Destinies': the Entangled Histories of West African Ethnic and National Identities. In *Ethnicity in Africa: Roots, Meanings and Implications*, L. de la Gorgendière, K. King, and S. Vaughan, eds. Edinburgh: Centre of African Studies, pp. 117-146.

Farred, Grant

2003 'Theatre of Dreams': Mimicry and Difference in Cape Flats Township Football. In *Sport and Postcolonialism*, J. Bale and M. Cronin, eds. Oxford and New York: Berg, pp. 123-145.

Fehérváry, Krisztina
2002 American Kitchens, Luxury Bathrooms, and the Search for a 'Normal' Life in Postsocialist Hungary. *Ethnos* 67(3): 369-400.

Fernandez, James W. and Mary Taylor Huber
2001 Introduction: The Anthropology of Irony. In *Irony in Action: Anthropology, Practice and the Moral Imagination*, J. W. Fernandez and M. T. Huber, eds. Chicago and London: Chicago University Press, pp. 1-37.

Ferguson, James
1999 *Expectations of Modernity: Myths and Meanings of Urban Life on the Zambian Copperbelt*. Berkeley, CA: University of California Press.

Fisiy, Cyprian and Mitzi Goheen
1998 Power and the Quest for Recognition: Neo-traditional Titles among the New Elite in Nso, Cameroon. *Africa* 68(3): 383-402.

Friedman, Jonathan
1990 The Political Economy of Elegance. *Cultural History* 7: 101-122.

F.[oimoukom], H.[onoré]
2005 Football des jeunes: la descente aux enfers: La politique de développement du football pour minimes, cadets et juniors est quasi-inexistante au pays des Lions Indomptables, *Le Messager*, November 30, 2005, p. 6.

Fombad, Charles Manga
2004 The Dynamics of Record-breaking Endemic Corruption and Political Opportunism in Cameroon. In *The Leadership Challenge in Africa: Cameroon Under Paul Biya*, J. M. Mbaku and J. Takougang, eds. Trenton, NJ and Asmara: Africa World Press, pp. 357-394.

Fonchingong, Tangie Nsoh
2004 The Travails of Democratization in Cameroon in the Context of Political Liberalisation since the 1990s. *African and Asian Studies* 3(1): 33-59.

Gal, Susan
1995 Language and the "Arts of Resistance". *Cultural Anthropology* 10(3): 407-424.

Gandoulou, J. D.
1989 *Dandies à Bacongo: le culte de l'élégance dans la société congolaise contemporaine*. Paris: L'Harmattan.

Gaonkar, Dilip Parameshwar
2002 Toward New Imaginaries: An Introduction. *Public Culture* 14(1): 1-19.

Gausset, Quentin

1999 Islam or Christianity? The Choices of the Wawa and the Kwanja of Cameroon. *Africa* 69(2): 254-278.

Geertz, Clifford

1973 *The Interpretation of Cultures*. New York: Basic Books.

2000 Thinking as a Moral Act: Ethical Dimensions of Anthropological Fieldwork in the New States. In *Available Light: Anthropological Reflections on Philosophical Topics*. Princeton, NJ: Princeton University Press, pp. 21-41.

Geschiere, Peter

1996 Kinship, Witchcraft, and the Moral Economy of Ethnicity: Contrasts from Southern and Western Cameroun. In *Ethnicity in Africa: Roots, Meanings and Implications*, L. de la Gorgendière, K. King, and S. Vaughan, eds. Edinburgh: Centre of African Studies, pp. 167-192.

Geschiere, Peter and Stephen Jackson

2006 Autochthony and the Crisis of Citizenship: Democratization, Decentralization, and the Politics of Belonging. *African Studies Review* 49(2): 1-7.

Geschiere, Peter and Francis B. Nyamnjoh

2000 Capitalism and Autochthony: The Seesaw of Mobility and Belonging. *Public Culture* 12(2): 423-452.

Giulianotti, Richard

1999a *Football: A Sociology of the Global Game*. Cambridge: Polity Press.

1999b Sport and Social Development in Africa: Some Major Human Rights Issues. www.ausport.gov.au/fulltext/1999/nsw/p18-25.pdf (accessed January 25, 2005).

2004 Human Rights, Globalization and Sentimental Education: The Case of Sport. *Sport in Society* 7(3): 355-369.

Goerg, Odile

2002 L'électricité, le pouvoir et le football en Guinée. *Politique Africaine* 88: 168-173.

Goheen, Miriam

1996 *Men Own the Fields, Women Own the Crops: Gender and Power in the Cameroon Grassfields*. Madison, WI: The University of Wisconsin Press.

Gordon, David F. and Howard Wolpe

1998 The Other Africa: An End to Afro-Pessimism. *World Policy Journal* XV(1): 49-59.

Gupta, Akhil
1995 Blurred Boundaries: The Discourse of Corruption, the Culture of Politics and the Imagined State. *American Ethnologist* 22(2): 375-402.

Guttmann, Allen
1994 *Games and Empires: Modern Sports and Cultural Imperialism.* New York: Columbia University Press.

Guyer, Jane I.
1981 Household and Community in African Studies. *African Studies Review* 24: 87-137.

Hadas, Miklós and Karády, Viktor
1995 Futball és társadalmi identitás. *Replika* 17-18: 89-119.

Hadas, Miklós
1999 Stílus és karakter: Futballhabitológiai traktátus. *Replika* 36: 125-144.

Handler, Andrew
1994 *From Goals to Guns: the Golden Age of Soccer in Hungary, 1950-1956.* East European Monographs. Boulder, CO and New York: Columbia University Press.

Hannerz, Ulf
1987 The World in Creolization. *Africa* 57(4): 546-559.

Hargreaves, Jennifer
1982 Theorising Sport: An Introduction. In *Sport, Culture and Ideology*, Jennifer Hargreaves, ed. London: Routledge and Kegan Paul, pp. 1-29.

Hargreaves, John
1982 Sport, Culture and Ideology. In *Sport, Culture and Ideology*, Jennifer Hargreaves, ed. London: Routledge and Kegan Paul, pp. 30-61.
1986 *Sport, Power, and Culture: A Social and Historical Analysis of Popular Sports in Britain.* New York: St. Martin's Press.

Haugerud, Angelique
1995 *The Culture of Politics in Modern Kenya.* Cambridge: Cambridge University Press.

Haynes, Jonathan
2003 Mobilising Yoruba Popular Culture: Babangida Must Go. *Africa* 73(1): 77-87.

Herzfeld, Michael

2001 Irony and Power: Toward a Politics of Mockery in Greece. In *Irony in Action: Anthropology, Practice and the Moral Imagination*, J. W. Fernandez and M. T. Huber, eds. Chicago and London: Chicago University Press, pp. 63-83.

Hobsbawm, Eric and Terence Ranger, (eds.)

1983 *The Invention of Tradition*. Cambridge: Cambridge University Press.

Hognestad, Hans and Arvid Tollisen

2004 Playing Against Deprivation: Football and Development in Nairobi, Kenya. In *Football in Africa: Conflict, Conciliation and Community*, G. Armstrong and R. Giulianotti, eds. Houndmills and New York: Palgrave MacMillan, pp. 210-226.

Holt, Richard, J. A. Mangan, and Pierre Lanfranchi, (eds.)

1996 *European Heroes: Myth, Identity, Sport*. London: Frank Cass.

Hutcheon, Linda

1994 *Irony's Edge: The Theory and Politics of Irony*. London: Routledge.

Hurault, Jean

1962 *La structure sociale des Bamiléké*. Paris: Mouton.

Jameson, Fredric

1988 Cognitive Mapping. In *Marxism and the Interpretation of Culture*, C. Nelson and L. Grossberg, eds. London: MacMillan, pp. 347-357.

Joseph, Richard A.

1977 *Radical Nationalism in Cameroun: Social Origins of the U.P.C. Rebellion*. Oxford: Clarendon Press.

Joseph, Richard, (ed.)

1978 *Gaullist Africa: Cameroon under Ahmadu Ahidjo*. Enugu, Nigeria: Fourth Dimension Publishers.

1999 *State, Conflict, and Democracy in Africa*. Boulder, CO: Lynne Rienner Publishers.

Jua, Nantang

1993 Production/Consumption of the Politics of Ethnicity and the Democratic Discourse in the Camerounian Electoral Process. Paper presented at the XXXVI Annual Meeting of the African Studies Association, Boston, 1993.

2001 Democracy and the Construction of Allogeny/Autochthony in Postcolonial Cameroon. *African Issues* 29(1-2): 37-42.

2004 "Spatialization" and Valorization of Identities in Contemporary Cameroon. In *The Leadership Challenge in Africa: Cameroon Under Paul Biya*, J. M. Mbaku and J. Takougang, eds. Trenton, NJ and Asmara: Africa World Press, pp. 299-334.

2005 The Mortuary Sphere, Privilege and the Politics of Belonging in Contemporary Cameroon. *Africa* 75(3): 325-355.

Kaplan, Robert D.

1994 The Coming Anarchy. *The Atlantic Monthly* 273(2): 44-76 (February).

Karlström, Mikael

2003 On the Aesthetics and Dialogics of Power in the Postcolony. *Africa* 73(1): 57-76.

Kirk-Greene, A. H. M.

1980 The Thin White Line: The Size of the British Colonial Service in Africa. *African Affairs* 79(314): 25-44.

Kodo-Ela, Jean-Claude and Mayamba Masika

nd *Il était une fois ... Les Lions Indomptables du Cameroun*. Yaoundé: Editions SOPECAM. Collection Hommes et Evénements.

Kofele-Kale, Ndiva

1986 Ethnicity, Regionalism, and Political Power: A Post-Mortem of Ahidjo's Cameroon. In *The Political Economy of Cameroon*, Michael G. Schatzberg and I. William Zartman, eds. (A SAIS Study on Africa). New York: Praeger, pp. 53-82.

Kom, Bernard

2007 Football africain: plaidoyer pour un entraîneur. From: http://centralepanafri.onlc.fr/index.php?page=17 (accessed January 10, 2007).

Konings, Piet

1996 Le "problème anglophone" au Cameroun dans les années 1990. *Politique Africaine* 62: 25-34.

2004 Opposition and Social-Democratic Change in Africa: The Social Democratic Front in Cameroon. *Commonwealth & Comparative Politics* 42(3): 289-311.

Konings, Piet and Francis B. Nyamnjoh

2003 *Negotiating an Anglophone Identity: A Study of the Politics of Recognition and Representation in Cameroon.* Leiden and Boston, MA: Brill.

2004 President Biya and the "Anglophone Problem" in Cameroon. In *The Leadership Challenge in Africa: Cameroon Under Paul Biya*, J. M. Mbaku and J. Takougang, eds. Trenton, NJ and Asmara: Africa World Press, pp. 191-234.

Krieger, Milton

1994 Cameroon's Democratic Crossroads, 1990-4. *The Journal of Modern African Studies* 32(4): 605-628.

Lanfranchi, Pierre and Matthew Taylor

2001 *Moving with the Ball: The Migration of Professional Footballers*. Oxford: Berg.

Last, Alex

2004 Containment and Counter-Attack: A History of Eritrean Football. In *Football in Africa: Conflict, Conciliation and Community*, G. Armstrong and R. Giulianotti, eds. Houndmills and New York: Palgrave MacMillan, pp. 27-40.

Lazarus, Neil

1994 National Consciousness and the Specificity of (Post)colonial Intellectualism. In *Colonial Discourse/ Postcolonial Theory*, F. Barker, P. Hulme, and M. Iversen, eds. Manchester: Manchester University Press, pp. 197-220.

Leite Lopes, José Sergio

1997 Successes and Contradictions in 'Multiracial' Brazilian Football. In *Entering the Field: New Perspectives on World Football*, G. Armstrong and R. Giulianotti, eds. Oxford: Berg, pp. 53-86.

2000 Class, Ethnicity and Color in the Making of Brazilian Football. *Daedalus* 129(2): 239-270.

Leite Lopes, José Sergio and J. P. Faguer

1994 L'invention du style brésilien: sport, journalisme et politique au Brésil. *Actes de la Recherche en Sciences* Sociales 103.

Lentz, Carola

1995 'Tribalism' and Ethnicity in Africa: A Review of Four Decades of Anglophone Research. *Cahiers des Sciences Humaines* 31(2): 303-328.

2000 Colonial Constructions and African Initiatives: The History of Ethnicity in Northwestern Ghana. *Ethnos* 65(1): 107-136.

Leseth, Anne

1997 The Use of *Juju* in Football: Sport and Witchcraft in Tanzania. In *Entering the Field: New Perspectives on World Football*, G. Armstrong and R. Giulianotti, eds. Oxford: Berg, pp. 159-174.

LeVine, Victor T.

1964 *The Cameroons from Mandate to Independence*. Berkeley, CA: University of California Press.

1971 *The Cameroon Federal Republic*. Ithaca, NY: Cornell Press.

1986 Leadership and Regime Changes in Perspective. In *The Political Economy of Cameroon*, M. G. Schatzberg and I. W. Zartman, eds. (A SAIS Study on Africa). New York: Praeger, pp. 20-52.

Lewis, Paul. (ed.)
2009 *Ethnologue. Languages of the World.* Dallas, Tex.: SIL International. Online version: http://www.ethnologue.com (accessed March 11, 2010).

Lobé, Lyé Kala
1977 *Douala Manga Bell: héros de la résistance douala*. Paris: ABC.

Malaquais, Dominique
1999 Building in the Name of God: Architecture, Resistance, and the Christian Faith in the Bamileke Highlands of Western Cameroon. *African Studies Review* 42(1): 49-78.

Malkki, Liisa H.
1995 *Purity and Exile, Violence, Memory, and the National Cosmology among Hutu Refugees in Tanzania*. Chicago, IL: The University of Chicago Press.

Mamdani, Mahmood
1996 *Citizen and Subject: Contemporary Africa and the Legacy of Late Colonialism*. Princeton, NJ: Princeton University Press.

Mangan, James A.
1986 *The Games Ethic and Imperialism: Aspects of the Diffusion of an Ideal.* London: Viking.
1987 Ethics and Ethnocentricity: Imperial Education in British Tropical Africa. In *Sport in Africa*, W. J. Baker and J. A. Mangan, eds. New York: Africana Publishing Company, pp. 172-195.

Mangan, J. A. (ed.)
1996 *Tribal Identities: Nationalism, Europe, Sport*. London: Frank Cass.

Marks, John
1999 The French National Team and National Identity: Cette France d'un 'bleu métis. In *France and the 1998 World Cup: The National Impact of a World Sporting Event*, H. Dauncey and G. Hare, eds. London: Frank Cass, pp. 41-57.

Martin, Phyllis M.
1991 Colonialism, Youth and Football in French Equatorial Africa. *International Journal for the History of Sports* 8: 56-71.
1995 *Leisure and Society in Colonial Brazzaville*. Cambridge: Cambridge University Press.

Mazrui, Ali A.

1983 Francophone Nations and English-Speaking States: Imperial Ethnicity and African Political Formations. In *State Versus Ethnic Claims: African Policy Dilemmas*, D. Rothchild and V. A. Olorunsola, eds. Boulder, CO: Westview Press, pp. 25-43.

Mazrui, A. A. and M. Tidy

1984 *Nationalism and New States in Africa*. Nairobi: Heinemann.

Mbaku, John Mukum

2002 Cameroon's Stalled Transition to Democratic Governance: Lessons for Africa's New Democrats. *African and Asian Studies* 3(1): 125-163.

Mbaku, John Mukum and Joseph Takougang, (eds.)

2004 *The Leadership Challenge in Africa: Cameroon Under Paul Biya*. Trenton, NJ and Asmara: Africa World Press, Inc.

Mbembe, Achille, (ed.)

1984 *Um Nyobe et le problème national camerounais*. Paris: l'Harmattan.

Mbembe, Achille

1986 Pouvoir des morts et langage des vivants: les errances de la mémoire nationaliste au Cameroun. *Politique Africaine* 22: 37-72.

1992 Provisional Notes on the Postcolony. *Africa* 62: 3-37.

1996 *La naissance du maquis dans le Sud Cameroun (1920-1960)*. Paris: Karthala.

1997 The 'Thing' & its Double in Cameroonian Cartoons. In *Readings in African Popular Culture*, K. Barber, ed. Bloomington and Oxford: Indiana University Press and James Currey, pp. 151-163.

2001 *On the Postcolony*. Berkeley, CA: University of California Press.

Mbembe, Achille and Janet Roitman

1995 Figures of the Subject in Times of Crisis. *Public Culture* 7: 323-352.

Mbono Samba Azan, Madeleine and Bernard Rouzet

1976 *Martin Samba: face à la pénétration allemande au Cameroun*. Paris: ABC.

Mbuagbo, Oben Timothy

2002 Cameroon: Exploiting Anglophone Identity in State Deconstruction. *Social Identities* 8(3): 431-438.

Mbuagbo, Oben T. and Robert M. Akoko

2004 Motions of Support and Ethno-regional Politics in Cameroon. *Journal of Third World Studies* 21(1): 241-258.

McKeever, Lucy
1999 Reporting the World Cup: Old and New Media. In *France and the 1998 World Cup: The National Impact of a World Sporting Event*, H. Dauncey and G. Hare, eds. London: Frank Cass, pp. 161-183.

Mehler, Andreas
2006 Political Discourse in Football Coverage – The Cases of Côte d'Ivoire and Ghana. *GiGA Working Papers*, No. 27.

Messang, Abed Nego
1995a Obsolescence, déchéance et fuite en avant. *Génération*, No. 22, January, 18-24, p. 13.
1995b Mécomptes et légendes de la World Cup. *Génération*, No. 38, June 14-21, p. 13.

Meyer, Birgit
1998 Commodities and the Power of Prayer: Pentecostalist Attitudes Towards Consumption in Contemporary Ghana. *Development & Change* 29(4): 751-776.

Mignon, Patrick
1999 Fans and Heroes. In *France and the 1998 World Cup: The National Impact of a World Sporting Event*, H. Dauncey and G. Hare, eds. London: Frank Cass, pp. 79-97.

Moadougou, Priscille G.
2006 Pierre Wome: Les tee-shirts qui fâchent. Le manager du joueur menace de porter plainte contre la Fédération ivoirienne de football. *Mutations* June 22, 2006. From http://www.camfoot.com/article.php3?id_article=7417 (accessed May 31, 2007).

Mohammadou, Eldridge
1988 *Les lamidats de Diamare et du Mayo-Louti au XIXe siècle (Nord-Cameroun)*. (African Languages and Ethnography XXII.) Tokyo: Institute for the Study of Languages and Cultures of Asia and Africa (ILCAA).

Mokeba, Harry Mbella
1989 The Politics and Diplomacy of Cameroon Sports: A Study in the Quest for Nation-building and International Prestige. Unpublished doctoral dissertation, University of South Carolina.

Monga, Célestin
1990a Roger Milla est-il l'intellectuel africain de la décennie? *Afrique 2000: Revue Africaine de Politique Internationale* 3: 121-125.

1990b La démocratie truquée. Lettre ouverte au president Paul Biya. *Le Messager*, No. 209, December 27.

Monga, Yvette Djachechi

2001 The Politics of Identity Negotiation in Cameroon. *International Negotiation* 6: 199-228.

2000 "Au village!": Space, Culture and Politics in Cameroon. *Cahiers d'Études africaines*, 160(XL-4): 723-749.

Monnington, Terence

1986 The Politics of Black African Sport. In *The Politics of Sport*, Lincoln Allison, ed. Manchester: Manchester University Press.

Moukoko Priso

2002 Au-delà de la débâcle. *Le Messager*, July 10, 2002, p. 10.

Mudimbe, V. Y.

1988 *The Invention of Africa: Gnosis, Philosophy and the Order of Knowledge*. Bloomington: Indiana University Press.

Nana, Walter Wilson and Innocent Mbunwe

2006 Why Mbarga Mboa was Dropped. *The Post*, September 28, 2006. From http//allafrica.com/200609280756.html (accessed January 12, 2008).

Ndjio, Basile

2005 Carréfour de la joie: Popular Deconstruction of the African Postcolonial Public Sphere. *Africa* 75(3): 265-294.

Ndogkoti, L.

2007 La malediction de Nfandena, December 22, 2007. From http://www.camfoot.com/La-malediction-de-Nfandena (accessed January 12, 2008).

Ngatsing, Laure

2005 La fin des illusions. *Le Messager*, October 10, 2005. From http://fr.allafrica.com/stories/200510110041.html (accessed June 20, 2007).

Nguini, Charles

1996 *Le Footoir Camerounais*. Yaoundé: Capel.

Nketcha, Jean-Calvain

1990/1991 Sport et Politique au Cameroun. Unpublished thesis, University of Yaoundé, Department of Public Law.

Nkwi, Paul Nchoji and Francis B. Nyamnjoh (eds.)
1997 *Regional Balance and National Integration in Cameroon: Lessons Learned and the Uncertain Future*. Leiden: African Studies Center and Yaoundé: ICASSRT.

Nkwi, Paul Nchoji and Bea Vidacs
1997 Football: Politics and Power in Cameroon. In *Entering the Field: New Perspectives on World Football*, G. Armstrong and R. Giulianotti, eds. Oxford: Berg, pp. 123-139.

Nsigué, Guy
2005 Après le match: Les coulisses, October 11, 2005. From http://www.camfoot.com/Apres-le-match-Les-coulisses.html (accessed January 12, 2008).

Ntonfo, André
1994a *Football et politique du football au Cameroun*. Yaoundé: Editions du Crac.
1994b Ethnie et sport au Cameroun. In *Ethnie et développement national. Actes du Colloque de Yaoundé 1993*. Yaoundé: Editions du Crac, pp. 148-157.

Nyamnjoh, Francis B.
1999 Cameroon: A Country United by Ethnic Ambition and Difference. *African Affairs*, 98: 101-118.
2000 "For Many are Called but Few are Chosen": Globalisation and Popular Disenchantment in Africa. *African Sociological Review* 4(2): 1-45.
2001 Delusions of development and the enrichment of witchcraft discourses in Cameroon. In *Magical Interpretations, Material Realities: Modernity, Witchcraft and the Occult in Postcolonial Africa*, Henrietta L. Moore and Todd Sanders, eds. London: Routledge, pp. 28-49.
2002a "A child is one person's only in the womb": Domestication, Agency and Subjectivity in the Cameroonian Grassfields. In *Postcolonial Subjectivities in Africa*, R. Werbner, ed. London: Zed Books, pp. 111-138.
2002b Cameroon: Over Twelve Years of Cosmetic Democracy. *Nordic Africa Institute News* No. 3. From http://www.nai.uu.se/publications/news/archives/023nyamnjoh/ (accessed June 10, 2007).
2005 Images of Nyongo amongst Bamenda Grassfielders in Whiteman Kontri. *Citizenship Studies* 9(3): 241-269.
2007 Theorizing Agency In and On Africa: The Questions Are Key. In *Strength Beyond Structure: Social and Historical Trajectories of Agency in Africa*, M. de Bruijn, R. Van Dijk, and J-B. Geward, eds. Leiden: Brill, pp. 340-344.

Nyamnjoh, Francis B. and Jude Fokwang
2005 Entertaining Repression: Music and Politics in Postcolonial Cameroon. *African Affairs* 104(415): 251-274.

Nyamnjoh, Francis B. and Ben Page
2002 Whiteman Kontri and the Enduring Allure of Modernity among Cameroonian Youth. *African Affairs* 101(405): 607-634.

Nyamnjoh, Francis and Michael Rowlands
1998 Elite Associations and the Politics of Belonging in Cameroon. *Africa* 68(3): 320-337.

Odendaal, André
2003 *The Story of an African Game: Black Cricketers and the Unmasking of One of Cricket's Greatest Myths, South Africa, 1850-2003.* Cape Town: David Philip.

Odhiambo, E. S. Atieno
1987 Democracy and the Ideology of Order in Kenya. In *The Political Economy of Kenya*, Michael G. Schatzberg, ed. New York: Praeger, pp. 177-201.

Ogola, George
2005 Popular Culture and Politics: Whispers and the Dramaturgy of Power in Kenya. *Social Identities* 11(2): 147-160.

Onana, Jean-Baptiste
2004a Cameroun: le sport contre les ethnies. *Outre Terre* 8(2004/3): 69-76.
2004b Entretien avec André Kana Biyik. *Outre Terre* 8(2004/3): 65-67.

Ondoa-Etoa, Vincent
1994 Je suis "béti," l'homme des "bêtises," on fera comment? *Le Messager*, 15th anniversary special issue, November 26, 1994, p. 39.

Ortner, Sherry B.
1995 Resistance and the Problem of Ethnographic Refusal. *Contemporary Studies in Society and History* 37(1): 173-193.

Poli, Raffaele
2006 Migrations and Trade of African Football Players: Historic, Geographical and Cultural Aspects. *Afrika Spectrum* 41(3): 393-414.

Poli, Raffaele and Paul Dietschy
2006 Le football africain entre immobilisme et extraversion. *Politique Africaine* 102: 173-187.

Population Reference Bureau

2006 World Population Data Sheet. From www.prb.org/pdf08/08WorldDataSheet.pdf (accessed August 2, 2009).

Pratt, Mary Louise

1992 *Imperial Eyes: Travel Writing and Transculturation*. London and NewYork: Routledge.

Ralph, Michael

2006 'Le Sénégal Qui Gagne': Soccer and the Stakes of Neoliberalism in a Postcolonial Port. *Soccer and Society* 7(2): 300-317.

Ranger, Terence

1983 The Invention of Tradition in Colonial Africa. In *The Invention of Tradition*, E. Hobsbawm and T. Ranger, eds. Cambridge: Cambridge University Press.

1987 Pugilism and Pathology: African Boxing and the Black Urban Experience in Southern Rhodesia. In *Sport in Africa*, W. J. Baker and J. A. Mangan, eds. New York: Africana Publishing, pp. 196-213.

1993 The Invention of Tradition Revisited: The Case of Colonial Africa. In *Legitimacy and the State in Twentieth Century Africa: Essays in Honour of A. H. M. Kirk-Greene*, T. Ranger and O. Vaughan, eds. London: MacMillan, pp. 62-111.

Ranger, Terence and Olufemi Vaughan

1993 Introduction. In *Legitimacy and the State in Twentieth Century Africa: Essays in Honour of A. H. M. Kirk-Greene*. T. Ranger and O. Vaughan, eds. London: MacMillan, pp. 1-28.

Rausing, Sigrid

2002 Reconstructing the Normal: Identity and the Consumption of Western Goods in Estonia. In *Markets and Moralities: Ethnographies of Postsocialism*, R. Mandel and C. Humphreys, eds. Oxford: Berg, pp. 127-142.

Regis, Helen A.

2003 *Fulbe Voices: Marriage, Islam, and Medicine in Northern Cameroon*. Boulder, CO: Westview Press.

Richards, Paul

1997 Soccer and Violence in War-Torn Africa: Soccer and Social Rehabilitation in Sierra Leone. In *Entering the Field: New Perspectives on World Football*, G. Armstrong and R. Giulianotti, eds. Oxford: Berg, pp. 141-157.

Rieff, David

1998 In defense of Afro-Pessimism. *World Policy Journal* XV(4): 10-22.

Robinson, Pearl T.

1994a Democratization: Understanding the Relationship between Regime Change and the Culture of Politics. *African Studies Review* 37(1): 39-67.

1994b The National Conference Phenomena in Francophone Africa. *Comparative Studies in Society and History* 36(3): 257-310.

Royer, Patrick

2002 The Spirit of Competition: Wak in Burkina Faso. *Africa* 72(3): 464-483.

Saavedra, Martha

2003 Football Feminine and Development of the African Game: Senegal, Nigeria and South Africa. *Soccer and Society* 4(2-3): 225-253.

Samnick, E. Gustave

2006 Merci Ghana. *Mutations*, June 23, 2006, No. 1681: 8-9.

Sanders, Todd

2001 Save our Skins: Structural Adjustment, Morality and the Occult in Tanzania. In *Magical Interpretations, Material Realities: Modernity, Witchcraft and the Occult in Postcolonial Africa*, H. L. Moore and T. Sanders, eds. London and New York: Routledge, pp. 161-183.

Sarro, Ramon

1999 Football et mobilisation identitaire: la "réinvention des traditions" par les jeunes Baga de Guinée. *Politique Africaine* 74: 153-161.

Schatzberg, Michael G.

1993 Power, Legitimacy and 'Democratization' in Africa. *Africa* 63(4): 445-461.

2000 La sorcellerie comme mode de causalité politique. *Politique Africaine* 79: 33-47.

2001 *Political Legitimacy in Middle Africa: Father, Family, Food*. Bloomington and Indianapolis, IN: Indiana University Press.

2006 Soccer, Science, and Sorcery: Causation and African Football. *Afrika Spectrum* 41(3): 351-369.

Schilder, Kees

1994 *Quest for Self-esteem: State, Islam and Mundang Ethnicity in Northern Cameroon*. Leiden: African Studies Center.

1997 Regional Balance in Northern Cameroon. In *Regional Balance and National Integration in Cameroon: Lessons Learned and the Uncertain Future*, Paul Nchoji Nkwi and Francis B. Nyamnjoh, eds. Leiden: African Studies Center: Yaoundé: ICASSRT, pp. 177-192.

Schler, Lynn
2005 History, the Nation-State, and Alternative Narratives: An Example from Colonial Douala. *African Studies Review* 48(1): 89-108.

Schneider, Jürg
2004 Speaking in Bubbles, Press Cartoons and Comics in Cameroon. In *African Media Cultures: Transdisciplinary Perspective*, R. M. Beck and F. Wittmann, eds. Köln: Rüdiger Köppe Verlag, pp. 59-81.

Schultz, Emily
1984 From Pagan to Pullo: Ethnic Identity Change in Northern Cameroon. *Africa* 54(1): 46-64.

Scotch, N. A.
1961 Magic, Sorcery, and Football Among Urban Zulu: A Case of Reinterpretation Under Acculturation. *Journal of Conflict Resolution* 5(1): 70-74.

Scott, James
1985 *Weapons of the Weak: Everyday Forms of Peasant Resistance*. New Haven, CT: Yale University Press.
1990 *Domination and the Arts of Resistance: Hidden Transcripts*. New Haven, CT. Yale University Press.

Shimada, Yoshihito
1984 *Dynamique politique des Etats traditionelles sous l'Indirect Rule: du pouvoir à l'autorité – étude de cas du Lamidat de Rey Bouba*. Africa 3, Shohei Wada and Paul Eguchi, eds. (Senri Ethnological Studies 15). Osaka: National Museum of Ethnology, pp. 289-359.

Shipton, Parker
1990 African Famines and Food Security: Anthropological Perspectives. *Annual Review of Anthropology* 19: 353-394.

Socpa, Antoine
2000 Les dons dans le jeu électoral au Cameroun. *Cahiers d'Études africaines* 157(XI-I): 91-108.
2003 *Démocratisation et autochtonie au Cameroun*. Münster: LIT Verlag.
2006 Bailleurs Autochtones et Locataires Allogènes: Enjeu Foncier et Participation Politique au Cameroun. *African Studies Review* 49(2): 45-67.

Southall, Aidan
1970 The Illusion of Tribe. *Journal of Asian and African Studies* 5(1-2): 28-50.

Spitulnik, Debra Anne
1994 Radio Culture in Zambia: Audiences, Public Words, and the Nation-state. Unpublished doctoral dissertation, the University of Chicago.

Stevenson, Thomas B.
1989 Sports Clubs and Political Integration in the Yemen Arab Republic. *International Review of Sociology of Sport* 24: 300-313.

Stoddart, Brian
1988 Sport, Cultural Imperialism, and Colonial Response in the British Empire. *Comparative Studies in Society and History* 30: 649-673.

Stuart, Ossie
1996 Players, Workers, Protestors: Social Change and Soccer in Colonial Zimbabwe. In *Sport, Identity and Ethnicity*, Jeremy MacClancy, ed. Oxford: Berg, pp. 167-180.

Sugden, John and Alan Tomlinson
1998 *FIFA and the Contest for World Football: Who Rules the Peoples' Game?* Cambridge: Polity Press.

Szörényi, Szabolcs and János Bródy
1970 Én nem tudtam azt, kérem. Hungaroton.

Takougang, Joseph
1993 The Post-Ahidjo Era in Cameroon: Continuity and Change. *Journal of Third World Studies* 10(2): 268-302.
1995 The Press and the Democratization Process in Africa: The Case of the Republic of Cameroon. *Journal of Third World Studies* 12: 326-349.
1996 The 1992 Multiparty Elections in Cameroon: Prospects for Democracy and Democratization. *Journal of Asian and African Studies* 31(1-2): 52-65.
2003 Nationalism, Democratisation, and Political Opportunism in Cameroon. *Journal of Contemporary African Studies* 21(3): 427-445.
2005 Strangers Among Us? French Cameroon Immigrants to British Southern Cameroons, 1916-1961. In *Tradition and Politics: Indigenous Political Structures in Africa*, O. Vaughan, ed. Trenton, NJ and Asmara: Africa World Press, pp. 327-351.

Takougang, Joseph and Milton Krieger
1998 *African State and Society in the 1990s: Cameroon's Political Crossroads*. Boulder, CO: Westview Press.

Tapa, Célestin
nd [2002] Colonel Moume Mbedi Pierre-Claude "Liberté" My scrutiny of Cameroon Football. *Learn English* 27: 6-7.

Tardits, Claude
1962 *Les Bamiléké de l'ouest Cameroun*. Paris: Editions Berger-Levraut.

Taylor, Charles
2002 Modern Social Imaginaries. *Public Culture* 14(1): 91-124.

Taylor, Lawrence J.
2001 "Paddy's Pig": Irony and Self-Irony in Irish Culture. In *Irony in Action: Anthropology, Practice and the Moral Imagination*, J. W. Fernandez and M. T. Huber, eds. Chicago and London: University of Chicago Press, pp. 172-187.

Thébaud, François
1998 Arbitrage et politique. In *Football et Passions politiques*, I. Ramonet and C. de Brie, eds. *Le Monde diplomatique: Manière de voir* 39, pp. 19-20.

Thornton, Robert
1996 The Potentials of Boundaries in South Africa: Steps Towards a Theory of the Social Edge. In *Postcolonial Identities in Africa*. R. Werbner and T. Ranger, eds. London: Zed Books, pp. 136-161.

Torres, Gabriel
1997 *The Force of Irony: Power in the Everyday Life of Mexican Tomato Workers*. Oxford: Berg.

Toukas, Dominique
2002 Les Lions se mettent en difficultés. *La Nouvelle Expression* 6.

Toulabor, C. M.
1981 Jeu de mots, jeux de vilains: Lexique de la dérision politique au Togo. *Politique Africaine* 3: 55-71.
1991 La dérision politique en liberté à Lomé. *Politique Africaine* 43: 136-141.

Tsanga, Soter
1969 *Le football Camerounais. Des origines à l'indépendance*. Yaoundé.

Turnbull, Colin M.
1972 *The Mountain People*. New York: Simon and Schuster.

Turner, Victor
1967 *The Forest of Symbols*. Ithaca, NY: Cornell University Press.
1974 *Dramas, Fields and Metaphors*. Ithaca, NY: Cornell University Press.

van Santen, J. C. M.

1997 Regional Balance and National Integration: A Historical Overview of Mafa Integration in National Politics In *Regional Balance and National Integration in Cameroon: Lessons Learned and the Uncertain Future*, Paul Nchoji Nkwi and Francis B. Nyamnjoh, eds. Leiden: African Studies Center and Yaoundé: ICASSRT, pp. 242-259.

Vaughan, Megan

1987 *The Story of an African Famine: Gender and Famine in Twentieth-century Malawi*. Cambridge: Cambridge University Press.

Verdery, Katherine

1996 Whither 'Nation' and 'Nationalism'? In *Mapping the Nation*, G. Balakrishnan, ed. London: Verso, pp. 226-234.

Vidacs, Bea

1985 Komaság és kölcsönösség Szentpéterszegen [Godparenthood and Reciprocity in Szentpéterszeg]. *Ethnographia* 96: 509-529.

2001 Olympic Mvolyé: The Cameroonian Team that Could Not Win. In *Fear and Loathing in World Football*, G. Armstrong and R. Giulianotti, eds. Oxford: Berg, pp. 223-235.

2006 Through the Prism of Sports: Why Should Africanists Study Sports? *Afrika Spectrum* 41(3): 331-349.

Vigh, Henrik

2006 The Colour of Destruction: On Racialization, Geno-globality and the Social Imaginary in Bissau. *Anthropological Theory* 6(4): 481-500.

Vincent, Joan

1974 The Structuring of Ethnicity. *Human Organization* 33(4): 375-379.

Vubo, Emmanuel Yenshu

2006 Management of Ethnic Diversity in Cameroon against the Backdrop of Social Crises. *Cahiers d'Études africaines* 181.

Warnier, Jean-Pierre

1984 Histoire du peuplement et genèse des paysages dans l'Ouest Camerounais. *Journal of African History* 25(4): 395-410.

Werbner, Richard

1996 Introduction. Multiple Identities, Plural Arenas. In *Postcolonial Identities in Africa,* R. Werbner and T. Ranger, eds. London: Zed Books, pp. 1-25.

Wolf, Eric R.

1966 Kinship, Friendship, and Patron–Client Relations in Complex Societies. In *The Social Anthropology of Complex Societies*, M. Banton, ed. London: Tavistock Publications, pp. 1-22.

Wolf, Hans-Georg

1997 Transcendence of Ethnic Boundaries: The Case of Anglophones in Cameroon. *Journal of Sociolinguistics* 1(3): 419-426.

2001 *English in Cameroon*. Berlin and New York: Mouton de Gruyter.

Young, Crawford

2002 Nationalism and Ethnicity in Africa. *Review of Asian and Pacific Studies* 23: 1-19.

Zoa, Anne-Sidonie

1995 *Les ordures à Yaoundé: Urbanisation, environnement et politique au Cameroun*. Paris: L'Harmattan.

Zsolt, Róbert

1978 *Labdarugók, sportolók*. (Magyarország felfedezése). Budapest: Szépirodalmi Kiadó.

CREDITS

The book contains somewhat modified parts of articles I have published elsewhere. I thank the publishers for having granted me permission to reuse these materials.

Palgrave Macmillan for granting permission to reproduce:

France in the Cameroonian Football Imagination, in Gary Armstrong – Richard Giulianotti (eds) *Football in Africa: Conflict, Conciliation, and Community* London: Palgrave Macmillan, 2004. Pp. 169-182.

Berg Publishers, an imprint of A&C Black Publishers Ltd, for granting permission to republish parts of:

Football: Politics and Power in Cameroon, with Paul Nchoji Nkwi, in Gary Armstrong – Richard Giulianotti (eds) *Entering the Field: New Perspectives on World Football*, Oxford: Berg, 1997. Pp 123-139.

Olympic Mvolyé, the Cameroonian Team that Could Not Win, in Gary Armstrong – Richard Giulianotti (eds) *Fear and Loathing in World Football.* Oxford: Berg, 2001. Pp. 223-235.

Postcolonialism and the Level Playing Field in the 1998 World Cup, in John Bale – Mike Cronin (eds) *Postcolonialism and Sport*. Oxford: Berg, 2003. Pp 147-158.

Taylor and Francis Group (http://www.informaworld.com) for granting permission to publish parts of:

Football in Cameroon: A Vehicle for the Expansion and Contraction of Identity. *Culture, Sport and Society* 2(3): pp 100-117.

The journal *Mots Pluriels* for granting permission to reproduce parts of the article:

Soccer and Anti-Colonial Sentiment in Cameroon. http://motspluriels.arts.uwa.edu.au/MP698bv.html

The map of Cameroon on page 31 appears courtesy of the University Libraries, The University of Texas at Austin.